Analyzing Popular Music

How do we 'know' music? We perform it, we compose it, we sing it in the shower, we cook, sleep and dance to it. Eventually we think and write about it. This book represents the culmination of such shared processes. Each of these essays, written by leading writers on popular music, is analytical in some sense, but none of them treats analysis as an end in itself. The book presents a wide range of genres (rock, dance, TV soundtracks, country, pop, soul, easy listening, Turkish Arabesk) and deals with issues as broad as methodology, modernism, postmodernism, Marxism and communication. It aims to encourage listeners to think more seriously about the 'social' consequences of the music they spend time with and is the first collection of such essays to incorporate contextualization in this way.

ALLAN F. MOORE is Professor of Popular Music and Head of the Department of Music and Sound Recording at the University of Surrey. He is author of *Rock: The Primary Text* and editor of *The Cambridge Companion to Blues and Gospel Music*. He is also co-editor of the journals *Popular Music* and *Twentieth-Century Music*.

Analyzing Popular Music

EDITED BY ALLAN F. MOORE

CAMBRIDGE
UNIVERSITY PRESS

WITHDRAWN

PUBLISHED BY THE PRESS SYNDICATE OF THE UNIVERSITY OF CAMBRIDGE
The Pitt Building, Trumpington Street, Cambridge CB2 1RP, United Kingdom

CAMBRIDGE UNIVERSITY PRESS
The Edinburgh Building, Cambridge, CB2 1RP, UK
40 West 20th Street, New York, NY 10011-4211, USA
477 Williamstown Road, Port Melbourne, VIC 3207, Australia
Ruiz de Alarcón 13, 28014 Madrid, Spain
Dock House, The Waterfront, Cape Town 8001, South Africa

http://www.cambridge.org

First published 2003

Printed in the United Kingdom at the University Press, Cambridge

Typeface Minion 10.25/14 pt   *System* LaTeX 2_ε [TB]

A catalogue record for this book is available from the British Library

ISBN 0 521 77120 X hardback

Contents

Acknowledgement

Permission to quote the REM song 'Nightswimming' is gratefully acknowledged from Warner-Chappell.

Contributors

ALLAN F. MOORE is Professor of Popular Music and Head of the Department of Music and Sound Recording at the University of Surrey. Author of *Rock: The Primary Text* (2nd edn 2001) and *The Beatles: Sgt. Pepper's Lonely Hearts Club Band* (1997), he has published articles on Yes, U2, Big Country, the Beatles, Frank Zappa, rock music theory and musical modernism and has contributed extensively to the revised *New Grove*. He is a joint editor of *Popular Music* and is on the editorial board of *Popular Musicology*.

ROB BOWMAN is the author of *Soulsville USA: The Story of Stax Records* which won the 1998 ASCAP-Deems-Taylor and ARSC Awards for Excellence in Music Research. In 1996 he won the Grammy in the 'Best Album Notes' category for the monograph accompanying the ten-CD box *The Complete Stax/Volt Singles vol. 3*, which he also co-produced. In the past ten years he has compiled and written liner notes for more than 100 CD reissues. He is Associate Professor of Music at York University, Toronto.

JOHN COVACH is Associate Professor of Music at the University of North Carolina at Chapel Hill. Co-editor of *Understanding Rock* (1997), he has also edited special issues of *Contemporary Music Review* and has written widely, particularly on Progressive Rock and on the philosophy of music.

DAI GRIFFITHS is Principal Lecturer in Music at Oxford Brookes University. He has published articles on songs by John Cale, Bob Dylan, Michelle Shocked, Bruce Springsteen and Anton Webern. Other recent papers have included book chapters on cover versions and on the history of pop music since punk.

STAN HAWKINS is Associate Professor of Musicology at the Department of Music and Theatre, University of Oslo, where he teaches courses in popular music. In addition to his book, *Settling the Pop Score: Pop Texts and Identity* (2002) he has published numerous articles and chapters in the field of popular music studies. He is currently chief editor of *Popular Musicology Online* and the Norwegian chair for the Nordic Branch of IASPM (International Association for the Study of Popular Music).

CHRIS KENNETT includes among his research interests pop music sociology, the cognition, perception and analysis of music in retail environments, and film music theory, in addition to his long-held interest in pitch-class set theory. He has taught at the Universities of Bristol, Reading, Nottingham, Exeter, Thames Valley and at Goldsmith's College, and is currently Researcher in Sound Media at the University of Westminster. He writes for journals including *Music Analysis, Popular Music* and *Computer Music Journal.*

ADAM KRIMS is Associate Professor of Music and Director of the Institute for Popular Music at the University of Alberta. Author of *Rap Music and the Poetics of Identity* (2000) and editor of *Music/Ideology: Resisting the Aesthetic* (1998), he has published numerous essays and articles on music, Marxism, urban geography and cultural theory.

ROBYNN J. STILWELL is Assistant Professor of Music at Georgetown University. Her main research interests lie in music as cultural text and in the interaction of music and movement. She has published on topics as diverse as Phil Collins, *Die Hard* and Torvill and Dean, and has recently edited a special issue of *Popular Music and Society* dealing with popular music and national and ethnic identities in the wake of recent political change. She is currently working on a book, *Recontextualizing Music: The Use of Pre-existing Music in Film.*

MARTIN STOKES is the author of *The Arabesk Debate: Music and Musicians in Modern Turkey* (1992), the editor of *Ethnicity, Identity and Music: The Musical Construction of Place* (1994), co-editor of *Nationalism, Minorities and Diasporas: Identities and Rights in the Middle East* (1996) and of a special issue of the journal *Popular Music* on the Middle East (1996). He has published articles in *Popular Music, New Formations, The British Journal of Ethnomusicology, The Journal of the Royal Anthropological Institute*, the *Middle East Report*, the *New Grove Dictionary of Music and Musicians,* and elsewhere. Currently he is an Associate Professor in the Department of Music at the University of Chicago.

ROBERT WALSER is Professor and Chair of the Musicology Department in the University of California at Los Angeles. He is the author of *Running with the Devil: Power, Gender and Madness in Heavy Metal Music* (1993), which won the Irving Lowens Award for distinguished scholarship in American music, and *Keeping Time: Readings in Jazz History* (1999). A recipient of NEH, ACLS, and Whiting Foundation Fellowships, he is co-editor of the Music/Culture series at Wesleyan University Press, and former editor of *American Music*.

1   Introduction

ALLAN F. MOORE

How do we 'know' music? Although music has a variety of distinct
audiences, one way of approaching a universally applicable response is by
looking at the activities we undertake in its presence. Most widespread, of
course, is listening. We may listen for pleasure, for identification, as an accompaniment to other activities (dancing, cooking), distractedly (as when
watching a film) and in many other ways. In pre-modern societies, listening
without any more active form of participation was rare indeed, whether that
activity focused on performing itself, on some form of dance, or even on
banter with the musicians: some would argue that in modern society too,
the musical experience is impoverished without such participation. Many of
us are either fortunate or wilful enough to insist on performing, and even
composing. All of these activities may be defined as ways of 'knowing' music,
even if that knowledge is not communicated verbally. We do, however, find
verbal communication about music a seductive activity: the scholar Nicholas
Cook even argues that words are indispensable in the process of our creating for ourselves meaning out of the music we listen to (Cook 1998a: 270).
Verbal communication is certainly necessary for the remaining activity we
undertake in respect of music – its study, the process of knowing it 'better'.

Twenty years ago, it was difficult to find any institution where popular music (as a field distinct from 'classical' or 'non-Western' musics or jazz)
could be found being taught to prospective musicians at undergraduate level.
It simply did not appear on the syllabus. Partly as a consequence, the music
was ascribed 'amateur' status, notwithstanding the evident professionalism
exhibited by its practitioners, and the revenue those considered successful
were able to generate for various stakeholders (agents and managers, publishers and recording companies, performance venues, record distributors, high
street outlets). At the turn of the century, the position has changed to such

1

an extent that not only are many undergraduate musicians enabled to study some aspect of popular music (whether that be its performance, its composition, production, sociology, analysis, its marketing or whatever), but there are even degree programmes devoted entirely to it. This has raised within the academic community inevitable questions of how it is to be taught and studied. It has become abundantly clear that to treat popular music as simply another activity (something else that is 'popular', that people indulge in) and to restrict oneself to investigating its institutions and practices is not sufficient for, as music, it appears to hold such a qualitatively distinct place in our lives. It has become equally clear that to treat popular music as simply another genre (as simply another sort of 'music' that people listen to) and to make use of the techniques developed for the study of the bourgeois music canon, is similarly insufficient. The issue is wider than this, of course, for even the techniques through which the 'bourgeois music canon' is addressed are no longer unquestioned. It is at the intersection of these three realizations that this set of essays originates. It will be useful, therefore, to begin by outlining both the archaeology of 'popular musicology' and the problematics which have become identified as the 'new musicology', or 'critical musicology'.

'Popular musicology' is an unfortunate, and potentially misleading, term for the discipline which is growing out of musicology[1] in order to address the need for an investigative methodology.[2] When musicologists first took the daring step of investigating contemporary popular music, the need for a separate methodology (i.e. the realization that 'popular music' was another sort of music) was not readily perceived. Thus, in his ground-breaking attempt to interpret the music of the Beatles, British musicologist Wilfrid

---

1 Musical scholarship in North America observes a disciplinary divide between musicology (which incorporates historical study, aesthetics, criticism) and music theory (which incorporates analysis). The UK (and Europe generally, it seems) does not, except where the North American influence is overwhelming. The term 'musicology' acts there as an over-arching term for all these activities. Here, I adopt the latter usage, in part because the former divide is senseless in a field (popular music) which as yet involves so few musicologists (in the broader sense), but so many from other disciplines (sociology, cultural studies, media studies, literary theory, etc.). There are other reasons, of course, which will become clear.
2 'Popular musicology' should be read as the musicological investigation of popular music, rather than the accessible investigation of music!

2

Mellers (1973) nonetheless employed his version of the standard discursive analytical practice of the time.[3] Indeed, the Beatles were among the first pop musicians to have called forth positive evaluations from the establishment.[4] The US anthropologist Charles Keil came to a related repertoire with a different set of questions to pose. While his study of the blues is informed by close, analytical listening, his aim was to discover the role the contemporary blues singer played within urban, lower-class Negro culture (Keil 1991: 1). His compatriot Charles Hamm adopted a more standard historical musicological approach to his unearthing of the history of popular song in the USA (Hamm 1979) and, as befits a historical musicologist, his work remains concerned with the relationship between that repertoire and both avant-garde and African musics. He proclaims elsewhere his indebtedness to an earlier study by Mellers (1965), which at the time 'concern[ed] itself more with jazz and other vernacular music than any book to that point' (Hamm 1983: ix). Three approaches, then, the analytical/interpretive, the anthropological and the historical, whose terms are taken from their parent disciplines. It is only in retrospect that these studies have taken on their own historical importance – at the time they were each perceived as marginal studies within music, just as within each of these approaches popular music remained a marginal field of study. It was only with the activities of British sociologists, and particularly the work emanating from the Centre for Contemporary Cultural Studies in Birmingham, that the study of popular music began to move closer to centre stage. Here, it was constructed most typically as a music of youth resistance via theories of subculture (see especially Hall and Jefferson 1976), a construction which is falling increasingly into disfavour. Frith's (1983) related emphasis on issues of opportunity and constraint within which access to popular music operated posed many of the important questions. In the background of all these studies (although a long way in the background in some cases) was Adorno's denigration of pre-war popular music (e.g. Adorno 1978) in favour of European modernism, in the attempt to construct an adequate

---

3 Middleton (1972) proclaims its indebtedness to Mellers, and actually appeared slightly earlier. It is not that well known and has been out of print for many years, but is a vastly under-rated book, largely free from the methodological problems inherent in Mellers's approach.
4 Rorem (1968) and the entire collection edited by Eisen (1969) are cases in point, even if the latter consists largely of journalism.

and musically informed sociology of music (see especially the critique of Adorno in Middleton 1990: 34–63). The diversity of approaches observed here might usefully suggest that the study of popular music is an interdisciplinary affair, the contributions of whose various fields were mapped in Richard Middleton's mammoth study (1990). In part, this interdisciplinary agenda was formative in the institution of the International Association for the Study of Popular Music (Tagg 1985), even if the polarization often encountered between 'musicological' and 'sociological' approaches has been no less apparent there.

The last two decades in particular have sown poststructuralist doubts deep within the close reading of music of all kinds, doubts which are directed not only at the authority of the composer but, perhaps even more strongly, at the identity, the coherence, the autonomy of the individual piece, work, song (however we choose to label it). The consequences of this move have broadly been of three types. Some have argued that the very practice of close reading, or analysis, has become fatally flawed in its inability to respond to the particularity of our responses to music.[5] Some, in reinforcing the division between humanities-based and science-based approaches to music, have simply denied the force of these objections.[6] Both these types of response are fast becoming entrenched. A third possibility is available, to divorce the practice of analysis from the fundamental assumption of the autonomy of the piece under analysis. Adam Krims (1998) has recently attempted to establish such a position within the field of the canon, on theoretical grounds. A similar aim underpins this collection, to which I shall return. However, it is the first of these three approaches which most requires acknowledgement at this time.

To differing degrees, both (US) New Musicology and (UK) Critical Musicology broadly embrace the conditional relativism embodied in Middleton's call to study 'the whole musical field' (1990: 7). They are marked not only by dissatisfaction with the methods (including conventional analysis) employed to undertake such study, but also by dissatisfactions with the exclusive divisions into which musicology falls, and with the exclusive

---

5 This is the thrust of Tomlinson's key (1993) article.
6 In distinguishing between 'humanities-based' and 'science-based', I make reference to the musicology/music theory divide. Agawu (1996) clearly expresses such a denial.

repertoire usually studied by musicology (and which develops outward from the encounter with Classicism). One of the strongest points of contact among interested parties is the acceptance of a notion of inclusiveness, the realization that musicologists can no longer afford to ignore a particular corpus simply because it is written, performed, studied, or just listened to by, say, women, by expatriate, foreign or isolated communities, by a particular social class or age group, or simply by 'others'. This necessarily implies a questioning of such notions as genius, canons themselves, universality, aesthetic autonomy and textual immanence, a questioning now routinely traced to Kerman (1980, 1985).[7]

So, at the centre of the debate concerning just how popular music is best studied is the status of the 'musical text' and the activity of 'music analysis'. I have identified this debate above as originating in 'poststructuralism', which may be understood as a group of methodologies which go beyond the seeking of solutions in the ways cultural products and practices are structured. This is an aspect of a wider cultural shift in industrial society, a paradigmatic change conveniently known as 'postmodernism'. Under 'modernism', within music discourse, notions of originality, authorship and autonomy were self-evident. 'Originality' in some respect distinguished the noteworthy from the mundane, and pursuit of the original ensured the continual progress of musical styles and techniques. Notions of 'authorship' meant that to understand a piece of music was to understand the composer's intention, or at least his (normally) workings.[8] And, since the creative artist functioned as an autonomous being (see Pippin 1991: 61–4), it was not necessary to delve outside his biography, or that of his music, in order to understand it. 'Postmodernism', however, has recognized that progress is quite possibly an illusion (an argument put elegantly long ago by the scholar Christopher Small – see Small 1977: 9) and that the authority long vested in the author is specious. No less so are, we believe, claims to musical autonomy.

In the words of the anthropologist Gregory Bateson, 'information consists of differences that make a difference' (Bateson 1979: 99). Analysis is

---

7 Some of the results of such questioning can be found in volumes such as Bergeron and Bohlman (1992), Pople (1994), Schwarz, Kassabian and Siegel (1997), Krims (1998), Cook (1998b) and Cook and Everist (1999).

8 In the study of music, the notion of the omnipotent voice of the author in his/her work was never so strongly held as in the study of literature.

very good at pointing out differences, whether stylistic (i.e. between similar pieces) or within pieces (varied repetitions, for instance). Although this is easier for the canon (where one has a visual text to refer to), it is nonetheless possible when analyzing the aural text (what it is that we hear). Even such a critic of formalist analysis as Charles Keil nonetheless pays great attention to objectifiable details of musical structures (Keil 1994: 59–67). The difficulty lies in deciding which differences do make a difference, which carry any interpretive weight. Thus, as we see it here, analysis is an issue of interpretation. But, interpretation of what? It appears to me that the reason we (communally) go out of our way to experience music is *simply in order to have been part of the experience that was that music*. It is thus, at root, the experience which is subject to interpretation. This formulation is pretty abstract, but I think that most of the reasons which tend to be offered for why people use music at all can be distilled into such a phrase. Now, the role of scholars is principally to formulate pertinent questions. From my own perspective, the most valuable question to follow this observation is something like 'why was the experience like it was?' As a musicologist, I would tend to narrow the question down further to 'why did the music sound like it did?' Although I am necessarily defensive about this bracketing off of many of what I would call the 'paramusical' elements of the experience (in that the hearing of music is the *sine qua non* for a communal musical experience to have taken place), I take refuge in the recognition that it is the responsibility of the entire community of scholars to provide an adequate study of the field, rather than that of individuals. Nobody can claim to see the entire picture. Although the question, 'why did the music sound like it did?' may seem simple enough, it opens the door to that whole host of more detailed questions with which scholars are often concerned. These would include 'how does it sound?' (and the associated 'who does the telling?', i.e. does my observation carry more weight than that of anyone else, and if so, on what grounds?), 'for whom does it sound like that?' (i.e. for whom do the differences we observe make a difference? – what levels of competence should be assumed? – are we taking an 'objective view', the performers' view, the active listeners', or whose?) and even, at last, 'why does it matter?' (i.e. how does people's use of music relate to their uses of other artefacts and experiences?).

It is, however, necessary to begin from some conceptualization of how the music sounds. The most important reason for this, I believe, is one of empowerment. Listeners everywhere are encouraged to conceptualize the invention of music as a branch of magic, to believe that musical actions and gestures cannot be subject to any level of explanation, and hence understanding, beyond the trivially biographical. This view, which might almost be described as a sort of 'popular modernism' (in the terms discussed above) is ultimately disabling and disenfranchising, in that it conveys to the conventionally 'unmusical' that their state is beyond any hope of change. That this belief in music as magic is shared not only by those in influential positions within the media (much popular music journalism, for instance), but also by those in positions of power within the leisure industry (see e.g. Negus 1992: 52–5), only makes the disturbance more acute. The view seems only too natural to those who have never made note-to-note musical decisions, and only too absurd to those who reflect upon spending their lives doing so.

To take full advantage of the interdisciplinarity that the study of popular music offers, means at least to begin from the understandings that relevant disciplines can provide (see Tagg 1991: 144). The interface between musicology on the one hand, and the social sciences and other humanities on the other, is often highly problematic, and will remain so unless we can be quite explicit about our normally unexamined assumptions: it has been a salutary experience to engage with scholars who spend their entire professional lives researching aspects of music, but who cannot accept that such a thing as a 'perfect cadence' or a 'gapped melodic contour' can have any bearing on the way listeners respond to music, because conceptualizing such things requires training those listeners have not had. Defending the practice of analysis in such circumstances can be an education in itself, especially when trying to sort out at what point objectivity intersects with intersubjectivity in such an enterprise. This seems such a crucial task as to make acceptable the risk of briefly sinking into pedantry. We hear a sound when our eardrum vibrates at, say, 440Hz, having been set in motion by sound-waves vibrating at that same speed. They, in turn, have been set in motion by the vibration of some material, again at that speed, even in the presence of conflicting vibrations from other sound sources (such a sound may, of course, be of very short duration indeed). This is an objective description of what happens. In saying this, I mean that any person with normal or near-normal hearing, from whatever culture they come, will have their eardrums vibrate at the same speed. They will not identify the 'sound' that the brain receives in terms of its speed – that would be too cumbersome. There is a code fairly widely accepted in Europe, North America, and latterly in other parts of the world also, which would call the sound 'A above middle C' and, in choosing whether to use that code or some other, we are entering into an act of interpretation, but it is an interpretation of the cultural context of the sound, of how to understand it, rather than of the sound itself. Our choice of code (how we make sense of the sound) cannot affect the speed of the vibrations, nor their interference patterns with vibrations from antecedent, simultaneous, and subsequent sounds. By subjecting this sound to analysis, we are in fact making an interpretation of the relationships apparent between it and antecedent, simultaneous, and consequent sounds, an activity into which it is impossible not to insert the self, because such relationships only become apparent in the presence of a perceiver.[9] Thus, an analysis is only one among a number of possibilities. This is an important point, since this book lays no claim to the provision of a single mechanism whereby musical meaning is enabled.

An analysis can be subject to at least two types of evaluation. An inherent evaluation would critique it on what might be widely recognized grounds: its economy; its rhetoric or communicative power; its misidentification of the irreducible facets of the object.[10] For example, if we could demonstrate that profligacy was of little value in any aspect of life, we would have a secure basis for evaluation on this ground (thus does aesthetics shade into ethics). Structural coherence used to be regarded as such a ground, of course. These days, however, it may well be that there are no sufficiently widely recognized grounds to permit such an evaluation. A pragmatic evaluation would recognize the question towards which the analysis was directed in search of an answer and use this as a starting-point. The weakness of the scholarship community lies in the fact that any analysis worthy of the name has to be based on, and give rise to, mutually agreed theoretical paradigms. In some areas of music (for instance eighteenth- and nineteenth-century tonal music, perhaps jazz, perhaps the Indian *raga* traditions, perhaps twentieth-century concert music) we have these. Despite a growing number of studies

9 To my mind, the most elegant demonstration of this observation remains that of Barfield (1988).
10 What Tagg (1991) usefully identifies as its musemes.

(Winkler 1978; Tagg 1982; van der Merwe 1989; Middleton 1990; Brackett 1995; Everett 2000; Moore 2001), Western popular music is one of the areas in which, as yet, we do not. What, however, is this objective sound? We cannot entirely take it for granted. It does not exist in any sort of written form but only, ultimately, in our (faulty) memories. All visual representations of it are just that – representations. The emphasis on sounds *per se*, rather than on representations of them, distinguishes the investigations in this book from that of much other analytical enquiry. In formulating this distinction, Theodore Gracyk has recently differentiated between the 'ontological thickness' of 'rock' (the very physical nature of the sounds we hear, and the richness of detail over and above what can be visually represented in codified form) and the corresponding 'thinness' of the scores of the European tradition, where a great deal of performance detail has to be inferred through familiarity with performance styles. The issue is complex: as I have argued above, notwithstanding the difficulty of representation the musical text does have a specificity – we do not go so far as Raymond Monelle's recent claim that the '[musical] text is whatever criticism observes' (Monelle 2000: 157). However much our idealism may cause us to rue the fact, the commodification of contemporary music culture is taken as read.

The proximate causes of this book are broadly twofold. In 1990, Richard Middleton argued that the wholesale importation of analytical methods borrowed from music analysis and applied to popular music could not be sustained (Middleton 1990: 104ff.). All the essays in this book are therefore, in some sense, essays in music analysis, even where they take a critical stance towards the practice of analysis itself. As I have stated above, analysis is necessarily interpretation, and these essays alone demonstrate the healthy divergence of practices which nonetheless do not prevent us from continuing to laugh with each other. As will by now be clear, however, they exclude the formalist interpretations developing from traditional modernist musicology (represented best, perhaps, by Forte 1995), such that nowhere is the practice of analysis its own justification. In each case, analysis is put at the service of answering some larger question. In 1992, I co-hosted the London conference *Popular Music: The Primary Text*, whose purpose was, in part, to debate the senses in which analysis was appropriate to popular music. Although none of these essays is as old as that conference, I first ate and drank with some of the current contributors at that event. This book is a subsequent snapshot of the analytic work being undertaken. It addresses a variety of genres, each of which is 'current' at the time of writing, but since no genre predominates within the collection, we endeavour to evade any sense of presuming to establish a 'canon'. Above all, we believe the book demonstrates the sheer range and vitality of contemporary close reading of popular music.

Since it was first conceived, three other comparable collections have appeared: it may be worth outlining how they differ. John Covach and Graeme Boone's *Understanding Rock* (1997) addresses a smaller repertoire (i.e. 'rock') and is aimed exclusively, to all appearances, at a North American audience. Its subtitle ('Essays in Musical Analysis') situates it clearly within the discourse mapped out above. Walter Everett's *Expression in Pop-Rock Music* (2000) succeeds it by only three years. In some essays (most notably those by Hisama and Fast), the social and the musical are seen to impact on each other, while elsewhere not only the utilization, but the conceptualization, of analytic method is foregrounded in a primarily aesthetic discourse. Richard Middleton's *Reading Pop* (2000) is a collection of key articles with a similar range to this, but encompassing a far more overt interdisciplinary approach, such that the question of analysis is rather downplayed. These collections indicate the growth in collective popular music scholarship, while they also lay out a domain within which this present collection moves.

So, what of the chapters in this book? Each addresses a different genre, and each is analytically founded, while each also addresses a different area of the problematics outlined above. The issue of autonomy is met head-on in Robynn Stilwell's discussion of the music to the cult TV show *The X-Files*. She situates it as a site of many boundary distinctions: between music for television and music for film, between aesthetic and commercial imperatives, and between music and sound design, each pair impacting on the others. She traces the show's precedents and argues that it inhabits its own distinct sound-world, strongly (and problematically) dependent on what everyday language describes as 'ethnic' music. She argues that, in its acceptance of a specifically televisual medium, the show adopts a greater continuity of scoring than has been the norm, in the process denying the music any strong sense of autonomy, but as a result increasing its effectiveness 'as mediator of the visual experience'. The interdisciplinary approach required by this chapter is explicit elsewhere, too. Dai Griffiths takes up an old issue, that

10

of the extent to which the lyrics to popular song can be considered poetry. Indeed, it was through this route that popular music made an early entry into the academy, in the guise of literary studies. Subsequently, the position turned to such an extent that the meaning of lyrics became discounted, both by musicians (he cites Bob Dylan, of all people) and critics (Simon Frith, among others). Griffiths develops a number of themes in arguing for a partial rehabilitation of the meaning, and articulation, of lyrics: verbal space (to do with the varying pace at which lyrics are delivered), the role of sonic elements (particularly rhyme and alliteration), and the ways grammar is toyed with. Signalling the crucial importance of subject position for the subsequent development of the understanding of ways lyrics operate, he insists that a variety of literacies are required for this understanding, of which attending to words in their own relation to song has been badly overlooked hitherto. My own chapter on the music of Jethro Tull takes as its starting-point Fredric Jameson's curious identification of the music of the Beatles and the Rolling Stones as modernist popular music. It thereby responds to the notion of modernism as an ideological apparatus enabling the discussion of music, but views modernism as a bundle of aesthetically based identifiers (crudely summarized as ambivalence, difficulty, alienation, historical consciousness, concentration on technique, fragmentation) indicative of a response to the conditions of modernity. It asks what a modernist popular music might look like viewed according to these parameters, and argues that the output of Jethro Tull goes a long way towards fitting the profile. Although acknowledging that these identifiers do not arise in a social vacuum (their congruence is dependent on the social organization we term 'modernity'), it demonstrates that the relationship between social base and aesthetic response is not causal, and thus that the meaning of the music is not fixed.

The social is also an overt presence in Robert Walser's theoretically inclined chapter. Walser develops answers to the question that underpins much of what I have said above – what should analysis, in the field of popular music, actually do? He attacks the journalistic drive towards 'music appreciation' arguing that instead of aestheticizing popular music (i.e. following a line adopted from the treatment of the canon), we should recognize the contingency of musical values across the board. He also argues that any understanding which does not take account of musical detail is not 'ignoring the irrelevant', but can only be partial: 'how does musical discourse articulate social meanings and produce particular pleasures?' he asks, since, without this understanding, we are unable to understand key social structures, identities and relations. He then develops a series of ideas to make our analytic practice more effective, focusing on such issues as inter-subjectivity, the falsity of disciplinary distinctions, the retreat from universality and the errors of formalism. Finally, he examines four recordings, comparing them not in terms of how good they are, but in what responses to them tell us about them, and about their listeners. That he has to focus here on issues of interpersonal violence reminds us of the pivotal role that music analysis may sometimes have to assume. It goes without saying that Walser treats music as something to which people respond, rather than as something which can be separated from those responses. Two further chapters take up this issue in different ways. Stan Hawkins's discussion of house music focuses on a particular track (Lil' Louis's 'French Kiss') through an overt analytical approach, but emphasizing that this analysis only makes sense when it takes place in relation to the social space in which the track, and the genre, is received. Having laid out the genre's historical location, and thus its key technological determinants, Hawkins uses these to view the track's 'internal mechanisms', particularly its temporal and timbral phenomena. Indeed, the temporal dimension proves problematic, for Hawkins argues that dancers' experience is crucially determined by the way that beats can be construed as functioning within the genre – he finds that metric organization is more strongly related to patterns of musical motion than individual accents. Chris Kennett discusses a related genre (drum'n'bass), but in the process develops a model for understanding the musical text under contingent circumstances. This is a vital move, since most writing on reception assumes, at least implicitly, that the experience was sought. Kennett takes issue with semiotic approaches to musical meaning in which he finds meaning appearing to inhere in the music – he supplies examples where this is clearly not the case. He thus supports Walser's drive to the historicization of musical pleasures, but he goes further in insisting that the presence of other, more demanding activities does not absolve us from considering the role of music in experiencing those activities. He offers two distinct case studies: music programming policy in the ASDA supermarket chain, and a thought-experiment based on studying individuals with particular demographic specificity in a High Street wine store, arguing for how different listeners will construct different listening texts. He discusses these by way of his cultural-acoustic model which investigates personal (time- and demography-specific), situational (intensity- and locus-specific) and intentional (producer task- and user task-specific) listenings.

The topic of Rob Bowman's essay relates to the difference posited by Gracyk (see above) between rock's ontological thickness and the comparable thinness of score-based music. He explores the differences between four different recordings of the Tin Pan Alley standard 'Try a Little Tenderness', recorded over a period of more than three decades. The now-dominant model of popular music as the authentic expression of one or more individuals, realized through their own authorship, is here challenged. Having outlined the song's origins, and the style of its earliest renditions, Bowman focuses in turn on recordings by Bing Crosby, Aretha Franklin, Sam Cooke and Otis Redding, calling attention to the performed differences, both subtle and gross, which exist between them. This enables him to cast light on the status of the notated text within popular music, arguing that with respect to these recordings, it is in performative domains, rather than those of melody, harmony and metre, that meaning is most strongly created. The consequence for this on legally enshrined concepts of copyright are obvious. It also enables him to address processes of cultural change, such that what can be characterized as 'Northern, urban, print-based, middle-class sensibilities' are clearly placed in opposition to 'Southern, rural, oral-based, working class aesthetics'. Cultural change is also, in part, the subject of John Covach's chapter, focusing as it does on the music of the 'new wave' in late 1970s rock. Covach argues that the new wave is best understood as a reaction, not only to earlier styles of rock, but also to the way those earlier styles generated meaning. He develops the concept of 'musical worlding', which he has employed elsewhere, to help explain how music by the bands Foreigner and the Cars respectively 'mean' in different ways. His conclusion reinforces the necessary historicity which surfaces in a number of these essays, in arguing that the irony inherent in the music of the new wave results in a romanticized vision of pre-hippy culture, a romanticization which could only come about because of the perspectives offered by that denigrated culture.

Very different perspectives are offered by the collection's remaining two chapters. Adam Krims's essay foregrounds the role, alluded to above, that Adorno's work has played in popular music studies. He argues, however, that it lacks sufficient historicization, particularly with respect to what he regards as key issues: standardization, and cultural imperialism, and this lack is also apparent in those who theorize cultural capital. In other words, the whole nature of the game has changed: 'the challenge now ... is how to theorize capital as simultaneously diversifying culturally and segregating economically and spatially'. He uses the example of rap music in order to explore how expressive culture can challenge this domination, finding the discourse of popular music as resistance wholly inadequate to this task. The collection closes with Martin Stokes's problematization of the practice of analysis itself. I sought his critical intervention here in order both to acknowledge and to demonstrate the open and ongoing nature of the debates in which we are engaged. Stokes is an ethnomusicologist, and his chapter calls for a rapprochement between ethnomusicological and musicological approaches. The key term in his discussion is 'culture' – what are we doing in trying to observe musical details as product of a culture? He begins by unpacking the distinction between Theory (what a few of us can indulge in) and Culture (which we all experience), seeking a proximate cause for the lack of agreement between current ethnomusicological and popular musicological approaches in the distinction between UK sources of study in concerns with the 'social' as opposed to the more flexible US sources in concerns with the 'cultural'. In the process, he critiques both psychoanalytic and Marxian analyses in the doubts they raise as to whether people, users of music, can be treated as authors of their own meaning. This concern has been raised in other chapters, as we have seen, but with more particular respect to individual examples. He provides detailed discussion both of his own work with Turkish 'Arabesk' (itself a 'popular' genre) and of Sara Cohen's (1991) ethnographic discussion of local music-making in Liverpool, allowing him to glimpse a solution, which hinges on us refocusing our gaze towards the everyday, toward the performative, and even toward possibilities apparent in contemporary cognitive psychology. He echoes Walser, Kennett and others in concluding that 'modes of knowing music compete, and only occasionally connect, with one another. It is, perhaps, music's semiotic multiplicity that makes it so valuable,

14

so pleasurable, and so consequential.' Thus the collection as a whole both argues and demonstrates the unviability of two assumptions: that music's meanings can be fixed, that they can be interrogated without some reference to those individuals who may hold them; and that such meanings can be specified and communicated without close attention to matters of difference between related sounds.

2 Popular music analysis: ten apothegms and four instances

ROBERT WALSER

About thirty years ago there was much talk that geologists ought only to observe and not theorize; and I well remember someone saying that at this rate a man might as well go into a gravel-pit and count the pebbles and describe the colours. How odd it is that anyone should not see that all observation must be for or against some view if it is to be of any service![1]

Introduction

What exactly constitutes 'analysis' of the texts, performances and discourses of popular music too often goes without saying. Indeed, the very idea of musical analysis has often been disparaged or defended as though it inevitably implies the deployment of ready-made models that had originally been designed to demonstrate the supremacy of German instrumental music or the underlying coherence of jarring modernisms. But basic questions of analytical method deserve to be continually rethought, since interpreting

Portions and earlier versions of this chapter were delivered as invited talks at the Claremont Graduate School, the University of California, Riverside, the University of Colorado, Northeastern University, Brandeis University, SUNY-Buffalo, the University of Girona, the University of Valencia, Gothenburg University, the University of Hong Kong, the University of Melbourne and the University of Munich, as well as at conferences of the American Musicological Society and the International Association for the Study of Popular Music (US Branch), the Cross(over) Relations conference at the Eastman School of Music, and the Discord conference at UCLA. I am grateful for the invitations to speak and for the productive dialogue that followed in each case. I would like to thank David Ake, Robert Fink, Susan McClary and Mitchell Morris for their helpful comments on the written version of this chapter; I am solely responsible for any faults they may have charitably overlooked.

1 Charles Darwin in a letter of 1861, quoted in Zinn (1990: xvii).

the musical texts and activities upon which pleasures and powers of popular music depend ought to constitute one of the central activities of popular music studies. And yet much of the popular music analysis that has been appearing lately simply applies methods that were developed for very different repertoires, without much explicit concern about the fit. This chapter is written in suspension, out of dissatisfaction with the recent burgeoning of formalist approaches to popular music analysis, on the one hand, and on the other, the conviction that despite the importance of scholarship that investigates other topics (the music industry, technology, criticism, artists, audiences), 'the study of popular music', as Susan McClary once put it, 'should also include the study of popular music' (McClary 1994: 38).[2] What follows are some reflections on the situation of musical analysis in popular music studies, a set of ten proposed axioms or aphorisms that might help generate some interesting new analyses, and a set of four analytical sketches of fairly recent popular songs.

Disciplines and values

Joseph Kerman predicted in 1985 that the most interesting areas for future music research would be found where disciplines compete for territory (Kerman 1985: 15). I doubt that he had popular music in mind, but the interdisciplinary community of popular music studies has come to exemplify perfectly his prediction. Over several decades, and particularly since the founding of the International Association for the Study of Popular Music in 1981, the academic study of popular music has evolved from a cramped and furtive enterprise, wedged in between jingoistic defenders of high culture and pathologists of adolescent deviance, into something exciting, ambitious and conflicted. The field can boast a top-notch scholarly journal, *Popular Music*, along with several contenders, as well as increasing visibility in less specialized journals across several disciplines.

Many debates over method and value within popular music studies stem from its mixed heritage: from sociology, Parsonian models that present the world as too static and unconflicted, and scholarship as too naïvely

---

2 See also McClary and Walser (1990). At present, our field is strikingly different in this respect from the study of the printed word, where many more scholars analyze printed texts than analyze the printing industry.

objective;[3] from music theory, formalist analytical methods that inevitably yield ahistorical results; from musicology, an inferiority complex that makes such methods tempting, as well as positivist research models; from English departments, a readiness to push aside the specific details, techniques and relationships of musical texts (however unthinkable it would be to do that with verbal texts); from ethnomusicology, the tendency to regard technologies and mediations as distortions of something more 'authentic', rather than as parts of the conditions of cultural creativity;[4] from fandom, the intensely felt desire for authenticity as compensation for the feeling that nothing escapes commerce; from rock criticism, the imperative to decide what is cool, what sucks, what to buy and recommend.

IASPM maintains valuable lines of communication, yet it has been a fractious society; its rocky history can usefully be understood in terms of struggle among those factions whose primary objects of analysis are texts, institutions and people. A number of scholars have been working to undermine this methodological separation by taking notes seriously – as traces of social activities.[5] Such work blurs the lines among historical, analytical and ethnographic approaches arguing, in effect, that musical texts and practices

3 Sociologists should be credited, though, with having studied popular music first, decades ago, because they weren't worried about whether popular music was 'art'; they knew it was socially important.

4 See Martin Stokes's chapter in this book [ed.]. Ethnomusicologists have long been suspended between openness to all musics (particularly those that have been neglected by Eurocentric musicology) and a queasiness about mass mediation. This is changing with, among other developments, the rise of 'urban ethnomusicology', which treats mediations and interactions as normal aspects of culture rather than as corruptions of autonomous traditions. Recently, ethnomusicologists have usefully championed ethnography within popular music studies; still, the discipline's principled opposition to ethnocentrism has had the corollary effect of disabling, except in a few exceptional cases, discussions of value and detailed analysis of musical texts. The best known of those exceptions would probably be Chernoff (1979), Seeger (1987) and Feld (1990). In this context, it's worth noting that none of these three scholars was trained primarily as an ethnomusicologist.

5 This approach owes much to the influence of Christopher Small and George Lipsitz, as well as to scholars of classical music who have developed new approaches to analysis, such as Susan McClary and Lawrence Kramer. In addition to these writers, I would suggest that the most successful examples of this sort of work have been produced by Richard Middleton, Philip Tagg, Susan Fast, Alf Björnberg, my colleagues Mitchell Morris and Robert Fink, and David Brackett.

are just as complex, and just as historically situated, as people are. But there are many conceptual and practical barriers before this sort of analysis, some of them quite recently erected.

For instance, two of popular music's most influential scholars have recently presented arguments that stand squarely in the way of attempts to develop popular music analyses that are both specific and consequential. Simon Frith's most recent book, *Performing Rites*, raises what he calls 'the value problem in cultural studies' (1996: 3). Frith argues that as cultural studies has taken up a wider range of texts for its cultural analysis – advertising, Madonna, comic books – scholars have lost sight of, or avoided, questions of value. In particular, he charges that many of us have neglected the importance of the arguments about value that take place among fans and critics. In effect, Frith argues that popular music deserves the sorts of aesthetic distinctions that are taken for granted in discussions of more elite forms of culture. Even more than that, he contends that we must establish value in order to be able to convince others to listen to what we like: 'If, in my own cultural practice, I prefer... Meat Loaf to U2, shouldn't I be prepared to argue the case for my values? Shouldn't I *want* other people... to listen to Meat Loaf rather than U2? Shouldn't I be able to persuade them...?' (1996: 16).

Frith's appeal should sound familiar to music scholars: he has just reinvented music appreciation, whereby people who have greater authority, cultural capital or rhetorical skills (teachers, critics) tell others (students, fans) what they ought to be listening to (classical music, authentic rock) according to a single scale of value. The presumption is that what they should be hearing is somehow better for them, although it is rare to find anyone attempting to explain just how or why this improvement will take place. Since Frith limits his concern to what he thinks people should be listening to, without examining the moral and ethical commitments that underpin such choices, his is not really a discourse of value as much as it is a discourse of power.[6] If, as Kerman alleged in a famous critique of formalism, 'analysis exists for the purpose of demonstrating organicism, and organicism exists for

---

6 As Virgil Thomson once characterized such a conflation of value and power, 'the German tradition is a perfectly good one, of course, as you can tell by all of the big names that are associated with it' (Thomson 1981: 128); the logic of this relationship is circular because it can be, given the economy of prestige within which it operates.

the purpose of validating a certain body of works of art' (Kerman 1980: 315), it seems that much journalistic criticism and academic work alike, however different their methods, exist for the same purposes.

Among the questions I want to raise here are whether the arguments of rock fans and critics provide the ideal model for what scholars should be doing, and whether the advocacy mission of music appreciation is the best model for cultural analysis and historical understanding. Frith quite rightly attacks the dominant model of cultural hierarchy, but I would argue that he's going the wrong way: instead of aestheticizing popular music, we should be historicizing all music and accounting in each case for the particular pleasures that are offered and thus for the values on which they depend and to which they appeal.

Even more fundamental to the problem of value, however, is the problem of signification. In *Performing Rites*, Frith credits my book *Running with the Devil* (Walser 1993) with having produced 'a wholly convincing musicological explanation' of how heavy metal musicians compose and perform. Yet, he wonders, do all of these technical details – modes, rhythms, timbres, harmonic progressions – tell us anything about what listeners experience? (Frith 1996: 64). Despite the fact that the book's analysis of heavy metal meanings was grounded in interviews with fans and musicians, analysis of the discourse of fans and critics, and historical accounts of musical signification, Frith remains unconvinced; he is essentially distrustful of music analysis.

That attitude is shared by cultural studies scholar Lawrence Grossberg, who writes that to understand rock music, 'it is necessary to explore effects that are not necessarily signifying, that do not necessarily involve the transmission, production, structuration, or even deconstruction of meaning' (Grossberg 1990: 113). One might mean by such a statement merely that we must understand musical signs within the social locations of the music and the people who are involved with it, but that's not Grossberg's point; he means to deny the operation of musical discourse. Not displaying any grasp of how musicians learn to produce affective responses through their negotiation of shared codes, he leaps to this:

> without the mediation of meaning, the sheer volume and repetitive rhythms of rock and roll produce a real material pleasure for its fans (at many live

concerts, the vibration actually might be compared to the use of a vibrator, often focused on the genital organs)....   (1990: 113)

No statement could better illustrate the need for musicologists to partici-pate in popular music studies. If we don't take seriously the technical and interpretive statements of musicians and music analysts, we're likely to end up mystifying music and dismissing musicological discussions as academic obfuscations. Such explanations – 'without the mediation of meaning' – ultimately trivialize and essentialize popular music and those who partici-pate in it, by implying that sounds work on selves that are unconstructed by culture, by not facing the question of why only some people get such pleasures (after all, not even vibrators produce pleasure for everyone).

Scholars outside music departments often mock the technical vocab-ulary musicologists use because they find it exclusive or unilluminating. This is partially due to the mysteriousness of musical signification for non-musicians – unlike language, music seems transparent, uncoded, not requiring translation. But it's partially our fault; as Alf Björnberg puts it:

> What in musicology is often termed 'analysis' often amounts to paraphrasing music-as-sound in some technical and formal symbolic language or other, the mastering of which requires special training. Such formal languages have been developed partly with the aim to invest musical analysis with an appearance of scientific 'objectivity', rather than 'mere' hermeneutic interpretation.   (Björnberg 1998)[7]

As Björnberg suggests, musicologists need to consider carefully the tools and goals that they have inherited from previous analysts if they want to produce illuminating accounts of how popular music works and what it means.

But analyze we must. Whatever else they do, neither Frith nor Grossberg offers us new ways of understanding how musical discourse articulates social meanings and produces particular pleasures; indeed, they imply that these are not useful or practical goals. In contrast, I argue that any cultural anal-ysis of popular music that leaves out musical sound, that doesn't explain why people are drawn to certain sounds specifically and not others, is at

---

7 This line of thought was acutely articulated in Kerman's (1980) earlier and broader critique of musical formalism.

least fundamentally incomplete.[8] Understanding of cultural pleasures is an unavoidable precondition to understanding social relations, identities, structures and forces, so we might as well confront the issue head-on: we are, despite the proverb, in the business of accounting for taste.

Ten apothegms

The methodological divisions and conflicts that have been affecting popular music studies (as well as musicology and cultural studies more broadly) have prompted the following ten apothegms. Despite their declarative tone, they are meant to be heuristic rather than authoritative, useful more than definitive. The test of their utility is simply whether they can lead to more illuminating analyses of popular music. The wording of the apothegms is mine, but the ideas have been stolen, derived, developed and twisted from the work of many other people, some of whom are acknowledged explicitly in notes.[9]

1 It's okay to write about music

It is often said that 'writing about music is like dancing about architecture', to which I would reply that dancing about architecture might be very illuminating, if we all danced as much as we use language.[10] Many scholars continue to argue that we need new terms and technologies as means for gaining greater analytical rigour. Technical terms for musical procedures and details are useful, of course, but we may not need as much jargon as we might

8 Such cultural analysis abounds, often in sophisticated form. A very recent example: 'This chapter has argued that the Yanni phenomenon is not primarily a musical one (based on artistic or aesthetic factors) but rather a socio-cultural and commercial phenomenon based on the mercantile, performative and cultural logics of twentieth-century capitalism. The Yanni phenomenon is partly a triumph of the commodification and technologisation of the exotic within the global cultural economy. It is also partly a triumph of the multi-media marketing of spectacle, privileging the ambience and formula over music *per se*' (Neuenfeldt 1999: 187). But can we really imagine that 'the Yanni phenomenon' would be unchanged in its scope and meanings if, for example, Yanni played electric guitar?
9 In particular, I'd like to acknowledge the impact upon my thinking of Small (1987), McClary (1991), Lipsitz (1990), Chernoff (1979), Lakoff and Johnson (1980), Marcus and Fischer (1986) and the writings of Seeger (1977 and 1994).
10 This anti-criticism apothegm is sometimes attributed to Elvis Costello, sometimes to Thelonius Monk.

suppose if we are to go beyond labelling to interpretation. Moreover, technical analysis hasn't made much progress in dealing with certain aspects of musical experience: how can we describe, let alone account for, such essential things as compelling qualities of motion or particularly affecting timbres? One answer is that we already have tools that we're not using as skilfully as we might. We have language, which is, like music, an incredibly powerful and nuanced system for making sense of things and communicating our understandings.

2 Unlike language, music often seems not to require translation

We don't imagine that we understand someone who is speaking a language with which we have no familiarity, but music can more easily be understood as interpretable within one's own discursive competency. We often hear unfamiliar musical systems as not having system at all, or as warped versions of the systems we know. That is why music enables great understandings and misunderstandings across cultural boundaries. This phenomenon is both a caution for analysis and an object for it.

3 Musical judgements can never be dismissed as subjective; neither can they ever be celebrated as objective

Since subjects are formed in culture, all understandings are intersubjective; since there is no way to stand outside cultural understandings, there can be no Archimedean objectivity. Thus we must work all the time with interpretations – our sense of what things mean and why they are the way they are. Musical interpretations are always open to refinement and contestation, but they are never arbitrary, and there is no way to avoid committing interpretation. So we work for the most illuminating ones, drawing upon our knowledge of history and of how music works and signifies. There is no one point of perfect perspective, and we can learn from other people, times and cultures so as to expand our individual understanding.[11]

---

11 Many philosophers and other scholars have developed critiques of objectivity. For my purposes, the most pertinent have been Lakoff and Johnson (1980) on objectivity; Marcus and Fisher (1986) on juxtaposition and Bakhtin (1981) on dialogism.

4 The split between musicology and ethnomusicology is no longer useful because its constitutive dichotomies – self/other, Western/non-Western, art/function, history/ethnography, and text/practice – are no longer defensible

What was once a progressive attempt to undermine ethnocentrism and elitism now reinscribes too many disabling binaries.[12] According to the implicit terms of this split, ninth-century French monks are 'us', while contemporary salsa musicians are 'others'. To be sure, many ethnomusicologists now define their field not by its objects but by its methods, in particular ethnography. The strength of ethnography is that it can teach us different perspectives, but because none of us understands fully the complex cultural forces and resources that have formed us, ethnography is as limited as any other scholarly technique. We seldom learn to be consciously analytical and articulate about the things that are most important to us, the things we take for granted, the things that seem natural. These limits imply that we should avoid fetishizing ethnography in ethnomusicology or any form of popular music studies.

5 Analysis is a relational activity; its success is relative to its goals, which analysts should feel obliged to make clear

As Darwin put it, 'all observation must be for or against some view'. Any analysis presupposes a host of choices that have been made by the analyst: what is worth studying? Which of its features are constitutive of its generic identity, uniqueness or efficacy? Why and how do the music and the analysis matter? Explicit answers to these questions are most successfully avoided when the legitimating presence of a powerful paradigm seems to obviate them. But all scholarship is dialogic, so analyses are invariably responses to other analyses or to their absence within particular intellectual communities.

12 As Charles Seeger put it forty years ago: 'All music is in culture so why do we need a term like "ethnomusicology"? The reason is that historians have hijacked the proper term, "musicology". Yet they study a very narrow band of world music and only part of that ... We had no choice but to use the title we now have, but we have patterned our constitution and organization on that of the American Musicological Society and when semantic sanity returns we must merge the two groups' (Seeger 1959: 101–2). See also Seeger 1961: 77–80 and 1970: 171–210.

24

6 The split between musicology and music theory has never been useful because its constitutive dichotomy – culture/structure – has never been defensible

People make music; it's something that they do. 'Structure' is a spatial metaphor that we often use to describe events that are experienced temporally. It has no real existence and it is a useful way of thinking only so long as we remember the people and the experiences. (See also apothegm 10.)[13]

7 Analysis is inevitably reductive, which is precisely why it's useful

Analysis maps, and like any map, it reduces and abstracts in order to show particular relationships more clearly. Two-dimensional maps cannot accurately represent three-dimensional surfaces; so too with prose mappings of music. Still, maps are useful because they conceal certain relationships in order to reveal others. All maps are drawn to serve specific purposes, to show relationships at a particular scale. Seemingly passive descriptions can be usefully understood as examples of analyses that conceal their purposes and goals.

8 'Popular music' and 'classical music' cannot be compared in terms of value because these categories are interdependent and actively reproduced

As a great deal of scholarship in cultural history has shown, cultural genres are always polemical rather than natural.[14] Moreover, both 'classical'

---

13 Some of the essays collected in Covach and Boone (1997), for example, proceed as though the music they discuss existed in a world that contained only musicians and analysts, none of whom have noticed the historical constructedness and conflictedness of that world.

14 There is an extensive and, within musicology and popular music studies alike, too little-known body of scholarship on the development of cultural hierarchy. See especially Levine (1988 and 1996), Jameson (1979), DiMaggio (1982a and 1982b), Huyssen (1986), Eagleton (1990) and Sieburth (1994).
    DiMaggio documents how urban elites in New England worked to isolate a high culture and to differentiate it from a popular culture during the last half of the nineteenth century. In so doing, they built themselves a private refuge from a world that was being transformed by new technologies and new immigrations, defining a new type of culture, and creating institutions to control its legitimacy. Levine shows how class conflict stimulated that elite's desire for a prestigious body of culture that would fix their own values as universal truths. Just as the growing materialism of an industrializing capitalist society helped develop the

and 'popular' repertoires contain too much heterogeneity to be stable. What internal features unite Gregorian chant, a Beethoven symphony, and the music of John Cage, or, on the other side, Stephen Foster, Little Richard, and Trent Reznor? The work of Lawrence W. Levine and others demonstrates that cultural hierarchy cannot be explained in terms of the internal features of texts or practices; 'the popular' is not defined by simplicity, shallowness, immorality or ephemerality, but by social processes of prescription and negotiation in the service of competing interests. Such findings have been confirmed by numerous studies focusing on how particular texts or practices (jazz, opera, film, the novel) move up or down the ladder of cultural prestige.[15]

9 'Twentieth-century music' is the music that twentieth-century people have made and heard

This problem mainly exists within university music departments, but it shapes them profoundly. It should be regarded as amazing, even scandalous, that the major textbooks that are used for courses in twentieth-century music do not even attempt to explain their exclusion of the vast majority of music that has been performed and heard during the twentieth century, even within the geographical areas they address; some do not even acknowledge that exclusionary choices were made.[16] The problem of determining

ideology of aesthetic autonomy, the problem of authority in social life 'found idealized resolution', as George Lipsitz puts it, 'in cultural practices that affirmed the supremacy of texts over contexts and art over audiences' (Lipsitz 1991: 520). William Weber (1977) has explained how this process began in Vienna early in the nineteenth century. See also Goehr (1992).

15 Those who object to the inclusion of popular music studies in the academy, either because they feel it disrupts a great and timeless tradition or because they fear its debasing effects, should recall how transient and negotiable our canons and curricula are. Levine (1996) reminds us that one hundred years ago, advocates of the Greek and Latin curriculum attacked those who pressed for the inclusion of English literature, including Shakespeare, which they saw as a threat to the seriousness of higher education. He points out that for most of the nineteenth century, courses in the sciences and in modern languages were unavailable for credit at the best US colleges, as were for the most part history courses.

On cultural hierarchy and popular music, see Tomlinson (1991), Gabbard (1993), Walser (1992 and 1999). All of this work makes indefensible the common distinction between 'commercial' and 'art' musics.

16 See Morgan (1991), Antokoletz (1992), Watkins (1988), Machlis (1979) and Simms (1986). Morgan mentions jazz, folk and popular musics, but says only that they have been excluded because of space constraints. Watkins remarks that 'some readers will note the omission of a rigorous treatment of the vernacular or

26

whose twentieth century will be taught, given limited pedagogical space and time, is a serious one, and we can no longer pretend that the answer is simple or obvious. Our textbooks record not any reasonable history of twentieth-century music but rather the history that some composers and musicologists wish had happened.

10 You only have the problem of connecting music and society if you've separated them in the first place

When analysts discuss musical texts, what usually goes unremarked is the tremendous cultural work that is required to textualize musical practices. What is patently a mode of human interaction that is enabled by particular histories and cultural ground is remade into an object with 'internal' properties. Texts are talismans of a lost provenance, the context of desires and dialogue that made their existence possible and meaningful. If that context is understood, a text can be analyzed as a kind of human utterance, in dialogue with other utterances.

Profound simplicity

By way of exploring some of the implications of these ideas, I want to examine briefly four contrasting recordings, all of which were released around the same time, 1991–92. Much more could be said than I will say here about all four, in terms of both the conventions they exemplify and the

jazz traditions that in recent decades has [sic] increasingly vied for the attention of the music historian. Partial redress is offered, however, in the repeated consideration of such repertoires for the composer of art music' (pp. xvii–xviii), which does not really explain anything. Machlis and Antokoletz say almost nothing about the choices they have made. Simms says nothing at the beginning of his book; at the end, the Beatles, Laurie Anderson, and the relation of popular music to minimalism fill two pages (including the startling observation on page 421 that Anderson's music 'relies upon sounds of the jungle').
   Despite the challenging precedent of Austin (1966), which included jazz among the musical styles it covered, as well as later work by Charles Hamm, Wiley Hitchcock and other music historians, these more recent authors (the majority of whom are composers by profession) still tend to take it for granted that 'music' can be used as shorthand of the scores of American and European modernist composers, and even that 'our' culture is modernism. Morgan makes this last point explicitly in his odd celebration of the 'pluralism' that exists outside 'our' culture in his introduction to Morgan 1998: 3–4.

things that make them distinctive. My purpose is not to produce analyses that even pretend to be exhaustive; the four have been chosen because of the musical contrasts they present and the different issues they raise.

My first example is 'Feed Jake', a country hit song and video of 1991 that helped the musicians who recorded it, Pirates of the Mississippi, win an award from the Academy of Country Music as the Top New Group of 1991. The lyrics relate the thoughts of a man on his deathbed whose last wish is that his beloved dog, Jake, be taken care of when he is gone. It is a song that is easily dismissed, because sentimentality is often mocked, however strong its hold on us might sometimes be. 'Feed Jake' also seems to offer little purchase for analysis, with its standard verse/chorus form, generic instrumentation, and conventional harmonies.

The song's form could be easily diagrammed, of course, which might give us a useful sense of its narrative progression, of how a listener experiences moving through time with the series of events it offers. This sort of imaginative work is, ironically, a mainstay of even the most resolutely 'objective' musical analysis, and it is often very illuminating to use form as spatial metaphor with which to represent temporal experience. In this case, though, identifying a series of verses, choruses, and other parts will not do a great deal to help us understand why many people found this song powerful. Similarly, a diagram that labels the chords that are used will not shed much light, except that it would confirm what we can already hear: that the song relies upon a concise and familiar chordal vocabulary (I, IV, V, VI, with many plagal and authentic cadences) to produce effects of plainness and clarity of direction. That this does not seem remarkable in itself should not distract us from realizing that it may be a crucial constituent of the song's coherent signification.

It is hard for analysts to resist seeking complexity (descrying and accounting for various kinds of complexity would seem to be the very purpose of analysis, after all), and if we are to satisfy that urge, we must look to other parameters than form and harmony – timbre, for example. The singer's voice is one that has been cultivated and presented so as to seem uncultivated and unmediated. We've heard this sort of voice before, from Bruce Springsteen among many others, and its power lies in its projection of sincerity, honesty, directness. A chorus of other voices chimes in periodically, affirming, as choruses so often do, that the singer's insights and feelings are widely shared. An

acoustic guitar provides the most prominent instrumental backing and contributes its own related associations: seemingly non-technological, used more
by placid folk musicians than raucous rockers, perhaps rural, it is congruent
with the vocals and supports them. So is the recording's straightforward,
economical bass playing, and its near lack of drums, which helps keep its
overall quality of motion gentle. But not every aspect is that simple: in addition to the acoustic guitar, we eventually hear a chorused electric guitar with
slight distortion, pedal steel guitar, and an orchestral string section. Strings
are often used in popular music as a means of adding poignancy, grandeur
or affective depth, and the pedal steel swells, fades and slides, modelling the
way emotions feel.

The pre-chorus and chorus contain the lyrics' most vivid imagery:

Now I lay me down to sleep
I pray the Lord my soul to keep
If I die before I wake
Feed Jake
He's been a good dog
My best friend, right through it all
If I die before I wake
Feed Jake

For many listeners, these lyrics invoke a childhood prayer – except that the
fourth line should be 'I pray the Lord my soul to take', not 'Feed Jake'. The
song exploits this bit of memory as its music supports and frames the nostalgic, familial, earnest tone of the prayer. That a revered collective memory
and such powerful semiotic weaponry have been deployed on behalf of a dog
might strike a listener as incongruous; it would be easy to dismiss the song
as trivial sentimentality, as cheap manipulation. But its power comes from
its invocation and musical dramatization of the most serious of issues. The
song's fundamental message is a plea on behalf of caring for others, and it
more specifically addresses these issues and values: fear of mortality, com-
passion, loyalty, danger faced bravely, hope of virtue rewarded. If we don't
recognize how the song invokes and appeals to these emotions and values, we
haven't analyzed it at all. No matter what else is done, with whatever sorts of
diagrams and technical terms, to stop short of reaching this level of analysis
is to produce only a partial description of certain abstracted features of the
performance, one that does not explain why people have been moved by it.

29

There is much more that could be said about those features, of course. We might dwell on the deft use of poignant 4–3 suspensions, on how the singer places his lyrics with rhythmic and accentual nuance, or on the pauses that occasionally interrupt the steady pace of the song – moments to reflect, or to draw a breath and prepare to go on. Once when I discussed this song during a public lecture, someone who turned out to be a bluegrass musician pointed out that the acoustic guitar playing that I had described as simple was in fact quite a complicated bit of finger-picking. It makes sense that this musician's attention was drawn to the subtlety of the guitar-playing, for which considerable craft was required. But that doesn't contradict the purposes for which that skill was deployed – the impression of honesty and directness it helped produce, its intensification of the sentiment that is invoked by the narrator's story and his prayer. Such challenges can strengthen analyses, when different ways of hearing music are accommodated. They underscore the fact that meanings are not random, yet the complexity of culture renders them not always predictable.

Fearing semiotics

The same bit of collective memory appears in another popular recording of 1991, Metallica's 'Enter Sandman'. We hear again that four-line prayer, this time growled by a low male voice and repeated, line by line, by a little boy. But the musical setting is strikingly different: heavily distorted guitars play power chords and percussive riffs, powerful drums lead a precise ensemble through a tight groove to unpredictable punches, a menacing vocalist sketches paranoid imagery, sometimes with the gravity of a funereal chorale doubled in parallel octaves; a guitar solo seems to scramble in futility for escape. The affect is grim, with not only a minor mode but Phrygian riffs that emphasize the claustrophobic relationship of the tonic and the flat-second scale degree.[17] A sudden key change, up a half-step at the end of each verse, adds to the tension. Unlike the gentle motion of 'Feed Jake', we experience a frantic but rigidly controlled drive towards the choruses:

17 On scrambling guitar solos, Phrygian claustrophobia, and the dialectics of control and freedom in heavy metal, see the more extensive discussions in Walser (1993).

30

Exit light
Enter night
Take my hand
Off to never-never land

The prayer appears here as an interlude, and the music frames and inflects it with drastically different effect. The scene is literally nightmarish; the boy seems forced to repeat the four lines, each of which has new implications suddenly revealed. The same bit of memory that was comforting in 'Feed Jake' becomes frightening, even morbid, in the dark world of 'Enter Sandman'. It is the latter setting that resonates most with my own experience as a boy: parts of summer vacations spent sleeping alone on the second floor of my grandparents' farm house, down the hall from rooms where people I'd never known had once lived and died; repeating, just before the lights went out, the lines of that prayer as my grandmother led me through them; thinking about dying before I wake; terrified. An analysis of a song such as this should, among many other things, grapple with how this prayer's deployment and contextualization depend upon musical semiotics so as to produce meanings that differ drastically from those of the preceding song. Even though our experiences of such shared bits of culture vary, music can be used to inflect and articulate such memories so as to produce vastly different evocations of seemingly simple material.

Is it good to have violent music?

Ice Cube mobilizes different sorts of complexity in his 1992 release 'When Will They Shoot?' The song prominently incorporates samples of previous music by Queen, The Watts 103rd Street Band, and X-Clan, so Ice Cube is in dialogue with these artists, their contexts, their audiences. He assumes of his listeners a particular kind of cultural literacy: if you don't catch the references, you can't hear the relationships. In addition to the effects of quotation, the harmonic conflict that results when songs in different keys are combined helps construct a noisy, urban soundscape of layers and clashing discourses. Turntable scratching contributes yet another layer of rhythmic intricacy and deliberate noisiness. The ponderous beat of the Queen sample is familiar from its use to underpin the chanting of crowds at sports events, and it similarly evokes collective determination here.

Ice Cube must shout to be heard above all this, yet as with most such music, much could be said about the rhythmic and linguistic virtuosity of his rapping, as he deftly phrases with and against the emphatic points of the groove.[18] In his lyrics, Ice Cube's main topic is racism; he denounces racist politicians such as David Duke and Uncle Sam, comparing himself to Malcolm X and John F. Kennedy as an outspoken critic whose life may be endangered.[19] He rejects the label 'African American' and mocks those who seem not to understand why racist violence provokes angry resistance. Other voices confirm his statements by reacting to them in something less formal, more overlapping, than straight call-and-response. Ice Cube is a rhetorician, delivering a verbal message of resistance, strength and craft through musical means that communicate those same qualities.

Songs such as 'When Will They Shoot?' often seem to provoke the question 'is it good to have such violent music?' with debates over censorship typically following as the answer. But that's the wrong question for musical/cultural analysis. In order to understand why these sounds have been arranged in this particular way, we must understand the context within which their composition seemed meaningful and urgent. That context is a place, the United States, at a time when the rate of infant mortality for African-American children is twice what it is for white children, and child poverty is three times as severe. Black youth unemployment quadrupled during the period between 1965 and 1990, while white youth unemployment was static. The level of violent crime is virtually identical for black and white populations, but three times as many black people are arrested for committing the same crimes. 13 per cent of US Americans are black, and 13 per cent of drug users are black, yet African Americans somehow earn 43 per cent of the drug felony convictions and serve 78 per cent of the prison time for such offences.[20]

---

18 On the virtuosity of rapping and its relation to grooves, see Walser (1995).
19 He also touches, in contradictory ways, on the subject of gender, bragging that a black woman is his manager but endorsing the motto 'treat 'em like a prostitute'.
20 See Lipsitz (1994: 18–19) and Wideman (1995); statistics vary slightly from study to study, but the overall picture is clear. On enduring differences in wealth as a cause of disparities between black and white portions of the population, see Oliver and Shapiro (1995). See also Lipsitz (1998), especially Chapter 1, and DeMott (1995).

Instead of censorship, demonization or hand-wringing about whether it is a good thing for us to have violent music, we might better ask whether it is a good thing to have social conditions to which violent music is an obvious and reasonable response. Such 'sociological' information is often taken to be quite distant from the concerns of musical analysis. But knowledge of these conditions of poverty and injustice is absolutely essential, because without it, the analyst cannot possibly understand why this music has taken the form it has.

Killing Kenny G

If it is sometimes simply assumed that violent music breeds violent actions while calm music ennobles, then one of the most striking counter-examples is saxophonist Kenny G, whose soothing music has often been denounced in the most vicious terms. When a newspaper columnist solicited reactions to the prediction that a giant asteroid would slam into the earth in 2028, Kenny G showed up in his readers' responses. One 'sought to make the best of a disastrous situation by having Michael Bolton and Kenny G duct-taped to the top of Mt. Everest so they'd be "the first to go."' Another suggested: 'Obliterate the asteroid with a kamikaze spacecraft carrying Kenny G, John Tesh, Alanis Morissette and assorted daytime talk-show hosts' (Rivenburg 1998). In another context, an angry reader protested a paper's coverage: 'To call the shit that comes out of Kenny G's horn "music" is an insult to music lovers everywhere. The old joke used to be: "Use an accordion, go to jail." It should be amended to: "Use a soprano sax, die by lethal injection!" It's the only humane thing to do' (Matteson 1998).

An innocent query about what sort of equipment Kenny G uses to produce his distinctive sound, posted to the 'Classicsax' internet discussion list, provoked this exchange (original spellings preserved):

'As a "classical" saxophonist, allow me to say that I find Kenny G to be Abhorrent and quite nasty. His technical abilities are nihl, his tone is bad, and all in all I think he sucks.'

'ALRIGHT, THIS IS REALLY GONNA PISS EVERYONE OFF BUT I DON'T CARE COLTRAIN, BIRD, DEXTER AND MOST OTHER JAZZ

SAXOPHONISTS SOUND LIKE A GOOSE THATS BEEN CAUGHT IN A
GARBAGE DISPOSAL.'

'Why are people talking about Kenny G on classicsax???!!?? He can't play
sax... And as for those comments on Bird and trane... I hope you burn in
hell. . . .'

'hmmmm sure is pretty famous and RICH for someone who can't play a sax
correctly...'

'so is bill clinton'[21]

What is most striking about these comments is their presumption. Classical
saxophone playing is an enterprise that is only tenuously established in the
academy, and for good reason: it exists nowhere else, and it has virtually no
audience beyond the players themselves. That classical sax players could dare
to muster scorn for artists such as John Coltrane, Charlie Parker and Dexter
Gordon reveals much about the power of music education to naturalize
particular musical techniques and senses of entitlement without any outside
corroboration. It seems to go without saying that Kenny G is not a good sax
player; even those who eschew violent imagery speak of, for example, 'fairly
mediocre skills as a saxophonist', which are used to produce 'a long lineup
of soupy ballads, played with quivering emotionalism by G's thin-toned
soprano and tenor saxophones' (Heckman 1996: 6).

As a sax player myself, I think it's clear that Kenny G's worth cannot
be decided at the level of technique; he is in fact a virtuoso of a particular kind. His intonation is flawless, even on the treacherous soprano sax.
He plays flurries of notes with tremendous technical precision. He controls his instruments perfectly, doing with them exactly what he wants to
do, particularly in the difficult altissimo register. He plays ornaments on
his ornaments, with nuances on his nuances; it's not surprising to learn
that he practices for three to five hours every day (Cole 1992: 22).[22] Yet
he is scorned and disparaged to a degree that few musicians have ever

21 http://www.classicsax.com/wwwboard/instrmessages; 'Re: "Kenny G" Sound',
posted May and June 1998; *sic* throughout.
22 Sympathetic posters on the classicsax discussion list have made some of the same
comments about Kenny G's technique that I make here. Some opponents then
counter by claiming that there is no 'emotion' in Kenny G's playing; others say
that the problem is that there is nothing but emotion. See, for example,
http://209.86.235.52/wwwboard/jmessages/879.html, posted 26 June 1999.

experienced: perhaps the problem is not with techniques but rather with sensibilities.

A good example of Kenny G's approach is 'The Joy of Life' (1992), the opening track of his album *Breathless*, the best-selling instrumental album in history. Throughout, care in crafting melodies is obvious, as he describes his compositional process:

> Then I ask, 'Should I end the verse here, or is it a bunch of notes, or does it continue to represent the theme of the song?' I will do it again and again to make the song that moves emotionally in the right way.   (Cole 1992: 24)

The mode is major with occasional bluesy touches; Kenny G's sound is smooth and his lines sinuous and seamless. He approaches high notes sensitively, often backing away as he ascends; he swells and fades and throbs with no trace of force, no pushiness; he quivers and soars. Digital reverb creates a warm, sensuous acoustic space for his utterances.

In terms of radio station genres, Kenny G is usually classed as 'Smooth Jazz', which currently has the fastest-growing advertising revenues of any format (Michaelson 1996; see also Kohlhasse 1997). The genre developed in the late 1960s and 1970s with musicians such as George Benson, Herb Alpert, Pat Metheny and Spyro Gyra, but it wasn't until the later success of Kenny G, Sade, Toni Braxton, Anita Baker, and other artists that a dedicated radio outlet developed for such music. Beginning in 1987 with KTWV in Los Angeles, the format has spread to over seventy stations in the United States, with a targeted audience of twenty-five- to fifty-four-year olds who, according to DJ Don Burns, seek soothing compensation in a troubled world, music that is 'comfortable', 'friendly', 'healthy' (Michaelson 1996). Kenny G's music is also popular in South America, Australia, Europe and particularly Asia, where his emphasis on smooth melodies fits well with dominant pop styles (Pride 1993).

Many jazz musicians and critics particularly despise Kenny G and, although their condemnations are usually couched in terms of technique, I think the real issue is sensibility. To be sure, part of the reason is that many people have come to associate the term 'jazz' with Kenny G and similar musicians; if he is counted as 'jazz', he is easily its biggest current star, which makes many feel that he has hijacked the label. Certainly there is resentment of his disproportionate financial success; he is easily positioned as another in the long string of white musicians who have grown rich by taking advantage of the fact that in a racist society, audiences often reward those who can deliver black music without the black people in it. Still, black 'smooth jazz' musicians such as Grover Washington have achieved great commercial success, and a complex history of cultural interactions makes defining 'black music' tricky. Moreover, 'smooth jazz' has the most integrated playlists of any radio format.

More to the point is that for people who want jazz to follow the model of John Coltrane – who is revered by many jazz musicians as perhaps the most important model for modern jazz – music is supposed to be adventurous, struggling, perhaps alienated. Miles Davis spoke of having played 'searching music' during the 1960s (Davis and Troupe 1989: 272). Kenny G, I would suggest, offers 'finding music'; there's no need to search for something better, because you're already there, in a warm, nuanced, free and secure acoustic space.[23] Yet if Coltrane and others have profoundly shaped jazz, has all jazz been searching music? Is 'The Joy of Life' so distant in affect from *Sketches of Spain*? Is the latter not closer to Kenny G than it is to 'Giant Steps'? 'Finding' yourself in music was an explicit concern of the great early jazz musician Sidney Bechet, whom post-Coltrane jazz musicians generally find irrelevant (they may acknowledge him as an ancestor without being attracted to his sensibility). 'Finding' has gone out of fashion because a certain type of jazz has successfully laid claim to embody the essence of the whole, complex tradition. Arguments about Kenny G among jazz musicians and critics are arguments about what jazz has been, is, and should be.[24]

In a larger context, Kenny G raises the question of whether we can respect people who respect beauty. Is this music mindless affirmativity that blinds us to history, pain and power? Is it the case, as Adorno argued, that 'to be pleased means to say Yes', to acquiesce in your own oppression? (Horkheimer and Adorno 1986: 144).[25] One critic asked Kenny G if he was ever going to play any 'challenging music', to which he replied: 'My answer

---

23 It's worth noting that Kenny G's first professional gig was with Barry White, another master of 'finding', and someone who can hardly be excluded from 'black music' (Cole 1992: 22–4).

24 On tradition in jazz, see DeVeaux (1991), an excerpt of which appears, along with other materials which address this set of issues, in Walser (1999). See also Ake (1998).

25 This theme, along with the possibility of affirmative critique, runs through Adorno's cultural criticism.

is that there is nothing more challenging than playing two or three notes that can touch people emotionally' (Cole 1992: 22). Violent reactions to Kenny G's music, as well as graphic fantasies about his demise, surely betray a widespread cultural discomfort with, even contempt for, sensitivity. For many people, to admit to being moved by this music would seem to betray manipulation and emasculation – which is just what Adorno wrote about the jazz of Louis Armstrong (Adorno 1981).

Of the critical and empathetic stances an analyst might adopt, the former is always easier. But millions of people make love to Kenny G's music; it reassures, comforts, promotes tenderness. Empathetically read, Kenny G's music is also a critique: its particular kind of beauty is meaningful for many people because it protests a world of too little tenderness, not enough nuance, too few caresses. If every critique implies an alternative, every affirmation is also a critique; its power depends upon its ability to address and redress pain and lack.[26] Not every affirmation gestures towards a more just or peaceful society, of course, any more than every critique does. My purpose here (*pace* Simon Frith) is not to promote Kenny G; whether he suits my taste or I can convince others to listen to him is not what matters. But music analysts need to be able to account for a music's appeal, and simply to ignore or vilify Kenny G and his listeners does nothing to help us understand contemporary musical culture, in which he has such a prominent place.

Analysis and values

My four instances – Pirates of the Mississippi, Metallica, Ice Cube and Kenny G – are very different, and despite my attention to values, I am not at all interested in saying which piece of music is 'best'; in the absence of a specific context, that would be a parochial and unproductive distinction. Of course, as Frith argues, we need to understand how and why fans and critics argue about value. But it's not enough to learn to think like a fan; we ought to be in the business of music history, not music appreciation. That doesn't mean abandoning questions of value in pursuit of some kind

26 Both Lipsitz's work and Jameson's (1979) germinal article analyze how the reifying tendencies of commercial culture could find no purchase if they did not evoke utopian fantasies produced by real experiences of oppression and disenchantment.

of neutral objectivity, such as strictly formal analysis seems to promise, but rather embracing values as crucial aspects of analysis and rehabilitating the concept of objectivity as the principled consideration of intersubjectivity. As Lawrence Levine puts it:

> Objectivity does not necessitate detachment; it does not entail the abandonment of passion or the emasculation of ideals. It means simply and profoundly the ability to keep one's mind open and to allow one's powers of empathy to range widely. It means, above all, the desire to understand.
>
> (Levine 1993: 20)

In the end, I am arguing for a more anthropological conception of culture in popular music studies, a stronger sense of history (not only in terms of historicizing our own analytical activities but also in that few people who write about rock music draw upon the perspectives offered by familiarity with earlier music), and a conception of analysis that is self-reflexive about methods and goals, tactical rather than absolute, less interested in describing or legitimating than in understanding how music works and why people care about it.

As Darwin pointed out with his parable of the gravel-pit, analysis is relational and purposeful. Since there are no autonomous people, there are no autonomous data, analyses, or pieces of music. This is a simple idea, to be sure, but one that has unrealized transformative implications for popular music studies. Ultimately, judgements of music are judgements of people. Analysis is thus not about structure; it is about people, because people make and perceive structures. Our commitment should be not to a certain set of methods, but rather to investigating music as something people do, something that they are enabled to do by the set of conventions and possibilities we call culture. Analysis requires a bifocality of perspective: enough insider's knowledge and empathy to understand a music's power, and enough outsider's critical stance and historical perspective to locate and explain that power within a larger context.[27] Only by adopting such a complicated stance can we do justice to the human complexities that are registered in musical sounds.

---

27 Rock critics often have plenty of the former but little of the latter; for academics, the characteristic imbalance is the opposite. I take this notion of bifocality from Fischer (1986) and from George Lipsitz's development of it in 'Cruising around the Historical Bloc: Postmodernism and Popular Music in East Los Angeles' (1990: 133–60).

3   From lyric to anti-lyric: analyzing the words in pop song

DAI GRIFFITHS

Introduction

The 'safesurfer' of Julian Cope's song is someone who sleeps around 'like HIV ain't never coming down'.[1] The record turns round a commonplace of rock music: that in song, words give way to music, a voice's emotion, a guitar's virtuosity. 'Safesurfer' lets its instruments loose at beginning and end, enclosing this risk-taking gigolo's statements.[2] When it arrives, his rap is determinedly prosaic, hard speech: senseless ramblings which create nothing but foreboding for what is to follow in the song. As his speech turns to song, to melody, he gets real: 'You don't have to be afraid, love, 'cos I'm a safesurfer, darling'. But he isn't: he's lying, and the record blisters and blisses and bleeps without words to its fade.

The safesurfer rides a wave between emotion and truth: full of feeling he may be, but what someone listening to him needs to know is the fact of his experience. What bothers sociologists about the words of pop songs is any presupposition that songs 'have inherent meanings which can be objectively identified, that the meaning of lyrics can be defined independently of their music, and that such cultural messages are effectively transmitted and received'. Peter J. Martin: 'none of these assumptions is easy to defend' (Martin 1995: 264). Simon Frith, too, is keen to blur any assumption of direct transmission and reception of words: songs, he says at one point, 'provide people with the means to articulate the feelings associated with being in love' (Frith 1996: 164). But the inarticulate speech of the heart should hardly *prevent*

---

1 Julian Cope, sleeve note to *Peggy Suicide*.
2 The song lasts just over eight minutes: the voice enters just after 2'50" and disappears after 4'54".

our observing and understanding words. Otherwise, well, I'm a safesurfer, darling.

Talking about the words in pop songs has had a hard time.[3] 'To be blunt', declares Theodor Gracyk, assuredly, 'in rock music most lyrics don't matter very much'. Called as Gracyk's witness: Bob Dylan who, yes, once told an interviewer that 'whatever I do . . . it's not in the lyrics' (Gracyk 1996: 65, 63). But this is *Bob Dylan*, right, who has recorded well over 350 songs, their words as well as their music: seeing all that effort behind him in the practice of bringing together words and music, wouldn't you be wary of bringing Dylan to the dock?[4] Maybe this is just an exercise in separating primary and secondary sources, trusting artist or tale, working out the conditions of reference to song and interview.[5] But I think there's more: this is to do with non-musicians – people identifying themselves as working in aesthetics, sociology, cultural studies[6] – convincing themselves that, because there are clearly situations where the words don't matter in the slightest – classically, 'when you're dancing this hard'[7] – this is enough to avoid attending to the words altogether. The rejection is compounded by a refusal to attend to music: songs without words are one thing; songs with neither words nor music are curious things indeed. However, a lot of ordinary talk about pop music depends on the words: to adapt Frith, words provide us with a means to articulate a response to the song. Also, people in some simple sense know the words: I have a tape of Oasis performing at Knebworth on which an audience in the dozens of thousands sings along with *every word of every song*. If sociologists have complicated reasons for suspicion and avoidance, for musicologists words are alien territory: they, one senses, have so many

3 The best writer on the general issue of words in pop music is Simon Frith: the article 'Why do Songs have Words?' (Frith 1988) is not entirely superseded by the chapter in Frith 1996. I suspect his sceptical attitude is revealed in a little footnote to the latter book: 'words have always been the least of my musical pleasures' (1996: 326, n. 47).
4 350 is a guess based on the albums. See Heylin (1996: 209–14) for an index. Dylan himself has said that he has '500, 600, 700 songs', *Uncut* (March 1999), p. 38.
5 Elsewhere, for what it's worth, Dylan said in a 1965 interview that 'words are just as important as the music. There would be no music without the words' (Miles 1978: 65, 69).
6 On sociologists and music, see Martin (1995: 12).
7 'Of course, the lyric was stupid and sexist but when you're dancing this hard, it can take a couple of years to notice' (Marsh 1989: 322 on the Rolling Stones' 'Honky Tonk Women').

battles simply in getting their colleagues to take pop music remotely seriously. In addition, their easy and assured technical certainty in the performance and explication of notated tonal music can make talking about words seem overly risky (see Middleton 1990: 228–32 and Brackett 1995: 77–89). If anything, the negligence most interesting is that of English, or literary criticism, where going on about words in pop music runs uneasily into the criticism of poetry:[8] in fact, poetry tends to be the dirty word of this subject-area, and it is worth a brief diversion to ponder why this should be the case.

Lyrics and poetry

Simon Frith has assiduously pinned down the problematic of the 'poetry of pop' to a particular period of pop music's history (Frith 1988: 117–18 and 1996: 176–7). The bringing-together of protest song and beat poetry by Bob Dylan, and his continuation of the 'heroic' merging of words, music, and their performance as singer-songwriter (following precursors such as Jimmie Rodgers and Hank Williams, Buddy Holly and Chuck Berry), acted as spur to a seemingly endless series of 'song-poets': Joni Mitchell, Neil Young, Van Morrison, Paul Simon. It is worth noting, *pace* Frith, that several singer-songwriters explicitly acknowledged this particular debt: Joni Mitchell has often emphasized the sense she felt that with 'Positively Fourth Street', Dylan's 1965 single, the pop song had 'grown up' (Russell and Tyson 1995: 554; Hoskyns 1994: 49). These primary sources vary, however, depending on who is talking, and to whom. John Lennon for instance, another of Gracyk's references, is someone who had a seething contempt for any idea of 'poetry': 'Dylan got away with murder. I thought, well, I can write this crap too. You know, you just stick a few images together, and you call it poetry' (Russell and Tyson 1995: 70). Van Morrison, however, who calls Dylan 'the greatest living poet' (Flanagan 1990: 411–14), is someone who seems always to have struggled *against* the idea of being a pop musician in favour of some deeper and possibly Celtic idea of what it is to be a poet. And yet, Frith is correct in

---

8 Day (1988) is an exceptional case of studying explicitly the *book* by Bob Dylan called *Lyrics 1962–85* (Dylan 1987). Aware that 'the sophisticated interplay between Dylan's words, voice and music needs always to be returned to and must remain centre-stage', Day is nevertheless making a 'claim that the words are not merely a part but the central part of a multi-dimensional art' (Day 1988: 5).

reading some of the critics as bringing to the singer-songwriter a romanticized conception of poetry, and furnishes splendidly excessive examples. One
gem which Frith overlooks is this snobbish comment of Michael Gray, which
takes Dylan as an opportunity to lay into the working class on their home
grounds of soccer and food: 'Before him [Dylan] you could say that pop was
like football. Millions of people liked it – millions of people like fish and
chips – but it didn't matter. Dylan made it matter' (Gray 1981: 115). To cut
a very long story short, I concur with Frith's evaluation of the romanticized
reading of rock lyrics. I would also suggest, first, that the general drift of rock
lyrics has indeed been towards a genuinely more romanticized melopoetic, a
conception of the rock lyric which depended less on rectitude and more on
individualized statement; and, second, that the great mistake of over-hyping
rock poetry was that it was taken to be sufficient ground for not attending to
the words at all. In considering the relation between the words of pop songs
and poetry, it is worth seeking out borderlines which can and do become
blurred. Since the Beatles, for instance, words have often been printed with
the record, and some songwriters have had their words printed as books:
Dylan, Shane MacGowan, Joni Mitchell among them; in fact, as published
poets who later became songwriters, Patti Smith and Leonard Cohen are at the
very edge of the line between published song and poem. Finally, the internet
has, at the time of writing, made lyrics massively available: for fans of The
Fall the appearance of homepages packed with lyrics was like having a
favourite and regular crossword puzzle suddenly and disappointingly sup-
plied with answers.

With such resistance firmly if rather purposelessly in place, the words,
innocently enough the single most consistent element of pop songs,[9] go by
with little to no systematic attention. What needs to happen, it seems to me,
is, first and crucially, that we stop thinking that the words in pop songs *are*
poems, and begin to say that they are *like* poetry, in some ways, and that by
extension if they are not like poetry then they tend towards being *like* prose: I
shall refer to these polarities as lyric and anti-lyric. I think we can then begin
to think systematically about how the words work, and historically about

9 The pop *vocalise* – the Cocteau Twins, My Bloody Valentine – never really got
anywhere: Reynolds (1990) is interesting, among many other reasons, for having
appeared when it seemed a distinct development.

42

how their position in the pop song has developed, what might be called 'word-consciousness'. My gamble here is that talking about pop songs from a word-centred perspective will help to configure the field more generally, itself reflecting recent arguments in the field of musical analysis *per se* (e.g. Guck 1994). My more general aim is straightforwardly to suggest things to think about when it comes to saying something about the words.

Verbal space

Verbal space is the pop song's basic compromise: the words agree to work within the spaces of tonal music's phrases, and the potential expressive intensity of music's melody is held back for the sake of the clarity of verbal communication. Tonal music's phrasing creates spaces which the words in performance occupy: we can visualize the combination of consistent phrasing and words producing *lines*, the line being a feature which pop songs to an extent share with poems. I call the function of musical phrasing in pop songs verbal space.[10] The idea is simple: lines can be full or empty, and words can be positioned at various points on the line; the line can be imagined as progressing left to right. The point at which a line begins and ends, the division of the musical phrase, can be imagined as being like a pillar in architecture, or as posts on a fence alongside the song's ongoing road: the return of the pillar or post can be a moment of some drama (for the sake of clarity, I shall use only the pillar metaphor here). The potential of verbal space depends crucially upon the speed of a song and the way it is phrased, but once these are established, we can develop ways of talking about the proportional relationships within the verbal space of any particular song.

What one takes to *be* a musical phrase is strictly speaking a musical matter, and one which it is not my aim to present here. Verbal and musical phrasing come together in aspects of rhythm: compare the discussion of musical phrasing in Lerdahl and Jackendoff (1983: 12–104) with Attridge (1995). As a brief example to consider take the song 'Please Please Me' by the Beatles, shown in Figure 3.1.

---

10 I first put the concept of verbal space forward in Griffiths (1992). My thanks to Simon Frith for having dug up this obscure reference on pp. 199–200 of *Performing Rites*.

X = two half-beats

Example 1	X	X	X	X	X	X	X
	Last night I	said	these	words to	my	girl	

Example 2	X	X	X	X	X	X	X	X
	Come on!	(Come on!)	Come on!	(Come on!)	Come on!	(Come on!)	Come on!	(Come on!)

Example 3	X	X	X	X	X	X	X
	I don't want to sound complaining but you know there's always rain in	my	heart	(in my heart)			

Figure 3.1: Beatles: 'Please Please Me' (opening)

This I take to consist of an eight-beat 'space', announced without words at the start of the song. It is possible to see the instrumental opening as two equal four-beat spaces, defined in particular by the repeated harmonica melody; but once the words enter, in terms of verbal space, it doesn't matter. In order to understand song's availability to words, it is worth noting the speed with which the song is proceeding. Again, though, once this is established the space, and its proportional occupation, will be, by and large, consistent. I should add that the pillar, described above, is the very first (left-hand side) beat: again, defining the pillar depends upon local circumstance.

The issue here is not, therefore, how we define that space but how the words occupy it, the relative density within and between each line. Example 1 in Figure 3.1 illustrates the first line of 'Please Please Me' arranged as verbal space. When the phrase, 'Come on', enters, as call-and-response, one could hear the space as drastically shortened to:

X   X
Come on! (Come on!)

this multiplied four times; but in fact, as Example 2 in the Figure shows, these four phrases add up to our earlier eight beats. The middle eight of the song is a classic case of doubling syllable count, so that for our earlier one- and two-syllable phrases: 'Last', 'night I', 'said these', 'words to', 'my' and 'girl'; and then, simply, 'Come on!', the middle eight has a series of four-syllable phrases: 'I don't want to', 'sound complaining', ' "but you know there's" ', and 'always rain in'. In Example 3, this effect is marked by a change in typography. In this final example, we observe a similarity between what Leonard Cohen refers to as a line's *syllabic density*,[11] and the musical idea of filling the space of a note with smaller diminutions, as sometimes occurs in the variation form.

A good example which displays the *filling* of verbal space – from lines being empty to being full – is the recording of Jim Weatherly's song 'Midnight Train to Georgia' by Gladys Knight and the Pips – the record rather than the song, as shown in Figure 3.2.

For this song's ideal presentation I advise that the reader has the record and a tape recorder. Tape the very first line of the song ('LA': Ex. 4 in Fig. 3.2);

---

11 '[T]he line of music is very influential in determining the length of a line or the density, the syllabic density', in Zollo (1997: 341).

X = half-beat

Example 4

	X	X	X	X	X	X	X
						pro——————ved too	

Example 5

	X	X	X	X	X	X
GK	-ways come true		Oh No!		Uh-huh	
Pips	Dreams don't al-	LA	-ways come true	Uh-huh	No!	Uh-huh

Example 6

	X		X	X	X	X	X
GK	(go)	for love	gonna board	board	on a	midnight	train to
Pips		for love	All aboard!	gotta board	on a	midnight	train to

Figure 3.2: Gladys Knight and the Pips: 'Midnight Train to Georgia' (1976)

then pick one from the end of the second verse ('Dreams don't always come true': Ex. 5) and the last few lines to the fade (Ex. 6). Finally, re-record the very first line.[12] After the gradual build-up of the song, the first line will now seem palpably and quite dramatically *empty* – no words, just two letters, L and A, in a space deserted, Pip-free. As the song progresses The Pips, as well as embodying 'pop's virtues and its politics' (Street 1986: 225), as well as fulfilling Chuck Eddy's 'Gladys Knight and The Pips Rule',[13] also function – notice how generously towards the sociologists I avoid saying first and foremost – as line-fillers, filling in the gaps between Gladys Knight's vocal line, the words of Weatherly's song, so multiplying the syllabic count.[14]

Some songs arrange themselves in this way as gradual build-ups in verbal garrulousness. Bob Dylan has a terrific example in the song 'The Groom's Still Waiting at the Altar': a verse which begins with a ten-syllable line, 'Cities on fire, phones out of order', and ends with the line, 'She could be respectably married, or running a whorehouse in Buenos Aires'. Same musical duration – four big beats – but in the one verse a remarkable doubling in syllabic density within the line. The pillar in John Cale's 'Leaving It up to You' becomes a wall into which his head is about to smash: the space formerly occupied by the desolate line, 'Looking for a friend, looking everywhere', is filled as 'And if you gave me half a chance, I'd do it now, I'd do it now, right now, you fascist', then, 'I know we could all feel the same like Sharon Tate, and we could give it all, we could give it, give it, give it all'. So not only is the syllable-count increasing, the whole nature and tenor of the words has shifted dramatically in the short but regularly divided time.[15]

---

12 Even though song words are generously available, especially on the internet, their usage is a matter of some contention: I thus quote only selectively and fleetingly, in order to illustrate a more general point. A detailed list of the records is included in the discography, and my advice is to track down all of the recordings.

13 'Rock 'n' roll works best when it seems both good for you and bad for you, nutritious and unnutritious, at the same time' (Eddy 1997: 173), and see Corbett (1994: 66, n. 15).

14 Syllabic count is clearly not something which one undertakes in precision whilst listening; but against the background of verbal space it is a key indicator of word-presence in the line.

15 An interesting example is found in Cale's pronunciation of the phrase 'the trouble with classicists' on the track 'Trouble with Classicists' on Lou Reed and John Cale, *Songs for Drella*. Between verse and chorus the music speeds up, rather less markedly than it may appear, making his phrase *appear* to be considerably faster and more squashed as verbal space.

Songs can do things with verbal space: change position, or extend and contract the line. I think something of the 'slacker' aspect of grunge had to do with the tendency of some songs to use relatively short, 'bored' lines starting from the pillar, the left side of the line: listen to Nirvana's 'Polly' or Hole's 'Doll Parts'. A good example of a song palpably engineering a dramatic change of position is found in the Sex Pistols' 'Pretty Vacant'. At the chorus, most of the lines *progress from* the pillar: 'We're so – ', 'Oh so – ', 'Va – (cant)'. The chorus progresses, until Johnny Rotten, padding time, says, '/Now', then, shifting position in order to *head towards* the pillar: ' – and we don't/Care', with 'care' stretched over a lot of verbal space.

While the phrasing of most pop music is consistent – close to saying that pop music is generally happy to stay in a key – there are exceptions. A lovely song of Jane Siberry, 'See the Child', has a perfectly visible, gradually stretching line (beginning *c.* 0.40), with one beat added each line: musically an increasing time-signature, visually the line is extending to its right-hand side. Readers may wish to compare, with reference to Figure 3.3, two hearings of the first verse of Elvis Costello's 'No Action' from *This Year's Model*. Allan Moore (1993: 176) is listening to this track *musically*, getting his bearings from correspondences in the structure of phrasing, and hears the verse as:

2 (touch) + 2; 2 (much) + 2.5; 2 + 1.5 + 2 (friends); 2.5 + 2 (hands).

Getting my bearings from the words, I hear it as:

$(4\times4) + (4\times4)$ (first two lines); 2 (telephone) + 8; 4 + 2 (just good) + 8; 4 + 4 + 2 (in my) + 8.

Verbal space is thus a key point at which music and words trade off each other's *rhythm*. Lou Reed begins 'Walk on the Wild Side' typically and pro- saically enough – 'Holly came from Miami, FLA'. During the song, though, he sees 'the coloured girls', and occupies the verbal space differently, dancing rhythm through a babble word: 'doot'.

Sound: rhymes and alliterations

There can be little doubt that many songs are invented from babbling sounds which eventually form into words. Paul Simon in an interview says of one line in 'Rene and Georgette Magritte with their Dog after the War': 'That's just the way that it sings – the EEE OOO EEE OOO sound: *e*-sily *loo*-sing *e*-v'ning *clo*', so presenting an interesting challenge of representation

48

(a) Allan F. Moore, *Rock: the Primary Text* (Buckingham: Open University Press, 1993), p. 176.

1 = per bar

I don't want to kiss you, I don't want to touch,
|2 |2

I don't want to see you 'cos I don't miss you that much   I'm not a telephone
|2 |2.5

junkie I told you that we were just good friends
|2 |1.5 |2

But when I hold you like I hold that bakelite in my hands   There's no
     |2.5 |2

action (etc.)
|4   (etc.)

(b)

1 = per beat

I don't want to kiss you, I don't want to touch
4   4   4   4

I don't want to see you 'cos I don't miss you that much.   I'm not a
4   4   4   4

telephone junkie I
2   8

told you that we were just good
4   2

friends   but when I
8

hold you like I hold that bakelite in my
4   4   2

hands there's no
8

action   (etc.)
8   (etc.)

Figure 3.3: Elvis Costello: 'No Action'

49

to his interviewer (Flanagan 1990: 322). In this discussion I shall look first
at rhyme and then, briefly, at alliteration.

Rhyme appears to be so central in pop music that it is surely a surprise
that there is little systematic discussion. Some songs, or sections of songs,
are driven by rhyme alone: the girl in Sleeper's 'Inbetweener' studies fashion, while her boyfriend, realistically enough, studies art; the true reason he
studies art and not, say, music, is in order to rhyme with 'smart' and 'start'.
And how could anyone get really annoyed about Niggaz With Attitude's
'Fuck the Police' when it includes rhymes as entertaining as: authority/to
kill a minority; teenager/gold and a pager; looking for the product/selling
narcotics; me and Lorenzo/rolling in a Benzo; fags or what/grabbing his
nuts?[16]

An emphasis on the sonorous quality of words arises from the idea of
lyric itself, the governing principle of the melopoetic relations of the popular
song. Hal David said of 'the ideal song' that 'it should seem not that two or
three people wrote it but that it came out of one mind' (Zollo 1997: 212).
Richard Rodgers is a musician who wants to make statements, Lorenz Hart
the magical maker of words in search of melody; Cole Porter is in some sense
the aesthetic condition towards which both aspire.[17]

In terms of verbal space, rhyme emphasizes the sense in which the line
can still be visualized as having a left- and right-hand side, being determinedly
the definition of the right-hand margin.[18] While the precise varieties of
rhyme are manifold,[19] my sense is that the recurrent types in pop songs,
until more taxonomic work is done, centre upon three: *full* rhyme; *near*

16 'In a pretty obvious way – that no reviewer seems ever to note, the metric,
   rhythmic possibilities the rapper's monologue explores are often what makes a
   particular cut driving and creative, in spite of – and see *because of* – the severe
   limitations of theme and near-cognate rhyme the genre imposes.' David Foster
   Wallace in Costello and Foster Wallace (1990: 95–6).
17 Jimmy Webb: 'if you're going to write songs and you really want to be a
   songwriter, write the whole thing. Write the words and the music. It's important
   to take English Literature and absorb as much poetry as you can' (Russell and
   Tyson 1995: 185).
18 See the draft of Samuel Johnson's 'The Vanity of Human Wishes' contained as an
   appendix to Fleeman (1971: 167–79). Johnson often has the rhyme ready while
   deletions remain in the 'left side' of many lines.
19 A fine introduction to rhyme is found in Brogan (1993). The twelve 'criteria for
   the analysis and categorization of rhyme types' at pp. 1054–9 are particularly
   illuminating.

rhyme; and deliberate *non*-rhyme in a rhymed setting. Most songs mix the first two. Here are some examples from which the reader might explore.

A sustained devotion to the *full* rhyme is found in the early albums of Jackson Browne: in the lovely song 'Fountain of Sorrow', the first chorus rhymes 'fountain of light' with 'fight', 'all right', and 'tonight'; the true compulsiveness of rhyme[20] emerges at the second chorus where from the same start, Browne rhymes: 'flight', 'fight', 'sight', 'right' and 'bright' – and all to the same interrupted cadence. One might then find justification for the rhyme in the song's subject. Here, perhaps, the rhymes in their fullness reinforce the delicately domestic, small-scale nature of the situation described, an impression possibly contained in the melodic line's rises to the upper tonic of the scale. In other words, and this is a possible tactic for the reader, one tries to link rhyme technique, or the lack of it, to the nature of the song. However, this is a tactic at best, and it is hard to generalize: as Browne himself began to address global concerns, to expect this to be reflected in rhyme technique would be to commit the worst excesses of homological mapping (and not a little preposterous); in fact, in a later song like 'Lives in the Balance', dealing with the political situation in Latin America, Browne's full rhymes are still intact – what changes is his use of more diverse instrumentation.

A great exponent of the *near* or *half* rhyme in pop song is Chris Difford of Squeeze, and the sustained, near-but-not-quite nature of the rhymes perhaps contributes to the sense of Squeeze's inhabiting a rather louche, downbeat world.[21] A splendid example is found in the song 'Labelled with Love', where an old drunk is observed as being 'like some kind of witch with blue fingers and mittens'. Now, what rhymes with mittens? ('Raindrops on roses, and whiskers on . . .'). Difford: 'She smells like the *cat* and the neighbours she sickens' – where the cat takes care of the kittens, leaving the line-end free for the rebarbative '*sickens*'.

The other thing possible is *not* to rhyme in a rhymed setting: here I think of Lou Reed. In 'There is no Time' on the *New York* album, there is one crunching no-rhyme, of 'turn your *back*' with 'learned *speech*'. Intended in

---

20 Browne says of rhyme that he used to be 'pretty obsessed with it. I didn't even want to rhyme a singular with a plural' (Zollo 1997: 417).
21 My thanks to David Roe for suggesting this line of enquiry, and to Christopher Ricks for responding to this point.

deadly earnest, the effect – especially as Reed enunciates it – is too close to comedy for comfort.

Proceeding from identification of rhymes to the question of evaluation, it may be worth rehearsing a formally conceived theory about value in rhyme. From his study of English poetry, and with special reference to Pope, W. K. Wimsatt (1954: 157) held that difference in meaning of rhyme words can be recognized in difference of parts of speech and in difference of functions of the same parts of speech, and that both of these differences will be qualified by the degree of parallelism or of obliquity appearing between the two whole lines of a rhyming pair. So in Costello's '(I Don't Want to Go to) Chelsea' on *This Year's Model*, the rhyme of 'tricks' and 'kicks', both nouns in the plural, is 'dullish', to use Wimsatt's term, whereas putting the number 'sixty-six' against the verbs 'licks' and then 'fix' is 'smarter' (Wimsatt 1954: 168).

Using Wimsatt's theory, I shall compare two songs, both by singer-songwriters, both of which utilize rhyme in different ways: Elvis Costello's 'Beyond Belief' from *Imperial Bedroom* and Rickie Lee Jones's 'Living it Up' from *Pirates* (Table 3.1).

There are two things we can observe from Table 3.1. First, very simply, there is a greater proportion of syllabic correspondences between the rhyming terms in Costello: eleven out of fifteen, as opposed to six out of ten in Jones. Secondly, using Wimsatt's idea, in 'Beyond Belief' many (ten out of fifteen) of the rhymes are grammatically similar; in Jones the number is considerably fewer (two out of ten). What matters now is how one wishes to interpret the data. The Costello rhymes seem to be more immediate and their pairing static. Jones, through the dissonance of the rhymed term, appears to push the thought forward, giving the pairing a sense of movement. However, this is not to say that the immediacy is what Costello intended, or that it isn't a good thing for this song, or conversely that Jones's contrasts are intrinsically good: this step depends upon the value judgement one is trying to make. The evidence, however, is there and can be observed.

Wimsatt's is a limited and rather specific idea, granted – 'the optimum instance of the theory', suggests Donald Wesling, tartly, 'may not be Pope but Ogden Nash' (Wesling 1980: 58) – and transferring directly a method derived from Pope to the pop song rightly invites scepticism. However, it may be that all we need to rescue is the idea of attending to similarity or difference in the rhyming correspondence: it is for us to work out which are

Table 3.1 Comparison of rhymes in two songs

Elvis Costello: 'Beyond Belief'	Rickie Lee Jones: 'Living it Up'
N(pl)/N(pl) conceits/defeats	**N/adv** crazy eye/pretty girl goes by
N(pl)/N(pl) issues/tissues	**adv/prep** nothin here to do anymore/something he's waiting for
N/N slick/nervous tick	**N/Np** picks up Eddie in the alley/they all look like Frankie Valli
N/N hovel . . . novel	**N/adv** her leg to her cigarette/he ain't come back here yet
Vpp/N tortured/orchard	**adv/adv** lost her job again/won't let her in
N/Np palace/Alice	**N/V** blue dress/lemme guess
N/adv jealousy/sweetly	**adv/V** then and there/they didn't care
N/adj malice/callous	**adv/Vpp** dreams let so many tickets through/somebody there they knew
V/N fit/identikit	**adj/adj** lights are blooming green/sad, a little mean
N/N fault/vault	**N/V** hotel/you couldn't tell
N/N barrier reef/belief	
adv/adv completely/discreetly	
adj/adj cunning/stunning	
Np/N(pl) Hades/ladies	
V/N wolf-whistle/thistle	

N: noun, pl: plural; Np: proper noun; V: verb; pp: past participle; adj: adjective; adv: adverb; prep: preposition.

the terms which matter in pop songs. One factor both these songs suggest is the collision of what Paul Simon calls ordinary and enriched language (Zollo 1997: 109), Costello's rhyme of 'ladies' with 'Hades' or 'alley' with 'Frankie Valli' in Rickie Lee Jones. A method, derived from Wimsatt, albeit in an adapted form, would at least offer a basis for taxonomic work.[22]

Alongside rhyme, and sometimes in opposition to it, alliterations can figure as a word-technique driven by sound. Mark E. Smith of The Fall is a great exponent here. 'Well, I didn't make the weekend', begins the 'Lie Dream of a Casino Soul', 'but I put the weight back on again'. 'Make/weekend' moves along its 'k' sound – Smith has extraordinary ways of emphasizing and elongating his consonants – and 'weight back on again' stretches 'weekend' into a sort of wreck of its original wholeness: 'weekend/way - k - n'. 'And Our

22 Preminger and Brogan (1993: 1056, para 4) appears to suggest that detailed taxonomic work is also lacking in the study of English poetry.

Kid got back from Munich', Muni - keh, as he'll say, 'he didn't like it much':
here 'Munich' is pulverized into 'much' as a sort of chip-paper residue, with
the 'k' sound propelled into 'like': 'Munich/like – much'. It's all like some
weird crossword puzzle.

As well as inhabiting the shouty prose of The Fall, alliteration can be
beautifully lyrical too. Transcribing the words to Van Morrison's great song
'Tupelo Honey', I figured the last line as 'Just like honey from the bee'. (I had
probably just listened to Cassandra Wilson's recording, which has this line
throughout.) Re-hearing Morrison's original recording, I knew something
was missing: the line should have been 'Just like honey, baby, from the bee'.
I'm sure that the missing word matters because of the internal run of the
line: baby to rhyme with honey, and to alliterate into bee.

Sense: word novelty and grammatical rectitude

They are really going to kill music if they keep it up, because they're not
writing songs anymore. They're only writing ideas. They don't really care
about repetition. They don't really care about a hook or melody.
(Phil Spector in 1969: Russell and Tyson 1995: 46)

I don't think songwriters listen to themselves talk. I think they sit down to
write a song and they fall into rock clichés, this kind of 'lyric speak'. That's
what I try to avoid.   (Aimee Mann in 1993: Russell and Tyson 1995: 133)

If rhyme is the key technique of lyric, then the removal of lyric as guiding
principle raises an interesting question about what occupies the space in
technique. Historically, anti-lyric arises as an extension of a tendency set in
Bob Dylan's songs of the mid-1960s; there is a return to the division of songwriting labour which we found Hal David commending earlier – one words,
one music – but this time lacking his principle of ensuring that both words
and music contribute to the one lyric unity. The relation of the words of Patti
Smith – to my mind a crucial figure in this development – to the piano and
guitar support of 'Piss Factory', or to the band on *Horses*, is of a very different
order to that of Lorenz Hart to Richard Rodgers: the music is a 'bed of
sound' upon which Smith performs, and in which the words are free to lose
the markers of lyric, rhyme and syllabic consistency, in favour of a looser
relation more akin to prose forms: less poem as analogy, then, and more
short story, novel, letter, confession, manifesto. Even some of the basic rules
of lyric can be broken. The Manic Street Preachers, for instance, maintaining

within the band a closed-shop division between the writing of words (Nicky Wire, Richey James) and writing music (James Dean Bradfield, Sean Moore), often break a basic rule of lyric concerning the correspondence of musical and syllabic rhythm. Read this line aloud: 'under neon loneliness, motorcycle emptiness'. The Manics: 'under knee-ón, lonely-néss, motorcy-kll, empty-néss' (on this, see Price 1999: 78–9).

Within the anti-lyric, the emphasis of a song shifts away from its sonorous rhyme towards the detail of its statement, away from *rectitude* of rhyme and rhythm towards the novelty or *interest* of words and ideas. Where in lyric one is following closely the progression of the right-hand side of the line, in anti-lyric one listens out for the striking detail, the unexpected word. Listening to The Gang of Four's *Entertainment!* – classic anti-lyric – the album's surprise lies partly in the fact that it contains so many unexpected words: 'ether', 'Long Kesh', 'H-bomb torture', 'Six Counties', 'contradictions', 'Rockall', 'corked-up' – all in the first track. Surely too the impact of The Smiths, as much as any band,[23] was due in large part to the sheer unexpectedness of the words. Here the idea of genre crossover is useful: the 'punctured bicycle on a hillside desolate' of 'This Charming Man' is like Wordsworth by way of Betjeman, and was for the pop song fresh and new.[24]

If we found Jackson Browne concerned earlier with the purity of rhyme, we may observe that both The Smiths' Morrissey and also Neil Tennant of The Pet Shop Boys are highly attentive to grammatical rectitude: with Tennant sometimes one can almost visualize the punctuation marks while listening to the song. 'Can You Forgive Her?', opening *Very*, is a good case, and here it is arranged as a prose passage:

> Another night with open eyes, too late to sleep, too soon to rise; you're short of breath – is it a heart attack? Hot and feverish, you face the fact you're in love, and it feels like shame because she's gone and made a fool of you in public again. You're in love and it feels like pain because you know there's too much truth in everything she claims. So ask yourself, now, can you forgive her if she wants you to? Ask yourself: can you even deliver what she demands of you?

23 John Peel describes The Smiths as 'an example – perhaps *the* example – of a band that arrived out of the blue without any apparent influences', in Gallagher, Campbell and Gillies (1995: ix).

24 For the classic literary theory of generic crossover, see Bakhtin (1981: 301ff.). My thanks to Rob Pope for this. See also Pope (1998).

Example 3.1: REM: 'Nightswimming' (reduction)

One of the things which helps the analysis of words in songs is thinking through their representation: sometimes it helps to preserve the verbal space of the song and map out the words; at other times it is helpful to decide between poetry and prose. The song 'Nightswimming' recorded by REM on *Automatic for the People*, with words by Michael Stipe, is a lovely illustration of a particular and current condition of anti-lyric, which could be described as the lyricism of anti-lyric. Musically, the song uses a procedure familiar in ground-bass technique: in relation to a repeating, six-bar chord sequence, the vocal line gradually develops melodic and rhythmic asymmetries. In terms above, the words shift position along the verbal space, with the vocal line carrying over the pillars, easily and languidly. The chord sequence itself is interesting, and if you play it you may find that, as on the record, it invites repetition (see Ex. 3.1).

The music's propensity to repetition may derive from the way that the melody line divides 4+2 as marked, but the harmony divides 2+4; the surprising reharmonization to V(7) of V at bar 4 second beat also seems to propel the music along. The 'ground bass' is repeated fourteen times in all, with occasional punctuation by a shorter phrase which is first heard as the 'intro', and later what I call the 'ground bass' itself, without words. Here are the fourteen lines:

> string 'splash'. *intro*
> 1. Nightswimming deserves a quiet night.
> 2. The photograph on the dashboard, taken years ago, turned around backwards so the windshield shows.

56

3. Every streetlight reveals a picture in reverse. Still it's so much clearer.
4. I forgot my shirt at the water's edge, the moon is low tonight. *intro*
5. Nightswimming deserves a quiet night. I'm not sure all these people understand.
6. It's not like years ago: the fear of getting caught, of recklessness and water.
7. They cannot see me naked. These things, they go away, replaced by everyday.
8. Nightswimming. Remembering that night. September's coming soon.
9. I'm pining for the moon, and what if there were two, side by side in orbit, around the fairest sun.
10. The bright, tight, forever drum could not describe nightswimming.
11. You, I thought I knew you. You, I cannot judge. You, I thought you knew me, this one
12. Laughing quietly, underneath my breath. Nightswimming. *intro + 'ground bass' × 1*
13. The photograph reflects, every streetlight a reminder. Nightswimming deserves a quiet night.
14. Deserves a quiet night. *'ground bass' × 2*

Table 3.2 shows the words arranged as verbal space.

This example shows many things: the word 'nightswimming' gradually shifting its position in the space, from three times in the first column to three times between the second and third; some lines packed and some more empty; a sense perhaps of a little culmination around the middle, announced by two noticeable full rhymes: 'go away' and 'everyday' (line 7), and 'soon' and 'moon' (lines 8–9). That said, beyond these little parameters and formal details, Stipe is characteristically able to do more or less anything he likes, with the freedom afforded by anti-lyric (see Gray 1996: 106–40). A few fingerprints are to be found: the demonstrative pronouns in lines 5 and 7, the suddenly pointed addressee in line 11, the limits of sense in line 10.[25] There's that very *prose*-like flatness, little metonymic details which contain and suggest their own radiance: 'the photograph on the dashboard', a 'shirt at the water's edge', 'recklessness and water', an 'orbit around the fairest sun',[26] the 'streetlight a reminder'.

25 Christopher Ricks, in 'American English and the Inherently Transitory', draws attention to a line of John Berryman ('Sort of forever and all those human sings' in *The Dream Songs*: 27) and its 'wistful wishful quality' (Ricks 1984: 434–5). Perhaps there's something of the same quality attending to 'forever' here.
26 The internet has 'fairest sun' which on hearing is right; I originally had 'ferris sun'. Although the internet lists thousands of song words, I advise transcription as the most direct and active way into the words of a song.

Table 3.2 'Nightswimming' arranged as verbal space

Phrase A	Phrase B	Phrase C
Nightswimming	deserves a quiet night	
The photograph on the dashboard	taken years ago	turned around backwards so the windshield shows
Every streetlight reveals a	picture in reverse	still it's so much clearer
I forgot my shirt at the	water's edge, the moon is low to-	-night
Nightswimming	deserves a quiet night	I'm not sure all these people under-
-stand, It's not like years ag-	-o, the fear of getting cau-	-ght, of recklessness and
water They cannot see me	naked, these things they go aw-	-ay, replaced by every-
-day, Nightswimming	remembering that night	September's coming soon
I'm pining for the moon	and what if there were two side by	side in orbit around the fairest
sun? The bright, tight,	forever drum could not describe night-	-swimming
You, I thought I knew you,	You, I cannot judge,	You, I thought you knew me, this one
Laughing quietly, under-	-neath my breath, night-	-swimming
The photograph reflects, every	streetlight a reminder, night-	-swimming deserves a quiet
night,	deserves a quiet	night.

This may end up merely the equivalent of saying that poetry such as that of Elizabeth Bishop or John Ashberry is able to attain a deep lyricism while being relatively flat and prosaic, but the historical journey of how the pop song reaches this point is perhaps as interesting as the destination reached. From the late 1970s onwards, the pop song had at its disposal a choice of bringing together words and music: following the demands of lyric, or making prose-like statements. At the time of writing, both tactics appear to be being followed in British pop: an emergent and winsome pop music from Scotland, exemplified by Belle and Sebastian's *The Boy with the Arab Strap*, seems to announce a return to lyric at its most fastidious, while in tracks like 'Dirty Epic', 'Born Slippy', 'Pearl's Girl' or 'Moaner', the techno group Underworld is, through Karl Hyde's shouty *paroles trouvées*, virtually typifying the anti-lyric.[27]

What is presented here can hardly claim to be exhaustive. Approaching the topic, a sociologist might rightly insist upon changes in technology and institution which affected the changing nature of words in relation to the music: the change in attitude to the words, or word-consciousness, reflects important shifts in the constituency of *the band* itself, a shift from the group being essentially music-lovers playing together to a more hierarchized model in which one, often the singer, became supplier and carrier of the words and the band's claim to attention. Of course, there are also all of the musical and performative issues with which the words are delivered (the musical setting to melody, production and voice), while the video of a song can radically affect a listener's understanding of the words. In fact, the whole question of meaning and words in pop song is another matter, one in which the question of subject position seems to me paramount (see e.g. Middleton 1990: 249–58; Cubitt 1984: 207–24; Bradby 1990: 341–68 or other examples of her work). But in conclusion it would be, and has been, erroneous, because of reasons such as these, not to attend to the words in their own relation to the song. Pop song, as an anti-disciplinary form, invites the strategic affectation of localized expertise for its understanding, and not one but a number of small literacies in order to express that understanding: musical, verbal, performative, technological, visual, cinematic, socio-cultural and political. This essay should be seen as a contribution to that analytical understanding.

27 The CD sleeve to Underworld's first album, *dubnobasswithmyheadman*, designed by the band themselves as part of the company Tomato, provides a suitable typolographical analogy to anti-lyric.

4 The sound is 'out there': score, sound design and exoticism in *The X-Files*

ROBYNN J. STILWELL

Introduction

While scoring for films is a subject which has finally, belatedly, been drawing scholarly attention, the television sound-world is still largely uncharted territory. The assumption is made, implicitly, that techniques are merely transferred from the big screen to the small. Although it is now widely accepted that visual codes are *not* fully transferable from one medium to the other – television has roots in theatre and radio, as well as in film – the study of sound, once again, lags so far behind that of image in television that it is practically non-existent.

Just as shot composition, editing, lighting, special effects, and acting are different in television and films – for various historical and technical reasons, television is thought of in terms of limitations *vis-à-vis* film (smaller screen, smaller budgets, shorter attention span) – sound is also different. Speakers are small and limited in reproductive range; stereo is a recent development and still dependent upon relatively poor quality and little or no practical separation, unless viewers invest in exterior speakers for their television sets. Therefore, frequency and dynamic range are restricted, and clarity of musical voice-leading is compromised.

Film and television *are* different. Television as it exists in most parts of the world is a commercial enterprise, a long flow of advertisements for products interrupted by a schedule of entertainments which in effect serve

My thanks to Ian Flindell of the Institute of Sound and Vibration Research, Southampton, for allowing me access to his knowledge of acoustics and perception; and to Nicholas Cook and Stan Hawkins for reading and commenting upon the draft.

as inducements for the real commodity – the consumers who are sold to the advertisers on the basis of the shows they watch. Film is also a commercial venture, though with a certain autonomy that allows the romance of the artwork to persist with less contradiction than in television. Neither film nor television are exclusively art or commerce (nor is music), but the slant of scholarly study tends to classify film as 'art' and television as 'commerce'; academia reflects this split, as film studies are frequently housed in the humanities, television studies in the social sciences. This disciplinary division is amplified by methodological differences, which means that relationships – the differences as well as the continuities – between these aesthetically related media are not always recognized. The scoring of narrative genres is a case in point. Television Westerns are generally scored similarly to film Westerns; television situation comedies, on the other hand, tend to be videotaped before a live audience rather than filmed and therefore usually have little or no music apart from the theme. *Star Wars* is frequently cited as a turning-point in science fiction film scoring, turning from electronic, futuristic styles to a swashbuckling one but in fact, John Williams had already accomplished that transformation some thirteen years earlier by scoring the television series *Lost in Space* as an adventure series rather than a futuristic one. The introduction of MTV in the early 1980s led to experimentation in video-style sequences in films like *Risky Business* and *Flashdance*, but it was in the television series *Miami Vice* that these sequences were fully integrated into the narrative and their dramatic possibilities realized.

The X-Files is a television series which forces consideration of many border crossings: television and film; aesthetics and commerce; and music and sound design are among the most critical. Each of these 'oppositions' (which need not be oppositions, but which are often perceived as such) has ramifications which affect the others. Economics and technology impact upon creativity, forcing aesthetic choices, but inventive artists can turn those imperatives to their advantage.

The X-Files started in the graveyard slot of a fledgling television network in 1993 and has become a cult favourite on a par with the *Star Trek* franchise, including a theatrical film release in the summer of 1998. The commercial background of *The X-Files* was a significant formative factor in its visual and aural aesthetic. In 1993, the Fox Network was still slowly expanding its weekly schedule: it had begun with a largely syndicated schedule with one night of original programming per week, gradually adding additional evenings. While Fox had produced successful comedies like *Married With Children, The Simpsons,* and *In Living Color,* its only drama success had been with the glossy soap *Beverly Hills 90210. The X-Files* was part of the debut line-up of the last night of the schedule to be filled, Friday night, and it filled a timeslot generally regarded as the 'death slot' of an American television schedule, 9.00 p.m. Eastern and Pacific time, 8.00 Central, when the target demographic of young, educated, affluent viewers is assumed to be out on the town. Creator Chris Carter was something of an unknown quantity, the cast unfamiliar, and the premise decidedly unusual. Fox was throwing all its support behind the 10.00 show, the surreal comedy Western *The Adventures of Brisco County, Jr.,* so no one expected *The X-Files* to survive.

Against such expectations, *The X-Files* was clearly fighting an uphill battle. Its initial budget was $1.1 million per episode, about average for a one-hour drama (Lowry 1995: 32), but with above-average technical demands. Extravagant special effects and an orchestral score were not going to be options, and aesthetic choices were carefully shaped to the budgetary limitations.

Stylistic precedents

Although the show has a distinct style of its own, a number of precedents are discernible. Visually and thematically, the most obvious and frequently cited source is *The Silence of the Lambs* – the modified documentary style incorporating subtly spectacular camera angles, the FBI milieu (including woodland settings balanced by clean, efficient offices, and a faintly Southern, courtly flavour to the characters' behaviour), monochromatic colour schemes that create an illusion of black-and-white photography, and most prominently the character and appearance of the female lead. But there are other precedents as well: Steven Spielberg's *Close Encounters of the Third Kind* for the realistic but poetic quality of the storytelling and the high-intensity light from focused sources piercing a generally dark screen; and a late 1980s science fiction television series from some of the producers of *Star Trek: The Next Generation* called *The War of the Worlds,* in which we may find the graphic interface typing time and location directly onscreen at the beginning of scenes, the oblique biblical references, the government conspiracy to

conceal the presence of colonising aliens, and the central dynamic of a sceptical female scientist and an eccentric male investigator wounded by an alien
experience in his family past (in Harrison Blackwood's case, the killing of his
parents in the 1953 invasion depicted in the classic science fiction film – the
show was unexpectedly virtuosic in its incorporation of previous versions of
the H. G. Wells story). It also had an atmospheric synthesizer score by Billy
Thorpe.

Some of the technical aspects of the visual style of *The X-Files* are
not only appropriate to the subject matter – and constitutive of its narrative
discourse – they are also cheap. Darkness covers a multitude of sins, including
rickety or inappropriate sets and very un-special effects. Bright lights from
flashlights, computer screens, car headlights, and alien spaceships are not
only thematically appropriate and stylistically distinctive, they do the same
job as darkness, blinding the viewer, particularly when diffused by smoke,
fog and rain (a near-constant thanks to the show's Vancouver locations).

The soundscape of *The X-Files* is equally distinctive and equally driven
by the necessity to be frugal. Therefore it is primarily provided by one person,
Mark Snow, and his synclavier. One of the most distinctive things about the
soundscape is its density. Not only is the show heavily scored (an average of
well over thirty minutes of a forty-three-minute episode are underscored),
but the sound design has a spaciousness and depth analogous to the dark,
deep-shadowed look of the show, and the border between music and sound
design is so permeable as to be non-existent. Although we may be able to
recognize 'music' at one end of the continuum and 'sound effect' at the other,
there is a very large, vague overlap in the middle.

The score normally has a very low 'musical' content by most traditional
standards, which means that conventional music analysis is both difficult and
almost always useless. As Mark Snow himself describes it, 'when the *X-Files*
television show started, the music was mostly atmospheric. It was ambient
sound effect music, with very little melody and little harmonic progression.
In the last couple of years, it has become more musical, more melodic, more
thematic' (Duncan 1998: 127). 'More' is always a relative term, and when
dealing with *X-Files* music, the differences can be very slight. Subtle distinctions force us to make clear differentiations between terminology often
used as interchangeable but which are not truly synonymous. In this essay,
ambient will refer to a soundscape which creates a sense of the space depicted

in the *diegesis*.[1] It is normally based on a low hum equivalent to room tone[2] (often even in exterior scenes) with sound effects, but though it is unmetered and irregular, it may incorporate musical elements such as focused pitches and musical timbres. *Atmospheric* designates passages which have a steady meter and/or melodic shape, including the loosely metric, meandering synthesizer pad over the ambient hum which might be called '*The X-Files* sound'. *Minimalist* will be used in a technical sense to describe cues which are metered and composed of repeated and/or slightly varied melodic cells.

Sound precedents

Like the visuals, the sounds have precedents. Strikingly, the two most obvious precedents are shows which, like *The X-Files*, have strong visual identities: *The Outer Limits* and *Miami Vice*.

The original series of *The Outer Limits*[3] ran in the United States in the early 1960s; although basically a monster show, *The Outer Limits* was sophisticated science fiction and usually revealed that the monsters are us, intolerant humans. The show had stunning black-and-white cinematography, and a moody, atmospheric score by Dominic Frontiere. Though an anthology series, with each episode normally having its own music, the show had one distinctive theme used under the voiceover at the beginning and end of each episode to lead us into and out of the narrative. Though in many respects the melodic or harmonic similarities between this theme and *The X-Files* theme are weak, the themes are gesturally similar (see Ex. 4.1a and b). *The Outer Limits* theme is composed of two musical gestures – a string figure that predominantly rocks back and forth between two notes a half-step apart, and a reverberant upward arpeggio on a vibraphone. *The X-Files* theme has a

1 The diegesis is the world created by the narrative; diegetic sound would be that emanating from a source visible onscreen (a shot from a pistol, salsa from a Latin band) or a source that could naturally be assumed to be present, even if not actually visible (typing in an office, a radio in a car). Non-diegetic sound would be that which comes from outside the realistic world of the diegesis (an omniscient narrator's voiceover, for example, or the typical orchestral film underscore).
2 'Room tone' is the basic ambient sound of a space, comprised of reverberation of even the slightest differences in air pressure off walls.
3 An updated version has appeared in the 1990s, but it bears little resemblance to the original.

Example 4.1a: Theme from *The X-Files*

Example 4.1b: Theme from *The Outer Limits*

Example 4.1c: Theme from *The Twilight Zone*

whistling tune that predominantly rocks between two notes a step apart, and an upward arpeggio on an echoing synthesizer sound. Both themes also bear more than a passing resemblance to Marius Constant's famous theme from *The Twilight Zone*, with its rocking semitone motion (see Ex. 4.1c) and a shrill upward flourish dominated by a piccolo shriek. (*The X-Files* theme is almost a direct inversion of *The Twilight Zone* motif.)

While the possibility of intentional or unintentional copying exists,[4] these gestural and timbral similarities suggest a certain cultural 'appropriateness' to the subject matter which demand a semiotic decoding. There is nothing too complicated here – the upward gesture with high levels of reverberation create a sense of floating, the possibility of falling, a detachment from the ordinary; the obsessive rocking in a narrow pitch band provokes claustrophobia, nervousness, even paranoia, similar to the cellular, motivic patterns used by Bernard Herrmann in his Hitchcock scores – and his scores to several episodes of *The Twilight Zone*.[5] They are tried and true musical mechanisms in American popular culture for this genre.

The similarity to *Miami Vice* lies in the synthesizer underscore. Although Jan Hammer was still working with themes (most prominently themes for Detective Sonny Crockett and Lt. Martin Castillo, but *not* for Detective Ricardo Tubbs), he also used minimalist segments and ambient synth pads. In comparison with *The X-Files*, however, *Miami Vice* used short cues, and there was not much score in an episode.

The occasional blurring of the diegetic and non-diegetic musical realms was one of the most blatantly surreal elements of a highly stylized show. An

4 Although to my knowledge neither Mark Snow nor Chris Carter has ever referred to *The Outer Limits* as an influence, this show was on television when Snow and Carter were impressionable children and young adolescents. It is extremely likely that it was absorbed into their aesthetic memories, creating a resonance when, after various false starts, Snow hit upon the 'whistling tune'. It seems that *The X-Files* tune has now supplanted *The Twilight Zone* in popular culture as a signifier of 'the weird': in an episode of the hospital drama *Chicago Hope*, a woman was brought in burned and pregnant, claiming her baby was fathered by an alien – cue the theme from *The X-Files*.

5 These qualities are emphasized by the imagery in the title sequences of each show: *The X-Files* with its superimposition of rising and falling ghostly silhouettes against photographs; the optical-illusion spiral and dolls, eyes, open doors, and equations floating among the stars in *The Twilight Zone*; and the manipulation of the television image by the 'control voice' in *The Outer Limits*.

indicative example is the opening of the episode 'Out Where the Buses Don't Run': a roller skater wearing a Walkman cruises down the pavement on South Beach, passing a number of interesting characters. The Who's 'Baba O'Reilly' plays; is it diegetic or non-diegetic? It could possibly be on the skater's Walkman, but then it would only be heard by him, and others on the beach seem to be aware of the song. The skater passes street percussionists; the rhythm of their conga-playing fits the Who's music. Little Richard plays a street preacher, standing at an organ; his preaching phrases match the rhythm of the music and his hands seem to be playing the distinctive chords. The actual kinetic connection between his hands and the chords is rather loose, but welded together by an effect sound theorist Michel Chion (1994: 63–5) calls *synchresis*, a combination of synthesis and synchrony, in which the mind links sound with action even if the match is not exact – an effect vital to the dubbing process, particularly when dubbing foreign language films, and to the soundscape of *The X-Files*. The occasional ambiguity between the diegetic and non-diegetic in *Miami Vice*, too, becomes fundamental to the style of *The X-Files*.

'Natural' sound

Other than the theme, each episode of *The X-Files* is its own sound-world, though there are similarities in the extensive dense sound, the meandering string pad, and a tendency to score everything *but* the sections of dialogue in which Scully is being scientific. Psychologically, it is tempting to conclude that the sound complex is there to cushion the delicate construction of realism in a narrative of 'extreme probability' (as Mulder would say). The extensive blanketing of the narrative in sound and the blending of sound design and music aids in this suturing of the audience into the narrative. By shortening the distance between the diegetic, 'objective' sound and non-diegetic, 'commentative' underscore, the sound design makes the suspension of disbelief easier to negotiate, like putting the rungs of a ladder closer together.

A comparison between a typical episode and the pilot show illustrates this. The pilot was the only episode blatantly to attempt realism. It opened with the legend 'This following story is inspired by actual documented accounts' and relied more heavily on Scully's field reports and autopsy technique to carry the narrative than other episodes. The score was more minimalist than ambient or atmospheric and significantly shorter, at just under twenty-four minutes. Yet the opening sequence set the precedent for one of the series' most prevalent methods of blending sound with music, 'synthesizing' nature.

Instead of providing a realistic soundscape, the sound designer, Mark Snow, or both,[6] create a simulacrum of one. Due to synchresis, it is easy to assume that we are hearing the sounds normally associated with a woodland scene at night. But closer listening reveals a highly synthetic soundscape. The artificial bird and insect sounds are not convincing on their own, but take on a realism when welded to the visuals. Even more typical 'sound effects' – the footsteps of a running girl, branches whipping around in the wind – are unrealistically forward in the sound mix, too closely miked, and either highly compressed or artificially produced.

Another feature of this opening soundscape is a low, rumbling sound that seems to enclose the space we see. Even if the space implied is as big as an aeroplane hangar, it creates a subtle sense of claustrophobia and impending doom. The sound could also invoke a massive, distant space ship, though my immediate impression is of enclosed space – individual perception may interpret the reverberant sound differently, but either interpretation is likely to provoke anxiety.

In contrast to the synthetic sound of the pilot's teaser, the opening sequence of 'F. Emasculata' creates a musical texture out of predominantly natural sound. Real, or at least realistic, sounds of birds and insects have evidently been sampled into a synthesizer to create the soundscape of the jungle scene. A distant, reverberant double hit on a bass drum organizes the apparently random screeches and chirps into a rhythmic pattern. The drumbeat forms the downbeat; the bird and insect sounds appear continually in the same sequence, in the same rhythm, entering on successive quaver beats. What prevents the sequence from immediately sounding artificial

---

6 Assigning authorship is difficult, if not impossible, without direct contact with the creators; however, this is not critical, as it is the effect that is of interest here. But the closeness of sound effect and sound design complicates even one of the simplest tasks, determining the extent of the underscore – is the pedal-drone ambient hum score or sound effect, for instance?

is the irregular meter and slight ritardando at the ends of some of the 'bars'.

Shifting the balance between sound effect and musical score, chase sequences feature frequently in the show and are often both the most stereotypically 'scored' sequences and the ones in which sound effects are most tightly integrated. Rarely are there blatant rhythmic connections between the sound effects and the action on the screen, but they create an atmosphere that loosely fits the dramatic situation and the physical space. They are therefore *ambient*, but much louder and more frenetic than is usually associated with that term.

Two separate chases from the same episode, 'Herrenvolk', feature different sounds. In the first, the highly reverberant, metallic percussion playing the busy 'hurry' music evokes the metal catwalk on which the chase takes place. The cue also incorporates a pulsating heartbeat rhythm on the synthesizer's typical electronic 'X-Files' patch when the camera focuses separately on Scully and Mulder stopping to catch their breath in the chase, an excellent example of empathetic scoring.[7] Even the breath sounds seem to be only loosely connected to the action depicted on the screen, but they nonetheless convey the panic and exertion of the scene. A later chase takes place on dried ground and stone, ending in a concrete bunker filled with bees: the reverberation is still unnaturally high, but not as high as in the first chase, and the percussion has shifted from metal pipes and pans to tom-toms and woodblock, ending with a buzzing string sound that throughout the episode replaces real bee sounds.

Similarly, in the episode 'Teso dos Bichos', a chase scene in an urban steam tunnel incorporates the sounds of rattling pipes and rushing air. A more extended use of this scoring technique was in the episode 'Død Kalm', most of which takes place on a submarine. The score is practically musique concrète, created out of the sounds of straining rivets and sheet metal, hollow metallic pings, sonar-like beeps, and the distant sound of water over the typical 'X-Files' synthesizer pad, treated with even more reverberation than usual.

---

7 A later, ambient synth cue in the episode of *Miami Vice* 'Out Where the Buses Don't Run', discussed above, also incorporates heartbeats, but these are real or realistic heartbeat sounds as opposed to these clearly synthetic chords.

Alien/other/exotic

The X-Files – as any X-Phile could tell you – divides into two kinds of episodes: the mythology shows, which further the overarching plot of Mulder's search for the truth that is 'out there' about the US government conspiracy to conceal the alien presence; and the stand-alone shows. The mythology episodes tend to be surpassingly bland in their musical content – consciously or unconsciously evoking the muffling layers of secrecy surrounding the labyrinthine plot – consisting primarily of the standard, meandering ambient synth pad. The stand-alones like 'Død Kalm' are much richer musical ground. For instance, the episode 'Drive', about a pathogenic subsonic sound-transfer technology, has a score primarily composed of complexes of sustained pitches, cueing us to the importance of sound long before the plot turns that way.

Snow does not completely abandon traditional compositional effects, but he incorporates their timbral qualities in the ambient textures he creates for the show, playing on their accrued symbolic meaning without fully exploiting their thematic distinctiveness. For instance, a highly artificial computer-morphed female shriek represents the banshee/succubus figure pursuing Walter Skinner in 'Avatar', while a New-Age-style piano represents his very human wife. This juxtaposition relies on an established distinction between the electronic/supernatural and the acoustic/natural. Orff-like *Carmina Burana*-inspired 'infernal voices' crop up in 'Die Hand die Verletzt' about a Satan-worshipping PTA group, as well as in 'Syzygy', a black-comic episode about astral alignment and the magical energy of two teenage girls. More subtly, wordless, lamenting female voices appear in two of the series' most emotive episodes, both dealing with the fates of young girls.[8] In 'Paper Hearts' it seems that Mulder's missing sister Samantha might not, in fact, have been abducted by aliens, but by a serial murderer of little girls: the recurrent, inarticulate angelic choir represents the unheard voices of all Roche's vulnerable victims, and carries the episode to the series' only musically unresolved ending. 'All Souls' deals with a seraphim returned to earth to retrieve his four severely disabled daughters, the nephilim: these girls provoke memories in

---

8 I explore the potent link between young girls and the voice in the underscore in my 'Adolescents and Angels: Girls' Voices in Recent Film Underscore' (in progress).

Scully of her own dead daughter, Emily, associated in the score with a similar angelic choir.

Because many of the episodes are based on some folkloric element, the issue of exoticism is unavoidable. In order to invoke a particular culture, Snow draws upon certain stereotypical musical sounds to reinforce a sense of atmosphere and depth that there simply is not time to establish otherwise. Therefore we have the panpipes and quena in 'Teso dos Bichos' about a Peruvian priestess's mummy, and Chinese percussion in 'Hell Money', set in San Francisco's Chinatown. A few examples, like these, border on the embarrassing because they are so 'on the nose', so obvious; but others have fascinating layers of meaning generated by the interaction of timbre and compositional technique.

The episode 'El Mundo Giro' teeters on the brink of patronizing Mexican migrant workers; the narrative structure is that of a folktale, which could be taken as a powerful metaphor for fantastic storytelling if not for the (possibly condescending) litany, 'These people love their stories'. The presence of noted Latin American musician and political activist Rubén Blades as 'La Migra', Immigration and Naturalization Service Agent Lozano, helps redress the balance, as does the fact that this is one of the few cases in which the audience and the migrant workers end up knowing more about the explanation of the mystery than do Mulder and Scully. The score might be dismissed as another example of the typical mix-up between Spanish and Mexican music, or it might be considered a subtle evocation of Mexican history, using a synthesized timbre that evokes a guitar in its lower register and a harpsichord in the upper. Beneath a possible explanation of a long-standing Mexican folktale of a goat-vampire ('el chupacabra'), the evocation of Spanish classical music – particularly the slow movements of minor key clavecin sonatas of Domenico Scarlatti – helps along this sense of antiquity. Yet this is an aristocratic image that does not mesh with the peasantry we are seeing on screen. Is this a mismatch, or is it meant to give dignity to the characters? Or, by evoking the colonial past of Mexico, does it remind us of the exploitation of these people over the centuries? In other, more intense situations in the story, we hear a rumba bass line that seems more earthy, sometimes combined with a marimba which begins to construct a mariachi band sound that never quite comes to completion. This fragmented, almost cubistic representation of a particular ethnic music is typical of many

Example 4.2: *Kethuk* pattern

Example 4.3: *Bonang* pattern

episodes of *The X-Files*, providing enough information to locate a story, while withholding enough to avoid the excruciatingly obvious.

Withholding to a remarkable degree, 'Ghost in the Machine' utilizes an Indonesian gamelan. The rationale is that the designer of the rampaging computer at the centre of the story has a deep interest in Eastern philosophy. Making the connection obviously demands that the listener has some sense of the gamelan sound as 'Eastern'. Mark Snow uses the metallophone orchestra in ways that demonstrate he knows something about the instruments. Two parallel scenes centre on Scully's home computer. In the first scene, she makes notes in her field diary; in the second, as she sleeps, the file is accessed remotely by the evil computer. In the second scene, Snow evokes the *kethuk* – a small knobbed brass pot-gong played with a string-wrapped beater giving it a slightly dead sound – played in typical fashion, a manual 'bounce' echo, or small, repeated after-beats (see Ex. 4.2). The kethuk is not normally used as a melodic instrument, however,[9] and this minimal melody may actually be played on a deadened *bonang*. The bonang – similarly shaped to a kethuk but slightly larger and more resonant[10] – is normally used as a 'decorative' element in gamelan, playing a semi-improvised pattern around the main notes of the balungan, or melody, and it typically uses a rocking pattern with a silent downbeat, a figuration evident in this cue (see Ex. 4.3). As with the fragmentation of the mariachi sound in 'El Mundo Giro', the individual elements of the thick gamelan texture are isolated and presented against the *X-Files* synthesizer pad, like jewels on a velvet backing.

9 There are only two *kethuks* in a gamelan, one for each tuning system (*slendro* and pelog) – see Lindsay (1979: 11).
10 A *bonang* is actually composed of a full range of pot-gongs, each representing a pitch of the scale (Lindsay 1979: 13).

Example 4.4: Rhythm of the lift

Snow detaches the instruments from their normal function in the gamelan, but he uses them with clear awareness of their distinctive methods of playing.[11] Therefore, the rhythmic pattern in another sequence is striking in that it includes a kind of syncopation completely alien to the traditional gamelan. This does not make sense until the sequence unwinds, following the computer designer from his home terminal, where he discerns a problem, to the office building, where he watches in horror as an FBI agent is plunged to his death in a computer-controlled lift. Snow has integrated sound with score in an unusual and unexpected way. Just before the drop, the lift's mechanical voice sticks between floors, and the rhythm of its repeated 'twenty-nine, thirty/twenty-nine, thirty' fits neatly with the syncopation (see Ex. 4.4). Snow apparently wrote this entire three-minute sequence backward from this moment. It is, of course, possible that the sequence was edited to the music, but Snow is normally given a completed episode to score (Lowry 1996: 59–60).

The connection between the gamelan and Eastern philosophy is at least logical, even if not automatic. One of the few recurrent sounds in *The X-Files* actually makes *no* sense if you know its provenance. One must reject recognition to make the connection to the sheer timbral power. The sound is the striking attack of a Bulgarian radio choir of women's voices, with its distinct hit, upward slide, open-throated yet nasal vocal quality, edgy timbre, and harmonies that sound dissonant to Western European ears. The sound was first used in the early episode 'The Jersey Devil', appearing at the point at which Mulder realizes that the Bigfoot-like creature they are stalking might possibly be female. It recurs several times in the episode, mixed deep into the reverberant synth pad and strongly associated with the presence of the beautiful, 'primitive' wild woman. This makes all sorts of ethnocentric, yet powerfully resonant, connections between the mysterious woman in the

---

11 This is something not discernible from merely listening to a gamelan.

episode and the vocal production of the Bulgarian radio choir, which is actually highly polished and superbly trained. It also partakes of a strain of American culture (at least) that perceives that sound as 'otherworldly'; this term, as well as the striking juxtaposition of 'earthy' and 'ethereal', crops up time and time again in describing the Bulgarian voices, helped along by the association with Marcel Cellier's celebrated collections released under the title of *Les Mystères des Voix Bulgares*. Preceding even this, however, was Carl Sagan's contribution to popular culture, the 1980 science documentary series *Cosmos*. Over the sequence describing the Voyager spacecraft and its recorded message to alien species sounds a Bulgarian shepherdess's song, one of the many pieces of music inscribed on the golden LP on the spacecraft.

That distinctive Bulgarian choir attack has clearly been sampled into Mark Snow's synclavier (in fact, it appears to be the very first sound of the first track of the first *Les Mystères* album, 'Pilentze Pee'), and it is a patch he uses, if not frequently, then with somewhat more consistency than any other such memorable sound. It has been used in two other episodes: 'Fresh Bones', in connection with the power of voodoo; and even more strikingly in the episode 'Teliko', about a sort of African vampire. At least voodoo has a strong female connection, its power resting largely in the hands of priestesses, but the Teliko is male. By this point in the series' run, it appears that the sound is simply connected to a powerful, supernatural force, a connection that seems based solely on its timbral qualities, not just its gender. It also becomes increasingly forward in the mix with each successive usage; by the time of 'Teliko', it is foregrounded prominently.[12]

The use of identifiably ethnic elements in the fragmented scores of *The X-Files* episodes demonstrates a politically dangerous but culturally potent slippage between 'others'. The depiction of an ethnic supernatural manifestation is linked to a musical representation of that ethnic group. A term

---

12 This distinctive sample has become a part of Snow's compositional vocabulary beyond *The X-Files*. The vocal attack and upward slide, with a less nasal vocal quality, also appeared in Snow's score of Carter's parallel series *Millennium* (1996–99), which overall has a warmer, more 'acoustic' sound; extending the association with female power, the sound symbolizes the diabolical Lucy Butler. Snow used a more extensive sample from 'Pilentze Pee' in an episode of the 2002 series *Haunted*, connected with the vengeful ghost of a voodoo priestess, harking back to *The X-Files*'s 'Fresh Bones'.

somehow drops out of this equation, and the ethnic becomes 'exotic' through the supernatural and its musical representation. In the case of the Bulgarian radio choir, the equation seems to shed terms indiscriminately – the ethnic (and female) becomes the supernatural other, and it is only a short step, then, to the alien, even the extraterrestrial. Music appears to be an efficient lubricant for such slippage.

Language and transformation

As his use of the Bulgarian voices hints, Mark Snow has largely created for *The X-Files* a music-sound syntax of its own. That grammar has now become established enough to make departures from the norm make sense, or even to make comedy. The use of the whistling theme-tune as the theme of Scully's 'alien autopsy' video in 'Jose Chung's *From Outer Space*' is overt comedy, particularly as it is in the major mode, but the pizzicato string accompaniment of other scenes is the direct opposite of the usual electronic, dense scoring of the series. It also bears resemblance to the accompaniment patterns of *opera buffa*, at odds with the scenes of alien torture or men-in-black invasions depicted on-screen, casting an ironic light over the dark proceedings.

More subtly, our sense of reality may be altered in the pre-title teaser of 'Paper Hearts', when Snow deploys one of his most overtly 'musical', if minimal, cues. Mulder is fetched out of his darkened apartment by a mysterious red light which flashes 'follow'. He obeys. A time ellipsis carries him to a State Park, where he sees a white mini-truck we will later associate with serial killer Roche. The red light spells out 'mad hat' on its side. Mulder runs into the woods, where he finds a little girl, apparently sleeping on a pile of leaves. As he approaches and looks down at her, the red light traces a heart on the breast of her flannel nightie, and she sinks into the leaves. Startled, Mulder sits up on his sofa, sweating from his nightmare.

Although this looks like a typical *X-Files* opening event, the music signals before anything else that it is, in fact, a dream sequence. The more lyrical music shifts it into a different register of discourse before the increasingly surreal and unlikely images and discontinuities do. However, this *is* the opening sequence; we must be aware of the show's general sound-world before we, however unconsciously, may process that information.

With such a distinctive look and sound already established – especially with a look so cinematic and a sound so appropriate to the subject matter – one would have expected the transformation to the big screen to be fairly straightforward. However, although the movie *looks* like *The X-Files*, it certainly doesn't sound like it. Given the budget and the expectations of a major motion picture, Mark Snow created a full orchestral score in keeping with a Hollywood summer blockbuster. The synthesizer is almost completely absent, though the ambient hum reappears, particularly in the underground sequences (but also in the corridors of the FBI Building in Washington, where Scully and Mulder are under administrative threat). In the extensive publicity surrounding the release of the film, it seems as though once the film was green-lighted, an orchestral score was understood by both Snow and Carter to be desirable and necessary (see for instance Duncan 1998, Koppl 1998). Amazingly, the possibility of a synthesizer score does not appear ever to have crossed their minds.

In the film, Snow works with melodic and thematic fragments far more than in any television episode. He even uses the harp-like arpeggios and whistle-tune, both independently and together, in the underscore. This was a tactic he had only used in the television series as a joke, as we have already seen. Other than the title sequence, in which the television theme slowly coalesces under expensive-looking, liquid metallic graphics, the tune first occurs in a lightly comic sequence. Mulder and Scully drive through the flatlands of North Texas, arguing over which direction to take at a T-section before Mulder takes an executive decision and drives off the road, straight ahead. Although their purpose is serious, this moment of comic relief and the lightly textured underscore encourages the connection of the narrative use of this music with the comic, which threatens to undermine the drama later in the film in much darker circumstances.

The difference between shot composition and editing in television and film also has ramifications for the scoring. One of the most 'cinematic' aspects of film is spectacle, particularly large-scale, panoramic views, like the pullback from Mulder and Scully's car, tiny in the flat landscape of North Texas, or the huge alien spaceship under the snows of Antarctica. Spectacle is inextricably associated with music in film – as the camera lingers on huge or complex or hugely complex visuals, music seems to be vital, providing some sort of cushion for the audience and/or depth to the images. It is in these

76

sequences in which the music of *The X-Files: Fight the Future* departs most dramatically from the score of the television series. On a smaller scale, but similarly transformative of the musical experience, is the difference in rhythm between an uninterrupted film and a multi-act television programme meant to have commercials.[13] The series of small cliffhangers, each with its own post-commercial resolution, typical of an *X-Files* episode generates similar musical gestures, with moderately quiet, open-ended cadential figures resolving into the string pad upon return from the adverts. A film simply is not paced or edited like that; action tends to escalate more quickly and intensely, and of course, is not usually interrupted. A typical sequence in *The X-Files: Fight the Future* is when the agents converge on the vending room where Mulder is waiting with a rigged drinks machine and Scully organizes the building's evacuation. Snow responds with what have become action movie clichés. As Scully realizes that Mulder is not joking about the bomb, she gets on the phone to the FBI while running down to the lobby; the strings pulse in a hesitant crotchet–quaver–quaver pattern and the orchestra crescendos to a *mf* into the jump-cut of Scully bursting through the lobby door. As the other agents arrive outside and streams of people leave the building, the strings change to a more insistent, steady crotchet pulsation at *mf*, building once more to a *ff* and a jump-cut, this time to silence as the camera tracks down the drinks machine loaded with C4 plastic explosives to the timer clock. At times like these, the distinctiveness of *The X-Files* is lost in its transformation from unique television experience to rather generic Hollywood blockbuster.

The oscillation between film and television is not complete with the movie, however. In the sixth season, after the release of the film, cinematic scoring becomes more prominent. This is most marked in the episode 'Triangle', a turning-point in the relationship between Mulder and Scully – or is it? Mulder is transported to the *Queen Anne*, a British ocean liner which disappeared in the Bermuda Triangle in 1939; though at first he thinks the ship and her passengers have been brought forward to 1998 (hence he makes an oblique joke about the Monica Lewinsky affair), in fact, he is back in 1939

---

13 When *The X-Files* is shown on British television, the rhythm is disturbed, whether through the lack of commercials on the BBC, or more profoundly, by the insertion of commercials in the wrong spots, as on Sky One.

and the ship has been boarded by Nazis. The passengers include a sassy OSS agent who is a dead ringer for Scully. Harking back to films like *Raiders of the Lost Ark* and *Titanic*, 'Triangle' features a sparky flirtation between Mulder and the OSS agent, ending in a passionate kiss – the first for stars Duchovny and Anderson, if not their characters[14] – filmed with a big-screen-style shot spiralling in on the couple. The episode also references 1939's classic film *The Wizard of Oz*: the *Queen Anne's* captain is named Yip Harburg, after the film's lyricist; the ship's singer is named Elvira Gulch; and the end scene, with Mulder waking up in the hospital, is a direct parody of the ending of *The Wizard of Oz*, with the Lone Gunmen standing in as the Scarecrow (Langly), the Tin Man (Byers), and the Cowardly Lion (Frohike).[15] Helping along the cinematic feel of the episode is its letterboxed format, mimicking Cinemascope, and a score as cinematic, if not more so than the theatrical film. The orchestral texture incorporates the whistling tune in a serious context for the first time in the series. If the film had not already broken that particular barrier, it might not have worked in the episode. The period aspects also allow a more 'classical' scoring style than the more exotic episodes through stylistic analogy.

Conclusion

One of the keys to the popularity of *The X-Files* is the variety of levels on which audiences may find entry into its world. It may be taken at face value by those who believe in alien visitation and government conspiracy. Like *Beavis and Butthead*, which celebrates ironically those it ridicules, *The X-Files* is at the very least ambivalent about the opinions and actions of its central characters. Other viewers may like its action or its links to horror genres, and that is not to underestimate the appeal of its attractive stars. Still others will enjoy it on a more intellectual level, spotting the references, ranging from dialogue to camera angles and lighting, borrowed from other famous horror and science fiction films. The music is similarly multi-levelled: even those who are not conscious of the score will be affected by the sheer sound, the

14 When, at the end of the episode, Mulder tells Scully at his hospital bedside that he loves her, her reaction is an exasperated groan.
15 This scene is a double reference, as there is a similar scene in *The X-Files: Fight the Future*.

reverberant hum, the ambient noise, the empathetic heartbeats and breathing; others will be aware of the music but not register its complexity; still others will recognize the specific musical aspects such as those dealt with in this chapter. A very small proportion of viewers is likely to recognize the gamelan references, for instance, yet the resonant traces of its intelligent use are there.

The X-Files partakes of a certain continuity of television scoring, drawing on stylistically outstanding precedents, but aware of the medium's technical limitations (particularly in the area of sound reproduction), and limited by the economic resources of its production circumstances. Those choices, aesthetically and practically determined, reinforce the show's visual and discursive style, setting it apart from the more typical science fiction fare, with their swashbuckling orchestral scores. Other recent shows like *Miami Vice, Star Trek: The Next Generation*, and *The Practice* have distanced television scoring techniques from cinematic ones, integrating the function more closely with that of sound than in most films. Technological and economic reasons no doubt generated this evolution, but aesthetics have been transformed along with function. The music may be less autonomous, but its effectiveness as mediator of the visual experience has, if anything, been increased.

5   Feel the beat come down: house music as rhetoric

STAN HAWKINS

It's 4 a.m. and you're speeding. On the crowded dance space, jagged flashes of strobe lighting fuse with the booming sound of the sub-bass to create a kaleidoscope of sensations. The sonic roar is driven by the fast pace of the 125 bpm beat, transporting you to a destination far removed from the grim realities of everyday life. Blood pressure rises as the temperature in the room intensifies and the beat takes control; all inhibitions are abandoned for euphoria. Lost in the music, you are aware of your feelings for all sharing the dancefloor as the serotonin in your body creates waves of depthless bliss. Suddenly the break section is upon us and the regular $\frac{4}{4}$ beat becomes layered with the amorous moans of a female vocalist lifting our emotions to a higher plateau. Next the rhythm and bass drop out leaving the voice on its own, raw, exposed, orgasmic. Flanged into the mix, pleasurable groans fill the air as the strobes dissipate into a flood of purple haze. You want to swoon, fall, float, as suspense in waiting for the return of the beat becomes an excruciating eternity. Caught in time, the crowd appears in a trance swaying with arms raised in response to the ecstatic moans of the female vocalist. Starting up again, then, slowly, the beat begins to pound through: the throb of the kick drum punctuated with stabs of metal-edged brass sounds on the off-beats. No longer are you listening, but feeling the overpowering beat as everyone starts jacking to the energy with a fluency that locks into the beat.

Musicological considerations

My approach in this chapter is to suggest ways for evaluating the track described above by identifying some of the organizing structures

I would like to express my gratitude to Bjarne Kvinnsland of NoTAM (Norwegian Network for Technology, Acoustics and Music) for generously affording his time to assist with sonographic readings of 'French Kiss', as well as discussing with me technological-related issues relevant to the development of popular music analysis.

and processes that are relevant to understanding its aesthetic.[1] Central to this analysis is a concern for examining style through a range of compositional features which systematize it.[2] Part of my study draws on reductive techniques to expose the details of structure and processing through which various parameters of rhythmic construction are presented as a basis for framing questions relating to musical composition and its communicative scope for expression. The main contention here is predicated upon a premise that many scholars of popular musicology have been anxious to emphasize: that the analysis of music only becomes meaningful when positioned in relation to the social space it is received in.

Accepting that house music is culture-specific, my argument proposes that its organization *musically* is a critical premise for working out its effect *musicologically*.[3] My purpose here is to discover and determine how some of the *internal mechanisms* of a house track function. Underpinning this investigation is a concern for how processes of composition can be identified in direct proximity to the technologies that produce them. In this respect, the DJ's task is to organize musical material through the imaginative application of technology. House music is generally based around simple rhythmic patterns which, when technologically manipulated, develop into complex sound-structures; variations on basic patterns of rhythmic, melodic

---

1 Throughout I have elected to employ the word track rather than piece or song as this is the term DJs commonly use. Note that Reynolds (1998) has suggested that track derives from the early stages of house where the music consisted of little more than a drum track and reel-to-reel tape and cassette.

2 Clearly, in undertaking any analysis of this kind, there is always the question of musical source. Turning to a recording of a dance track immediately separates the musical text from the context of its social space: the club setting, the sound-system, the mood of the crowd. In this sense, the recording is only representative of the sounds and processes the DJ has produced. However, in the case of the track, 'French Kiss', to be analyzed in this chapter, the rather unusual exception of this being a hit (in commercially recorded form) needs to be taken into consideration.

3 Also see Tagg (1994) who provides numerous important reasons for taking rave music seriously from a musicological position. Tagg's concern is that questions of musical structures in dance music should be recognized as different from 'rockology' in order to effectively and accurately assess their socialization strategies. Perhaps most significant is his claim that techno-rave ends nearly 400 years of 'the great European bourgeois individual' which begins with Peri and Monteverdi and ends with 'Whitney Houston and the TV spot for Bodyform sanitary towels' (Tagg 1994: 219).

and harmonic ideas is central to the compositional character of a track. As all the DJ's skills in mixing and editing are thrown together, the sound-object becomes the focal attention for response through dance. Importantly, the openness of house arrangements affords the DJ time and space to measure the dynamics of participation at the social event; the potential for social involvement is where the purpose of musical performance in house music is located through the unlimited mechanisms of sound reproduction.

There is little doubt then that house music refers to a complex set of social circumstances linked to specific practices and developments in musical production. Any musicological consideration of this genre, therefore, should not overlook the connection between the sounds emanating from studio-based production and their social reception. On this, Paul Théberge has insisted that in no other field has the 'link between "sound" and musical genre been so intensely formed' as in dance styles since the 1980s (Théberge 1997: 196). The relationship between sound and DJ[4] can be considered an act of ritual which discloses what is at the core of music production and consumption. In this sense, understanding dance as a response to house music is about the recognition and utilization of evolving technologies and cultures.

'French Kiss': on the wave of the Chicago phenomenon

Historically, house music, an immediate descendant of disco, originated in the clubs of the US in the late seventies.[5] Deeper and rawer than disco, it attracted large crowds who flocked in their droves to venues like the Warehouse Club in Chicago, often as a gesture of solidarity and cultural protest. Simon Reynolds explains:

4 A detailed and useful account of the role of DJs in the music industry has been provided by Tony Langlois who emphasizes the system of marketing house music. In order to keep in touch with the recent developments in house, DJs are often employed in other areas of the music industry, such as in record shops, journalism, event organizing, and studio-based work. DJs are constantly trying out new tracks in their clubs through the promotional channels of 'white label' singles. See Langlois (1992: 232–3).
5 Traces of house are found as far back in the New York underground scene before disco. New York DJs such as Francis Grosso, Steve D'Aquisto, and Michael Capello in the early seventies were already joining up tracks to create non-stop grooves which focus on the rhythmic track.

Chicago house music was born of a double exclusion, then: not just black, but gay and black. Its refusal, its cultural dissidence, took the form of embracing a music that the majority culture deemed dead and buried. House didn't just resurrect disco, it mutated the form, intensifying the very aspects of the music that most offended white rockers and black funkateers: the machinic repetition, the synthetic and electronic textures, the rootlessness, the 'depraved' hypersexuality and 'decadent' druggy hedonism.

(Reynolds 1998: 15)

Reputed by some to have derived its name from the Warehouse,[6] house started off as a culture with DJs at the helm competing with one another for the most exciting effects and mixing tricks in production. It was during this period that DJ Lil' Louis started up a club called Horizon West which became famous for its punk-type Sunday events.[7]

By 1983, the radio had assumed an important role by airing the various styles and grooves that clubbers wanted.[8] Notwithstanding the sheer diversity of stylistic tendencies and influences, a house style gradually emerged. And it was through the first house records that the style initially caught on as fierce competition soon fired up between the labels, Trax and DJ International in their efforts to release the best records.

While by 1989, a number of cities in the UK[9] and other parts of Europe had become centres for the rave and techno scene, having imported

6 In terms of coming up with a definition of 'house' I'm inclined to turn to the Detroit DJ, Juan Atkins, who claimed that house was derived from the record one would hear in a particular club. Carefully selected, the DJ would play a record, often an import, which was as unique as possible to his/her club, and this would become known as a 'house' record. As a result this led to the concept of DJs creating their own records which would then be completely exclusive. In a more general sense the term 'house', at least up to 1989, was used to include rave music. More recently, the proliferation of sub-genres in house has resulted in countless labels to describe its stylistic orientation. Also see Hawkins (1993); Thornton (1995); Kempster (1996); Rietveld (1997, 1998); and Reynolds (1998).
7 By 1983, numerous venues had sprung up in and around Chicago, not least, Ron Hardy's club, The Music Box. Hardy soon became a central person to whom other DJs would take their tracks to for testing out the public's reaction.
8 As a result of this the Imports Etc. record store in Chicago was inundated with requests for records to be played on radio. It was out of this context that the first major house hit by Farley 'Jackmaster' Funk, 'Love Can't Turn Around', was released in August 1986.
9 For example, London and the northern cities of Manchester, Liverpool, Blackpool, Sheffield and Leeds.

83

and transformed many ideas from the States, house music in the USA had developed into four distinct styles: deep New York and Chicago house; Detroit techno; sample-based hip house, minimal jack tracks and acid house.[10] And, by the end of the eighties, a deeper kind of sound was typifying Chicago house which eventually led to a more hardcore scene. On the wave of this, a 'sex track' phenomenon emerged resulting in hits such as 'French Kiss' by Lil' Louis, the track I will focus on in this chapter. When Lil' Louis introduced the first mix of this track at one of his parties (attracting between 5,000 and 8,000 people a night), little did he realize that it was going to be a commercial hit. Finally released two years later in 1989, this became house music's first million seller on both sides of the Atlantic. Banned by the BBC and a number of New York clubs, its tumultuous popularity was almost assured as it 'stole into the nation's collective consciousness during the strange not-quite summer, before the 1980s metamorphosed into the 1990s' (in Kempster 1996: 27). But, perhaps most compelling and memorable was its complete slowing down to a halt in the middle, exposing a series of orgasmic utterances. According to Tim Barr, this track pulled dance music 'into an interior world of jacked-up eroticism and sensual, hip-tugging grooves' (Kempster 1996: 27) encapsulating the sexual explicitness of Chicago house music in the late eighties.[11]

Editing and mechanizing the 'beat'

As already intimated, the evolution of house music can be traced through the music technology that has produced it. In the beginning, house tracks, basic in their conception, consisted of a drum track, a straightforward bass line, synthesizer keyboards, and occasional vocals. Gradually the development of new, flexible technologies resulted in the hybridization of house

---

10 Interestingly, Reynolds emphasizes that it was Black America that had generated these four full-formed styles. On being exported to Europe these sounds would then mutate 'through a kind of creative misrecognition on the part of the British and Europeans' (Reynolds 1998: 33).

11 Rietveld provides the following account of this trend: 'In night clubs which catered to dancers who enjoyed experimenting with their sense of sexuality, these often melancholic tracks, driven by deep rolling bass sounds and filled with sentiments of desire and lust, fitted perfectly' (Rietveld 1997: 128).

and other dance styles.[12] In particular, the programming of drum sounds and rhythms on state-of-the-art drum machines, MIDI, and sampling tools, would rapidly establish a range of stylistic norms which concentrated on the 'mechanization' of the 'beat' (see Goodwin 1998: 126).

In terms of musical editing, drum programming would have far-reaching implications in the formation of dance trends. As Goodwin has emphasized, the advantage of a new type of flexibility through the application of technology greatly enhanced this mode of performance. Indeed, it was the creative application of music technology that spelt out the aesthetic of house. Despite what 'technophobes' might perceive as the rigidity and machine-like senselessness of repetition, improvisation is an important part of the DJ's intentions. In club music, at least, how the feel and meaning are generated is best understood as a process of continual improvisation rather than 'progressive' development (also see Keil and Feld 1994: Chapter 3). As Lil' Louis has emphasized, there is far more to editing and production than the pushing of pre-set buttons: 'A lot of people look at editing as a mechanical process but it isn't. It's definitely a *feel* thing' (in Kempster 1996: 29, emphasis added).

Inevitably, Louis's above comment not only raises questions concerning the processes of music-making and the claims made by DJs concerning their selection of equipment, but also how music is received and evaluated. Notably, Chicago and Detroit DJs have tended to prioritize the creative manipulation of low-level equipment above the latest, up-to-date gear. The interesting point here is that aspirations to musical innovation and 'authenticity' are often located in the imaginative control of obsolete equipment and an interest for its sonic possibilities; analogue synthesizers, for example, are preferred to digital machines because of their 'warmth' in sound. On this, Lil' Louis has claimed: 'Generally I concentrate on sounds rather than particular instruments.... Music should be wide open. I try to display the fact that it doesn't have to be this instrument or that instrument,

12 See Andrew Goodwin (1998) for a useful study into issues concerning the programming of machines in relation to drumming. Also see Rietveld (1998) for a detailed discussion of music technologies used in house. Notably she emphasizes the economic consequences of the rise of a DIY market based on affordable recording technology, all of which made home production possible. The production of 'white label' could also be used by DIY producers as a marketing tool to try out the market.

or all live instruments or all synthesized. It can be anything' (in Kempster 1996: 29). For the purpose of the following musicological critique then, Louis's statement serves as a fitting point of departure for evaluating the properties of compositional processing found in a house track.

Stripping it down! Beats, hypermetric units, CGPs, and processes in 'French Kiss'

Producing musical ideas in house is contingent on the DJ's sensibility for processing patterns that convincingly spell out the stylistic idiom. In numerous ways, the DJ's role might be likened to that of the 'master drummer' in certain African cultures where the individual's responsibility for producing the grooves determines the social success of the event (Chernoff 1979). Through moulding together diverse layers of rhythmic textures and timbres, the musical outcome is ultimately measured by its ability to 'move' the community. And, as Christopher Small has stated: 'At the convergence of essence and form stands the master drummer, not creating new rhythms but giving order and organization to those already there' (Small 1987: 295). House's *intensional* quality is thus located within similar processes of inflection, repetition and development that are intrinsic to African music. In particular, its sensations are felt through the looping of grooves into polyrhythmic patterns which stretch time into one continuous plane.

A good deal of the appeal in 'French Kiss' lies in the creative processing of rhythmic regulation which forms an important point of consideration when evaluating this house track's compositional content.[13] In addition,

13 Mounting a most contentious argument around the question of 'musicianship', Langlois (1992) insists that this, at least in its 'generally accepted sense' is 'virtually non-existent' in house music. By this he implies that digital production and processing, involving the use of software tools, samplers, MIDI and computers, makes the job easier for composers with a DJ background. As I understand Langlois, his position on the creative evaluation of house music rests on the premise that technological processing 'eases' the process of composition, and, thus, as some might deduce from this assertion, reduces the degree of 'musicianship' required. While Langlois quite clearly recognizes the 'value' of such creative processing, he fails to make a case for 'musicianship' on the terms of the genre he analyses. As a result, his critique easily panders to the general suspicion surrounding the question of expertise or skills in the 'popular' composer and the general problematics of assessing musical value.

the control of the filtering and phasing of sounds, through editing functions, provides the music with its energetic charge. By connecting everything to the beat, DJ Louis produces different feelings from each machine to 'bounce' off the other. For Lil' Louis, the creative application of technology is more important than the type of latest technology one might use. This might explain his preference for multi-track recording over computer-based sequencing. As he claims:

> Music happens because of ideas – they're the important part of the process. I can take any piece of equipment and make something beautiful happen with it. There are a lot of times when I'll be in a music shop and I hear something from a keyboard and I just know it's going to be magic, but I'm not so much a stickler for that kind of thing. I do prefer older equipment – I like analogue stuff a lot better than the newer stuff. With analogue, you can't really miss. There's just no way of beating that pure sound and most of the digital stuff is just imitating that.
>
> (Tim Barr's interview with Lil' Louis in Kempster 1996: 32)

Such sentiments highlight the DJ's approach to the track's production and his processing of musical ideas in 'French Kiss'. But, for the purpose of this study, I want to concentrate primarily on the features that relate to rhythmic processing and metric structure. My commitment to music analysis here is located in the approaches and methods employed to explore the characteristic traits of the beat and its musical organization.

The beat, in its most identifiable form, is the basic unit of temporal measurement, which, in its regularity, is associated with a certain release in energy; in effect, the force of the beat shapes the energy flow. While beats occur in all types of intervals and permutations, they are essentially felt on the four-in-the-bar accents – usually on the kick drum – with their *predictability* expressing a principal aesthetic of house. There is, however, as I will argue, more to the beat than just the properties attached to its quantitative value. As my analysis emphasizes, any consideration of the beat needs to take into account its qualitative implications as well. Thus, the extension of the beat towards other structural levels of understanding, in terms of effect, is necessary in determining the overall rhythmic character of a track.

Constructed around highly repetitive structures, house tracks are usually divided into polyrhythmic loops which sculpture the groove. Responsible for the kinetic flow of material, the groove functions as a unifying unit, transporting with it a sense of regularity crossed with syncopation. In particular, its 'hypermetricity' forms the basis of what Tony Langlois has described as the 'internal logic' of house tracks. Importantly, as Langlois insists, house music is not intended for repeated listenings:

> On first hearing, the lack of predictable connection between musical elements is both confusing and exciting – the steady beat provides a solid background against which to appreciate them. On second or third hearings the internal logic of the piece becomes apparent, it no longer shocks and the meanings are clearer. By the sixth or seventh hearing, most records have already become stale and their meanings exhausted. Because of various re-mixes and performance techniques, however, one is quite unlikely to hear the same record being played the same way twice (Langlois 1992: 235).

From this it would seem that working out the 'internal logic' of a track depends on considering the function of repetition which, in turn, raises the question: repetition from what perspective? As the music analyst Nicolas Ruwet (1987) has emphasized, repetition needs to be comprehended through the many assumptions that define it (also see Keil and Feld 1994).[14] If we accept this premise, determining how repetition works in house is about verifying procedures of repetition in order to illuminate their different functions. To address this I have displayed numerous structural processes of repetition in 'French Kiss' in Table 5.1. As recourse to designating structures of segmentation, the representations of sound in the wave form snapshot of the entire track in the lower section of Table 5.1 serves to verify the rhythmic structures and their overall energy curves in the track.

With reference to Table 5.1, the structural outline of the track consists of a short intro and coda flanking three main divisions: Phase A (beginning at 5''), Phase B (6'10'') and Phase C (7'18''). The term 'phase' is employed

---

14 Cf. Nicolas Ruwet's application of methods (1987) of analysis to procedures of division based on the principle of repetition. Another perspective on 'reading' repetition is made by David Brackett in his study of James Brown's 'Superbad' in which he emphasizes the need for competence when responding to 'grooves': 'a groove exists because musicians know how to create one and audiences know how to respond to one. Something can only be recognized as a groove by a listener who has internalized the rhythmic syntax of a given musical idiom' (Brackett 1995: 144).

Table 5.1 Processes of repetition in 'French Kiss'

to denote the distinct periods in the unfolding of the musical material.[15] Lasting just under ten minutes (9′53″) in total duration, the track consists of approximately seventy units of repetition (excluding the non-rhythmic, ad lib, rubato passages) referred to as hypermetric units, designated in the next section of Table 5.1. Comprising sixteen crotchet beats (four bars), these units are also experienced as part of larger cellular groove patterns (CGPs) which regulate different scale proportions through constantly changing patterns of repetition. Altogether I have identified eleven CGPs (see Table 5.1) which are determined by a range of musical features (see Table 5.2) that signal their transformations. The application of my procedure for identifying these CGP grooves and their structures in Table 5.1 is twofold: (1) to confirm the processes of repetition at work; and (2) to provide structural evidence of the music's symmetrical and asymmetrical properties.

In the shifts between all the phases, CGPs, hypermetric units, single bars, it is essentially the beat, the hypermetric units, and CGPs that regulate the track's musical logic. As a result, the 'beat' is experienced as part of a single bar as well as of a larger hypermetric unit. While there is much room for debate on how one might define grooves and riffs, for the sake of this study I have chosen to categorize them by their groupings according to the musical data that determines their transformations. Generally, while we might easily perceive one main groove running throughout the track, there are also grooves within grooves; it is this aspect of musical organization that ultimately provides the alternating levels of intensity that define the track's syntax.

Given that the characteristics of grooves and beats are central to any taxonomic conception of rhythmic structures in house music, let us consider in more detail the rhythmic procedures employed in 'French Kiss'. From Table 5.1, we can see that the first seven cellular grooves, CGP, CGP(a), CGP(b), CGP(c), CGP(d), CGP(e) and CGP(f) in Phase A constitute the longest section (6′6″) in which each CGP undergoes transformations due to various compositional procedures: entries of musical ideas, effects processing, tempo regulation, textural manipulation. With the arrival of the break section (Phase B), there is a disruption to the CGP series

---

15 Responses I have measured suggest that there is a clear awareness of three distinct phases, as my analysis points out. The Norwegian dancer and choreographer, Odd Johan Fritzøe, interpreted Phase A as the warming up section, Phase B as the revving up period, and Phase C as the hi-energy, jacking-to-the-beat phase.

Table 5.2 Features determining CGPs

Time Duration	Hypermetric units	Groove	Form	Dominant Musical Features
0–4″			Intro	strings/space sounds
5″–59″	1–7	CGP	Phase A	synth/kick drum/hi-hats
1′00–1′30″	8–11	CGP (a)		synth/k.drum/hi-hat/shakers
1′31″–2′02″	12–15	CGP (b)		brass stabs (panned and filtered)
2′03″–2′42″	16–20	CGP (c)		reverbed hand claps on two & four
2′43″–4′26″	21–34	CGP (d)		four-pitch melodic synth motif
4′27″–5′28″	35–41	CGP (e)		modulation down a maj. second/ long sustained string note
5′21″–6′09″	42–45	CGP (f)	▼	slowing down of tempo/entry of female vocal moans and grunts
6′10″–6′22″	46–47	none	Phase B	no drum sounds/vocal utterances accompanied by slowed down brass motif (panned with heavy effects)
6′23″–7′09″	48–53	CGP (g)		entry of groove (synth + kit) – gradual speeding up
7′10″–7′17″	54	fermata	▼	no kit – filtered brass sounds and vocal utterances
7′18″–8′13″	55–61	CGP (h)	Phase C	return of main 'beat'; motif/ further increase in tempo/ vocal moans layered/pitch modulation in brass motif
8′14″–8′41″	62–65	CGP (i)		snare drum rolls mixed in
8′42″–9′19″	66–71″	CGP (j)	▼	full arrangement of all parts/ entry of long string note
9′27″–9′53″		none	Coda	no rhythm/string note exposed/ entry of ring modulated phasing effects in fade out.

(hypermetric units 46–7). Upon its return, the groove's (CGP(g)) tempo is considerably slowed down exposing the metric details of the rhythmic organization in 'slow-motion'. Then, following the free-floating fermata moment (hypermetric unit 54), Phase C starts up again with the first of three more variants of the cellular groove – CGP(h), CGP(i) and CGP(j) consisting of the hypermetric units, 55–61, 62–5 (see Ex. 5.2, below) and 66–71. As the musical ideas transported by each CGP are never identical, a certain sense

91

of expectancy results through the anticipation of changing effects in the CGPs' progression. Put differently, the compositional techniques of regulating repetition through the organization of the CGPs invoke a complementary sense of contrast versus constancy, which, on closer inspection, increases our understanding of rhythmic articulation through metric organization.

In most music, metre has a direct bearing upon how we interpret features of rhythm and beat duration, while the relationship between adjacent and non-adjacent rhythmic events is integral to the procedures of structural transformation determined by metric organization. Prevalent in 'French Kiss' are different strata of rhythmic motif that exist in the hypermetric articulation and beat configurations. Perhaps it is worth stressing here that metre is an abstract temporal construct for determining types of rhythmic movement. In this sense, metre might be best understood as conceptual in its function (see Coker 1972: Chapter 6). On this same point, Blom and Kvifte (1986) have argued that experiencing metre is based on inferential processes in the minds of the respondent. This would imply that metre is more in the mind than the music, as Kvifte insists:

> one and the same sound can be perceived in more than one meter by different persons, or by the same person at different times. That is: *meter is something one uses; a way of ordering sounds in a musically meaningful fashion.* . . . (This is) also obvious from the fact that metrical signs in written music – time signatures and barlines – are not represented by distinctly audible features in the music . . . barlines can only be inferred, not directly perceived. (Blom and Kvifte 1986: 495)

From my perspective, the metric organization of beats in house is situated in the articulation of recurrent patterns of motion as much as in the individual units of accentual stress. Indeed, the units denoting the beats determine their quality of movement through their schematic groupings into metrical measurements. Main beat-types in the groove appear on and off the beat. While the kick drum pounds out regular beats, four to the bar, the superimposed organ synth accents strong and weak beats with a syncopated couplet pattern that captures the stereotype idiom of house music – the melodic feature described by Philip Tagg as the 'almost obligatory syncopated keyboard chordal rhythm figure' (Tagg 1994: 214). Mapped against the regularity of the beat, the cross-rhythmic metric tension between the steady kick drum

Example 5.1: Sonogram

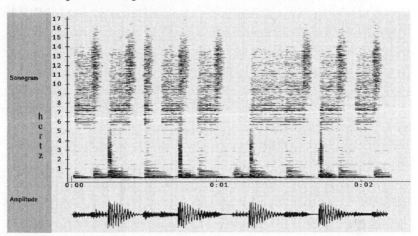

pulse and this melodic cliché ultimately spells out house music's aesthetic (See Ex. 5.2).

Inasmuch as we might be able to instantly recognize the succession of metronomic pulses, there are nevertheless many different ways to rationalize the beat. Above all, the impact of rhythmic articulation through the process of production, together with the relative amplitude of the beats,[16] considerably affects the ways we feel the rhythm. In stark contrast to many other forms of music, the beat in house music is tightly regulated to create a sensation of machination. Yet, as the sonogram of one of the first single bars of 'French Kiss' suggests (Ex. 5.1), the distribution of energy through rhythm, texture and timbre, perceived on a microstructural level, is complex. The energy in the kick drum and organ riff, concentrated in the lower part of the graph, often drops below 1,000Hz. Between 1,400–5,000Hz the overtone spectrum of the high string pitch which arches over the introduction into the first CGP is visible in the sparseness of texture displayed in this mid-region. The density of the hi-hat's energy, like the bass, spans most of the sonogram with its concentration occurring between 6,000–17,000Hz. Closer scrutiny of this sonogram also discloses the gaps in the sonic texture and the intricate spatiality of rhythmic punctuation. Between 150–500Hz the synth organ

16 Dirk Moelants (1997) refers to the relative duration and amplitude of beats as microstructures, claiming that this is necessary to clarify the differences in metric movement in music of contrasting styles.

sound is sparse in comparison to the bass, while the hi-hats foregrounding in the mix, like the bass's range, occupy the upper region, in concentrated levels between 6,000–17,000Hz. From the sonogram and the wave form representations of Example 5.1, it is clear that the overall effect of each of the four kick drum beats in the mix, together with the inflections of other timbres and textures, comprise the most dominant feature. Additionally, the sonogram displays how tension is regulated through the control of the strong and weak components of the metre. Most of all, the rhythmic traits of organization are clearly perceivable in the vertical layers of sonic representation, which, in effect, hold the clue to the chemistry of the groove. Significantly, the sonogram suggests that metric organization in the track is never *absolute*[17] as a result of the variable qualities of the beat.

As first listening of 'French Kiss' betrays, the gradual manipulation of tempo to a virtual standstill in Phase B occurs at the point of entry of the vocal utterance. Gradually, with the working up of the textures after the breakpoint, the track's moment of transcendence occurs during Phase C's outburst of blissful charge (7'18"). Here, the continuous repetition of the pounding bass beats and the fresh juxtapositioning of ideas in the tightly controlled levels in the production produce the most concentrated spurts of energy. Programmed on a TR-808 drum machine,[18] the drum sounds are tightly controlled through their positionings in the mix. Moreover, the compositing of musical layers enhances the hypermetric details of tension and release, focusing our attention on the intricacies of the production; such as the subtle differences in the organ attack, the vivid timbral contrast between the deep bass sounds and the high-pitched splash of open and closed hi-hats, all of which shade in the dynamics of the groove. From this it is evident that the transformations of CGPs within all three phases instil in the track a sense of primary musical charge. With the introduction of

---

17 This point is also raised by Coker (1972) in his conceptualization of the pulse as a unit of temporal measurement.

18 The Roland TR-808 drum machine signified a breakthrough for producers of dance music as it enabled them to program rhythms and process drum sounds separately. In other words, it became a serious compositional tool which could store up to thirty-two patterns on two banks, as well as providing space for over 700 bars for use. Also see Théberge (1997) for a useful discussion of the capabilities of drum machines, such as the TR-808, and their influence on the emergence of musical styles in dance culture.

each CGP, new features are introduced which affirm meaning. As illustrated in Table 5.2, it is the entry of percussion sounds, melodic ideas, and studio effects (filtering) that produce alterations in the CGPs' syntax. In addition, while creating a sense of progression, each change in the CGPs constantly transforms the rhythmic syntax of the track.[19]

Notably the extreme alterations in tempo in Phase B underline the prominence of the beat. While the beat remains mostly constant during the tempo-changes, additional qualities of metric manipulation induce variation.[20] These are most discernible in the tempo fluctuations, the fermatas, the break section (Phase B (hypermetric units 46–7)), the different cross-rhythmic pulsations (see CGP(i) in Ex. 5.2), all of which allow for an extensive range of emotive possibilities on the part of the dancer/listener. As we can see in Table 5.1, the effect of the complete alteration of the musical material at 6'10'' is verified by the amplitude readings of the wave-forms which indicate an acute lapse in energy level, with the focus on the mid-range intensity of the vocal utterances.

The intricate elements of rhythm, metre and repetition thus reveal interesting traits which mould the musical material into an organic unity.[21] Furthermore, the organization of all the CGPs bears directly upon the signification of beat structures and their metric construction. And, it is the impact of all the musical events entering and exiting the mix at specific points that determines the fluctuating currency of the beat; the result being that while the beat maintains a sense of regularity throughout, it is never stable. Continuously transformed through editing processes and metrical distribution, the beat controls how the energy in the track is compositionally

---

19 For a useful discussion of this, see Headlam (1997), who raises questions concerning perception of metre in his analysis of blues transformations in Cream. He emphasizes how the analysis of rhythm in country blues becomes problematic through a confusion of perspective in terms of deciding whether metre is regular or irregular.

20 This observation has also been made in a useful study conducted by Dirk Moelants (1997) into the subsymbolic aspects of metre.

21 Here it could be argued that the structural properties and 'banality' in repetition that define house are not that dissimilar to those of minimalism in 'high' art and contemporary music. Not only can parallels be found in the developmental techniques employed, but also through the music's disembodiment from many of the traditional procedures commonly associated with rhythmic, harmonic and melodic control in Western musical practice.

Example 5.2: Transcription of first and last bars in CGP(i)

expended. When we fix on the regularity of bass beats per bar, we are not only aware of how the tempo controls the energy flow, but also how the multi-dimensionality of the beat is always a fluid structural feature (see Ex. 5.2). Shorter and faster durations signal a more rapid flow and greater force in rhythmic energy as the full throttle of rhythmic propensity releases the power of musical momentum in the final lap of Phase C. It is at this point in 'French Kiss' that the functionalism of repetition triggers off all those physical reflexes which create the sensations of an imaginary space and an urgency to dance.

From Example 5.2, it is clear through transcription how the distribution of metre in 'French Kiss' is manifested in a rhythmicization of events. In this instance, transformation of the rhythmic material hitherto is derived from the brass stabs (Cm 11) in the last bar of CGP(i) on weak and strong semiquaver beats. Such a gesture has its origins in funk and certain jazz styles and can imply a familiar reference point for the dancer. Here, the regularity of the kick-drum, handclaps and hi-hats (open and closed) are heard differently due to the total effect of this brass idiom. In this context it should also be noted that the effects used on the brass stab further accentuate its edge in terms of rhythmic and timbral flavour. In this way, through studio production, a greater emphasis is placed on the beat as it defines the musical characteristics of the hypermetric unit and ultimately the structure of the CGP. From this example, we can see that while repetition proceeds on one level (in the kick drum, organ continuum and hi-hats), variation is an omnipresent element through the introduction of other musical features (brass stabs, vocal moans, new percussion lines, synth fragments). Gesturally, then, the function of repetition could be understood as *oppositional* in that it results from the relationships between gradations of linear and vertical principles of rhythmic development. At the same time, though, the rhythmic organization is goal-orientated in its linearity due to the constant confirmation of CGP alteration. In broad terms, this seems to tie up with the ideological imagination of a musical aesthetic that relates directly to new modes in dance experience, an issue I will address in the next section.

In sum, so far, the total effect of the processes of rhythmic organization around the beat is what results in pent-up action on the dancefloor. Moreover, the arrangement of the sounds in a meaningful fashion is what makes musical sense for persons 'into' house. Feeling the full weight of the beat, clubbers lock into house music's rhetoric, which, as Sarah Thornton has pointed out, always 'resides in a rich, full, emotive and embodied sound' (Thornton 1995: 73). With this in mind, let us now turn to considering the implications of these musical structures and processes and how they are encoded within the social context of dance.

'Jacking', desire and house aesthetics

House culture possesses its own aesthetics, which, from many vantage points, can be problematic for the traditional musicologist to grasp, especially given that this music might *seem* to lack 'materiality', offering 'no food for thought' (Reynolds 1998: 376). Importantly, its interpretation possibilities lie in the interface between respondent and DJ; clubbers know this is central to how house functions. How one dances to music *is* about interpretation. Moreover, basic sensory experiences originating from a kinaesthetic awareness of musical exertion, exhilaration and abandonment are manifested in individual responses to the beat and groove patterns (CGPs). The symbolic exchange of the beat always equates with the cyclical flow of erogenous material. And here, it seems as if our personal notions of time are dependent on instinctive responses to the dispersion of rhythmic pulsations.

Lest we forget, trends in dancing, when 'French Kiss' was first played in 1987, had changed quite considerably since the courtship style of disco. Pleasure in the intense sexual explicitness of much house music had a resonance in a freestyle form of dance known as 'jacking' where the entire body replaced the thrusting movements of the pelvis in a type of delirium. Interpreting the etymology of this term, Simon Reynolds explains:

> 'jack' seems to be a corruption of 'jerk', but also may have some link to 'jacking off'. The house dancefloor suggests the circle jerk, a spectacle of collective auto-eroticism, sterile *jouissance*. 'Jacking' also makes me think of jacking into an electrical circuit. Plugged into the sound-system, the jacker looks a bit like a robot with epilepsy (itself an electrical disorder of the nervous system).
>
> (Reynolds 1998: 21)

In hyper-sexual tracks, 'jacking' would ensue during the build-up of energy in passages, such as in Phase C of 'French Kiss'.[22] Relentless yet exhilarating, the stomping of the beat *is* the sexualized trademark of the track, its intention being to 'jack' the crowd into a state of excitement. Almost as if depersonalized in its aesthetic intention, the sublime effect of the beat is to mechanize the dancer into a collective entity which often involves the reconstruction of identities through carnivalesque display. In this sense, the idiomatic gestures of house convey a religious and political sense of purpose for its congregations. Hence, a notion of togetherness is mediated through the vitality of musical style which becomes an embodiment of dancefloor aesthetics.

Musically, the skills (on the part of the DJ) invested in controlling the beat and the crowd are what frames the aesthetic of house. Indeed, the grooves provide the prime stimulus for the DJ realizing music in 'real time', as if insisting that clubbers should party to the point of complete immersion in the beat (see Rietveld 1998: 148). Importantly, it is the unfolding of all the musical events – drum loops, beats, vamps, sound textures, special effects,

---

22 Although by the time this track was released two years later, dance styles had transformed. Rave was enormous in the UK and crossover was increasingly popular. Yet, 'French Kiss' was still able to 'move' fans on both sides of the Atlantic.

bass lines, melodies – that thrills, excites and drugs the dancer.[23] Moreover, physically responding to the beat builds up a sense of anticipation for what sounds and musical events will be superimposed over the pulse next.[24] In many ways, it would seem that the disciplinarity of the beat, located within a pool of changing timbres and textures, is what spells out house's rhetoric. Reading the beat in dance then empties out a wealth of gestures and inner details that expose its syntax.

In studying the effects of house music and its sub-genres, the combination of dance with drug intake cannot be ignored. The mood-enhancing influence of the drug 'Ecstasy', as research has indicated, is central to the hedonistic-based club experience. Its impact on the body results in a sense of euphoria which accentuates the sexual feelings of the clubbers. Losing one's inhibitions within the social context of the club is an important part of the escapist nature of dance, and, not surprisingly, Ecstasy's effect on the reactions to musical sound has led to it being celebrated as the 'flow drug'. According to Reynolds:

> it melts bodily and psychological rigidities, enabling the dancer to move with greater fluency and 'lock' into the groove. The energy currents that MDMA releases in a flood through the nervous system could be compared to the notion of a life-force promulgated by various 'vitalist' philosophers, mystics, poets and physicians from the eighteenth century to the present: Mesmer's 'magnetic fluid', Whitman's 'body electric', Reich's *orgone*.
>
> (Reynolds 1998: 410–11)

Turning to the issue of gendered identity in house music, it is interesting that while Ecstasy is often experienced as a type of aphrodisiac, it somewhat ironically causes impotence in males by focusing attention on 'sentimentality rather than secretions'. And, as Reynolds continues, 'it also gets rid of the thinks-with-his-dick mentality, turning raves into a space where girls can feel free to be friendly with strange men, even kiss them, without fear of sexual consequences' (Reynolds 1998: 411). Controlled by this drug and the music, the crowd becomes united through a utopian form of ritualistic

---

23 The important elements of timbre and texture are the least transcribable in music analysis and therefore, as many studies have indicated, the easiest to gloss over.
24 See Walter Hughes's (1994) discussion of disco music and his discourse on the 'troping' and 'inversion' of the beat.

display of erotic response that discards the restrictions of everyday 'fixed' identity.[25]

Perhaps the main point here is that dance is about *socially* interpreting musical styles. In Simon Frith's words, dance 'is an ideological way of listening; it draws our attention (not least in its use of space and spaces) to arguments about its own meaning . . . to dance to music is not just to move to it but to say something about it . . .' (Frith 1996: 224). Building on Frith's idea further, the meaning of house music is located in the ways that clubbers respond to it. In other words, modes of dancing mirror an array of shared values which always articulate a social function. To submit to the beat is to become part of an egalitarian community entrenched in a type of religious mysticism. Stylized trends of address in club culture relate directly to the ways in which body movements interpret music in specific social spaces without any recourse to clarification through words. So, while dancers are able to focus on their own individuality, their physical motions function to establish a 'communal ethos' which, in turn, define the event, genre and context. In this respect, the house event 'generates a "liminal" existence, ritually separating, by various means, the ordinary world from the dance environment' (Langlois 1992: 236). Moreover, while bodily gestures are controlled by the groove, they are also about blissful escapism, about letting go, about becoming 'one' with the music, about reshaping communities.[26] And, in this sense, every house event presents a different experience based on its own unique set

25 During the period in which I have researched the effects of dance music, starting in Manchester in 1989 and continuing in Scandinavia at the time of writing this chapter, my discussions with numerous people involved in club culture, as well as my own personal experiences of house music, have revealed that the individual's sexuality and gendered identity fades into insignificance within the context of the event. While the implications of a 'genderless' crowd are clearly far reaching and problematic, the idea of abandoning the restrictions of traditional and patriarchal 'states of being' is one of the most compelling features of house.

26 Emphasizing this quality of dance in relation to subjectivity, Rietveld (1998) problematizes the notion of identification by referring to comparable metaphors. Experiences of dancing, she explains, are frequently likened to religion, theatre, aspects of Shamanism and the carnivalesque, in which there is an 'ephemeral sense of community' which is not realized only through dancing: 'technologies of consumption and of space pull a crowd together through procedures of (physical) exclusion and inclusion' (Rietveld 1998: 204).

of qualities where the musical thrill becomes *tangible* through the interaction of the human body with its sonic-rhythmic surrounds.

As a regulating stimulus then, the beat in house music functions as a vital clue to the gestures and attitudes embraced by trends in socialization. In this respect, the whole question of bodily display, like music, is genre-specific and linked to modes of communication that are culturally disseminated. In the perceptual process of response, clubbers evoke in themselves a 'rhythm of feelings'. So when they 'feel the beat' they are aware of the control of their feelings by the immanence of musical events with the realization that there is always organization in the transience of affective conditions emanating from musical sound. As the felt qualities of volume, mix, timbre, sound-system and groove produce the stimuli for dance, so the affective force of energy flows through the beat into the body, eliciting powerful emotional responses. Ideologically, house music advocates an aesthetic that is both hedonistic and provocative in terms of the signification of musical stimulation. This much said, the onset of dance is primarily a spontaneous response to rhythmic gestures, based upon an intrinsic awareness of structure and processing, wherein we experience those valuable moments to feel the bliss through the force of musical energy.

Conclusion: deep meanings or just 'cheesy' clichés?

House tracks musically encode the dynamics of club culture where the blend of identities create the impulse for expressing a wealth of shared sentiments. Feeling the beat is thus linked to a sensibility towards cultural context as much as style; if the chemistry of the groove is right, it will succeed in arousing pleasures and passions that ritualize reality. What is at stake when responding to house is the simultaneous mapping of one's erotic identity onto the beat. As a determining factor of stylistic syntax, the intricate structures and processes of the beat become the guiding principles for evaluating how music feels. Importantly, understanding how organizational principles of sound work puts into place mechanisms of identification, which, at least for the discerning musicologist, should test all those ideological predispositions our discipline has historically had towards the essentialization of the body.

101

Finally, by returning once more to 'French Kiss', I should make reference to the more humorous dimension of the track. Any reading of this track cannot avoid the *inclusive* semantic weight of the parody found in a chain of banal, or cheesy (as some might have it), musical clichés. While the obvious message of sleaze teases out the erotic aesthetics of this track, it seems to me that it also does a lot of other things with compelling ironic intent. In the light of the ever-present opposition of the Establishment towards lewd expressions of sexuality in forms of pop, especially in tracks such as 'French Kiss', the enforcement of moral values continues to uphold dominant ideology and challenge pop culture. Whereas, diametrically opposed to this, the graphic, expressive nature of 'French Kiss' serves as a powerful reminder of how musical *jouissance* functions to build new emotional, erotic and political bridges between diverse groups of people. Effectively, an impression of erotic intimacy constitutes the ironic edge of 'French Kiss', situated very much at the centre of its fun-like, deviant musical rhetoric. Ending on a somewhat utopian upbeat, I am most keen to emphasize that it is through its vitality and reconfigurative nature that house music's survival in the twenty-first century seems assured.

6 The determining role of performance in the articulation of meaning: the case of 'Try a Little Tenderness'

ROB BOWMAN

The early history of 'Try a Little Tenderness'

Although folklorists for several decades have been interested in trying to understand variations of a given text over different performances, this is a much understudied phenomenon within popular music scholarship. This chapter presents a case study which explores the range of variation in four different versions of the Tin Pan Alley standard 'Try a Little Tenderness', recorded over a span of thirty-three years. Ultimately, such an exploration forces one: (a) to question how and in what parameters musical meaning is articulated; and (b) to grapple with the collision between written and oral culture and private ownership in the form of intellectual property.

The genesis of this chapter goes back about fifteen years to the point when I first found out that one of the all-time classic soul recordings, Otis Redding's 'Try a Little Tenderness', was in fact a cover version of a Tin Pan Alley standard. This was a revelation for me on a number of levels, as the Tin Pan Alley and soul traditions seemed light years apart temporally, geographically and socially. I had first bought the Redding recording in 1966 when I was ten years old. At the time I implicitly assumed that the song was an original composition and, in later years when I began to actively wonder about such things, I explicitly assumed that the writers listed on the record's label, Connelly, Woods and Campbell, were obscure soul writers that I had not encountered, most likely black and from the Southern United States. I could not have been more incorrect.

Reg Connelly and James Campbell were English songwriters who had a number of hits in the United States in the 1920s and early 1930s. Examples

103

include 'If I Had You' (1929), 'When the Organ Played at Twilight' (1930) and 'Goodnight Sweetheart' (1931). More often than not, the two British composers collaborated with a third composer, in this case the American Harry Woods (1896–1970). Woods was a native of Massachusetts, educated at Harvard, who composed a number of Tin Pan Alley hits in the 1920s and 1930s including 'Paddlin' Madelin' Home' (1925), 'I'm Looking Over a Four-Leaf Clover' (1927) and 'When the Red Robin Comes Bob-Bob-Bobbin' Along' (1926).

White clarinettist and band leader Ted Lewis was the first to record a hit version of 'Try a Little Tenderness'. In February 1933 Lewis's Columbia recording entered the pop charts peaking at No. 6 (Whitburn 1986).[1] A month later, Broadway torch singer Ruth Etting entered the charts with a version recorded for Melotone that settled at the No. 16 spot. Bing Crosby recorded the song in January for Brunswick but his version failed to chart. Frank Sinatra was to record yet another pop version of the song in the mid-forties. In 1962 Aretha Franklin recorded the first version that I know of by a black artist for her third Columbia LP, *The Tender, the Moving, the Swinging Aretha Franklin*, while Sam Cooke recorded it as part of a medley with another Tin Pan Alley standard, 'For Sentimental Reasons' (a 1946 hit for Nat King Cole), and his own 1957 smash 'You Send Me', on his 1964 *At the Copa* live album.

Otis Redding recorded 'Try a Little Tenderness' in 1966 originally for his *The Otis Redding Dictionary of Soul: Complete and Unbelievable* LP released on Volt Records, a subsidiary of Memphis's Stax Records. As with virtually everything recorded at Stax in the 1960s, Redding was accompanied by the label's house band, Booker T. & the MG's, augmented by Isaac Hayes and the Memphis Horns. MG guitarist Steve Cropper recalls Redding and the session musicians listening to both the Cooke and Franklin versions prior to recording. Subsequent hit versions have been recorded by Three Dog Night in 1969 and The Commitments in 1991.

1 Despite ongoing efforts I have never been able to find a copy of the Lewis recording. If anyone reading this is able to supply either the actual record or a tape of Lewis's recording, I would be indebted if you would write me at York University, Music Department, 235 Winters College, 4700 Keele Street, Downsview, Ontario, Canada M2J 1P3.

The Etting, Crosby, Sinatra and, presumably, Lewis versions all fit squarely within the Tin Pan Alley genre. As such they are similar to each other, sticking fairly closely to the melodic pitches contained in the original sheet music as written by Campbell, Connelly and Woods. The Franklin and, to a lesser degree, the Cooke versions are transitional in nature, the reasons for which will be discussed below, while the Redding version completely redefined the nature and meaning of the song and became the model for the later versions by Three Dog Night and The Commitments. At the dawn of the twenty-first century, the Redding version is probably the one most associated with the song by the broadest cross-section of the populace.

The remainder of this chapter will undertake a close reading of the Crosby, Franklin, Cooke and Redding recordings, ferreting out differences in the approach to, and ultimately meaning of, each performance. The case will be made that Redding's, and to a lesser degree Franklin's, versions transform the meaning of the song to such a degree as to problematize the notion that meaning is primarily located within the constituent compositional parameters of melody, lyrics and harmony. Instead, it becomes quite clear that musico-socio meaning commonly is located within what could broadly be termed performance practice. The logical corollary of this finding is to begin to question the rationale upon which composition is legally defined for the purposes of intellectual copyright, and, by extension, financial remuneration and historical recognition.

Structure

The original composition by Campbell, Connelly and Woods was written in $\frac{4}{4}$ time and consisted of a four-bar instrumental introduction and an eight-bar introductory 'verse' followed by a single thirty-two-bar AABA 'chorus'[2] (with both the A and B strains being eight bars long). Bing Crosby's version maintains exactly the same structure and then adds a second AABA chorus. As Campbell, Connelly and Woods only wrote one chorus worth of lyrics, in the second AABA section Crosby scat sings his way through the

---

2 In Tin Pan Alley parlance the terms 'verse' and 'chorus' have different meanings to those they have in contemporary pop music. In Tin Pan Alley it is commonplace to refer to the typical introductory, usually eight-bar, strain as a verse, and the subsequent thirty-two-bar AABA section as a chorus.

first two A sections, singing only the lyric for the concluding 'try a little tenderness' refrain that bridges bars 6–7 of each A strain. For the final B and A sections, Crosby simply repeats the words from the original chorus.

Franklin refashions the song into $\frac{6}{8}$ time,[3] in the process transforming the eight-bar A and B strains of the chorus into sixteen-bar units, and she dispenses with the eight-bar spoken introductory verse. While Crosby's version is set at a jaunty 108 crotchets per minute, Franklin dramatically slows the tempo down to fifty-four beats per minute and consequently has no need to repeat the AABA section. Her complete performance, then, consists of an eight-bar instrumental introduction (consisting of an arching string melody over quaver piano arpeggios with a string bass marking every crotchet) followed by a solitary sixty-four-bar AABA chorus.

While Sam Cooke's version of 'Try a Little Tenderness' is also cast in $\frac{6}{8}$ time, he takes it at a slightly quicker tempo (78 crotchets per minute). Sandwiched as part of a medley between 'For Sentimental Reasons' and 'You Send Me', Cooke sings only the first and last A sections, each one being sixteen bars long.

Otis Redding puts the song back into $\frac{4}{4}$ time but, like Franklin and Cooke, doubles the length of each strain, transforming the eight-bar A and B sections of the original into sixteen-bar units. Redding also, à la Franklin, omits the eight-bar spoken introductory verse included in all the Tin Pan Alley versions. This is not surprising as Redding, having learned the song at the Stax studio from the Franklin and Cooke recordings, probably didn't know such an introductory section even existed.

Completely unique to Redding's version is the addition of a concluding 'C' section, which is essentially a repeating eight-bar tag that breaks down into two four-bar sections (see Ex. 6.1). The first four bars of the C section double the preceding harmonic rhythm, with the band changing chords every two beats as they ascend chromatically through a,[4] b, C, C♯, D, D♯, E, F and F♯ before finally reaching the tonic G major chord in bar 5. The intensification of harmonic activity in this section is reinforced by Redding's improvised ad libs and the introduction four bars earlier (for the first time in the entire

---

3 Franklin's choice of $\frac{6}{8}$ time reconfigures the song into a groove that is emblematic of the African-American gospel tradition.
4 Lower case indicates minor triad, upper case indicates major.

Example 6.1: Bars 69–76 (first 8 bars of the first C section) as performed by Otis Redding

performance) of the full drum kit with snare and bass evenly marking all four beats of each bar. (Up to this point Stax session drummer Al Jackson Jr., had limited his time-keeping arsenal to hitting a closed hi-hat on quavers and the rim of his snare drum on crotchets.) The tension of these first four bars is further reinforced in the call-and-response relationship between Redding's vocal ad libs and the Memphis Horns who play on all four off-beats of each bar. While these four bars progressively increase the tension, winding the listener up through the quicker harmonic rhythm, introduction of chromatic harmony, call-and-response at close intervals and Otis Redding's increasingly manic and consistently syncopated vocal ad libs, the second four bars of the C sections calmly descend through the tonic G major chord in bar 5 to a G^7 chord over an F root in bar 6 to an E^7 chord in bars 7 and 8. Reinforcing the

ROB BOWMAN

sense of resolution and release in the second half of this section, beginning on the anacrusis to bar 5, Redding sings the song's title/refrain 'try a little tenderness', and for the first time in the C strain, he sings a series of attacks directly on the beat.

The third time through the C section, the whole song climaxes with an explosive two-bar break in bars 3–4 consisting of Redding's vocal, bass drum, hi-hat and, in the second half of bar 4, snare drum. The effect is cataclysmic.[5] Redding's approach to tempo also differs from that of the other versions analyzed. He sings the first two A sections at 96 crotchets per minute and hits the concluding C sections at 114 crotchets per minute.

Melodic interpretation

For the most part, the published sheet music of Tin Pan Alley compositions is fairly simple so as to facilitate home performance by a large number of potential amateur consumer/players. This was purely a pragmatic result of the nature of the political economy of the music industry pre-World War II where through the early 1920s there was more money to be made from sheet music sales than there was from the sale of records (Sanjek 1983: 13). From the mid-1920s into the rise of rock and roll of the 1950s sheet music sales remained a substantial and important revenue stream within the music industry.

The sheet music for 'Try a Little Tenderness' was no exception in this regard. The published bass line emphasized root motion primarily in minims while the melody was, for the most part, conjunct, moving in quaver and crotchet notes with a smattering of simple quaver syncopations. The melodic lines of the three A sections in the printed sheet music are exactly the same with the exception of their final note. The first A ends on the dominant while the second and third A sections cadence on the tonic.

Not surprisingly, Bing Crosby stays very close to the melody as published, engaging at a few points in small-scale pitch variation. For example, in bar 3 of the first A section (bar 15 overall), he omits an upper neighbour

---

5 Note that Isaac Hayes, who plays organ on this version of 'Try a Little Tenderness', took the groove of this two-bar break and used it as the basis five years later for his 'Theme from Shaft'.

Example 6.2a: Bar 17 (bar 5 of the first A section) as printed in the sheet music

(a)

Example 6.2b: Bar 17 (bar 5 of the first A section) as performed by Bing Crosby[6]

(b)

note on the second degree of the scale, repeating the tonic instead. Similarly, in bar 5 he omits lower neighbour-note motion on the second degree of the scale, repeating the third instead (see Ex. 6.2). In bars 6–7 on the word 'tenderness', where the sheet music moves from the sixth degree of the scale all the way to the seventh before jumping back up to the dominant, Crosby simplifies the gesture by descending from the sixth to the third before moving up to the dominant.

In the succeeding sections Crosby engages in similar small-scale variation, which does not alter the melody in any substantive fashion.

While Crosby stays exceedingly close to the composer's pitch choices, he takes a few liberties with their placement in time, commonly delaying the beginning of phrases and thereby setting up small-scale syncopation. For example, in the original sheet music, bars 2 and 6 contain a non-syncopated ascending figure consisting of four quavers, beginning on beat 1. Crosby sings exactly the same pitches but doesn't start the gesture until beat 2 and therefore sings semiquavers instead of quavers to make the phrase fit. Departing even further from the sheet music in terms of the placement of the melodic notes

---

6 While Crosby's performance is in the key of A, I have transposed the examples into the key of C (which the original sheet music was written in) so as to facilitate comparison.

Example 6.3: Bars 8–10 of Sam Cooke's performance (compare with the analogous material in Ex. 6.2a and 6.2b, above)

And oh———————— if she gets wea-ry

in time, Crosby rhythmically extends and displaces bar 3 of the original sheet music starting on the off-beat after beat 2 in bar 3 and continuing through beat 4 of bar 4.

Sam Cooke stays even closer to the sheet music, singing the exact pitches as published for the first two lyric lines of the first A section (bars 1–4 of the first A section in the sheet music, bars 1–8 of the same section in Cooke's performance). Lyric line 3 in Cooke's version contains some variation, although all the main pitches are still there. For the concluding line 4 (the refrain 'try a little tenderness'), Cooke again sings the exact pitches as printed, with the exception of the penultimate note. Here, instead of dropping a seventh to the leading tone and concluding the strain on the dominant as in the original sheet music and Crosby's performance, he descends a fourth to the third degree of the scale where he remains. Cooke engages in the same kind of small-scale non-substantive pitch variation through the rest of his short performance. In both of the A sections that he includes in his medley, he recasts the pitch material in time. This is partially a necessary corollary of the shift from ¼ into ⅜ time that characterizes both Cooke's and Franklin's performances. It is also a result of Cooke's dynamic and complex sense of time and his penchant for lyric/vocal interpolations such as 'oh' in Example 6.3.

In comparison with Crosby and Cooke, Aretha Franklin departs substantially from the published sheet music. Her variations take three forms: small-scale variation; extensions of the originally written melodic phrases that incorporate all of the important notes but that also add substantial new material; newly created lines. Examples of small-scale variation abound. On the words 'shabby dress' in the first A section, Franklin moves from the dominant to the third with a quick appoggiatura on the second degree of the scale, while Crosby simply descends from the sixth degree of the scale to the third. The original sheet music, likewise, moves from the sixth down

Example 6.4a: Bars 28–30 (last bar of the second A and first bar of the B section) of the original sheet music

Example 6.4b: Bars 39–43 (last two bars of the second A and the first three bars of the B section) of Aretha Franklin's performance

to the third, touching on the fifth along the way on the second syllable of 'shabby'.

In the case of extensions of original melodic phrases, Franklin routinely elongates and decorates lines through virtuosic melismas, lyric/vocal interpolations and/or the repetition of words within a phrase. Example 6.4a, from the beginning of the B section, is a perfect example. While the melody as originally written moves from the tonic note up to the sixth degree of the scale, includes a lower neighbour-note gesture to a sharpened dominant, returns to the sixth and then moves up to the leading tone,[7] Franklin extends the first syllable 'I' over a bar-and-a-half, similarly extends the words 'may be' over another complete bar, then pauses for three-quarters of a bar before repeating the words 'I may be' over three semiquavers before singing the last word, 'sentimental', of the lyric phrase over another full bar (see Ex. 6.4b). Included within this virtuosic performance are all the pitches that comprised the original setting of this line but the gesture is so elaborately decorated as to be virtually unrecognizable.

Franklin increasingly deviates from both the sheet music and Crosby's version as she moves through her performance. As a result, with the exception

---

7 Crosby hits exactly the same pitches, with the exception that he sings a non-sharpened dominant.

Example 6.5a: Bars 17–18 (bars 9–10 of the first A section) of Aretha Franklin's performance

Example 6.5b: Bars 13–15 (bars 9–11 of the first A section) of Otis Redding's performance

of the 'try a little tenderness' refrain, the final A section on Franklin's recording is virtually newly composed.

Otis Redding departs even further from the original published melody which, of course, he would have never seen. He was, though, intimately familiar with Sam Cooke's version which, as has already been discussed, is pretty faithful to the original sheet music. Redding also had Aretha Franklin's more elaborated recording to draw on as an alternative prototype. As was typical with most material that Redding covered, he shows little interest in replicating any pre-existing model. Instead, he substantially refashions the melody to suit his personal inclinations of the moment. This often involves the alteration of significant pitches. For example, while all other versions of the song begin the first vocal phrase on the third degree of the scale, Redding, after an opening quaver 'oh' on the dominant, begins the melody proper on the fourth scale degree. Similarly, while all other versions of the song end the first A section on the dominant, Redding cadences on the third scale degree.

As was the case with Franklin, Redding also routinely extends vocal phrases via elaboration and the interpolation of additional words and syllables. For example, in bars 6–7 of the second A section, he repeats the word 'never' four times in immediate succession. He also extends the register of several lines. While the lyric line 'But when she gets weary', from the first A section, is written in the original sheet music and sung by Crosby, Cooke and Franklin descending from the third to the tonic, Redding starts the phrase

112

Example 6.6a: Bars 65–7 (bars 9–11 of the final A section) of Aretha Franklin's performance

Example 6.6b: Bars 61–2 (bars 9–10 of the final A section) of Otis Redding's performance

on the fourth degree of the scale and then moves up to the sixth, before descending to the tonic (see Ex. 6.5).

Further alteration occurs as Redding rhythmically recasts virtually every vocal statement, his whole performance being much more syncopated than Franklin's, Cooke's or Crosby's on both a general level and micro levels, with most dynamic accents occurring on off-beats.

As was the case with Franklin, as Redding moves through his performance he diverges further and further from earlier versions of the melody. His final A section is nearly wholly newly composed (Ex. 6.6).

Redding's performance is improvised/process-driven to the point where, in addition to engaging in significant melodic alteration, he deviates substantially from the written lyric text. What was 'And a word that's soft and gentle' in the original sheet music becomes, in Franklin's performance, 'and just a good word soft and gentle'. It is the latter lyric that Redding learned from. He transforms it to 'but the soft words they all spoke so gentle, yeah'. All three variations contain the core ideas of 'word' and 'gentle', but their specific realization has little in common. While Franklin's line maintains logical linear continuity with the ongoing lyric and is grammatically correct, Redding's version and his subsequent lyric line, 'it makes it easier to bear', mixes singular and plural constructions, is convoluted and undermines literal lyric narrative sense. Tellingly, the two out-takes that exist by Redding similarly exhibit substantial variation from the released version in terms of pitch, rhythmic placement and lyrics. Clearly, much of his performance is spontaneous/improvised/of the moment.

113

Bars	1	2	3	4	5	6	7	8
Sheet music	I	V^7	I	VI^7	II^7	V^7	I	ii^7 V
Crosby	I vi	ii^7 V$^{7\text{-}9\text{-}13}$	I v/vii	VI^7	II^{13}	ii^9 V^7	I IV^7	I I^7

Bars	1-2	3-4	5-6	7-8	9-10	11-12	13-14	15-16
Franklin	I vi	ii^7 V	I v/vii	VI^7	II^7	ii^7 V^7	I III^{13}	♭VI^7 ♭I^7
Cooke	I ♭III^7	ii V$^{7♭9}$	I v/vii	VI^7	II^7 ♭III^7	ii V$^{7♭9}$	I vi	ii^7 V$^{7♭9}$
Redding	I IV/vi	ii V	I v/vii	VI^7	ii	V	I/v	ii V^7

Figure 6.1: Different chord progressions for the first A section

Harmonic setting

All four versions of 'Try a Little Tenderness' that are analyzed here flesh out the rudimentary harmonies of the A section as published in the original sheet music (see Fig. 6.1).[8]

With the exception of the turnaround, Crosby and Franklin employ the same harmonic progression. With the exception of a ♭III^7 chord in bars 2 and 10,[9] Cooke constructs his version of the song around the same chord progression. Typically, Redding and the Stax house band take a more idiosyncratic approach. In bar 2 where Crosby and Franklin move to a minor-sixth chord, the Stax house band moves to the subdominant,[10] albeit in first inversion to maintain the sixth in the bass. In bars 9–10, where the other three versions and the sheet music have a major chord built upon the supertonic,

---

8 Nomenclature here is standard – upper case indicates major chords, lower case indicates minor; a slash indicates a chord imposed over a non-root bass (i.e. I/v in C indicates a C chord over a G bass).

9 Substituting the ♭III for vi is a common bebop substitution.

10 Stax recordings, in general, make liberal use of the subdominant chord. This is undoubtedly a result of the substantial influence of African-American gospel music on soul.

114

Redding opts for a minor supertonic, and in bars 11–12 where the other three versions use a minor two chord before moving to the dominant with various upper extensions, the Stax house band moves immediately to a simple major triad on the dominant. Analogous changes occur in the B section where Redding's performance substantially diverges from all others in bars 7–14.

Timbre, dynamics and playful voicedness

The differences with regard to the domains of timbre, dynamics and general playful voicedness in the four vocal performances of 'Try a Little Tenderness' contribute greatly to differences in aesthetics and meaning between the four versions. Bing Crosby, operating within what is in many senses a bel canto aesthetic, exhibits little playful voicedness, timbre or dynamic variation in his 1933 recording. He predominantly sings in a wide-open voice typical of crooners of the era, employs a light vibrato on held notes, and completely avoids all traces of sibilance on words such as 'possess' and 'tenderness'. The net effect conveys a sense of effortlessness which, in turn, can be read/interpreted as conveying emotional distance or non-engagement with the subject matter at hand.

This kind of vocal performance can also be understood as articulating values of mastery and control where the latter is predominantly manifested through constraint (mastery of emotions to the point that they are publicly kept in check) and lack of strain (mastery of one's voice and vocal performance). Such effortlessness marks Crosby as a consummate professional who has learned his craft to the point where he could give this performance in his sleep. This is a level that non-professionals simply do not reach.

Aretha Franklin takes a very different approach to her performance of the song, deploying three recognizably different timbres: a thin head voice; a fuller throat voice; and a sparingly used third voice primarily produced in the nasal cavity. She juxtaposes these three voices one against another in an exceedingly dynamic and fluid fashion, evincing a great sense of play throughout the performance. A good example of this is the way she draws out the natural alternating assonance of the 'o' and 'e' sounds in the lyric 'women do get weary' in bar 4 of the first A section (bar 12 overall) by using the thinner head voice on 'wo' and 'do' and the fuller throat voice on

Example 6.7: Bars 29–32 (bars 5–8 of the second A section) of Aretha
Franklin's performance

'men' and 'get'. Further manifestation of this propensity for timbral play
is the way she inflects the word 'weary' differently all three times that it appears in the lyric of the first A section, and draws out the assonance of 'ten'
and 'ness' while playing with the alliterative possibilities of the consonant 't'
when she sings the refrain 'try a little tenderness' in bars 11–14 of the first
A section. This latter micro moment of high density virtuosic display gives
way to a breathy, sibilant caress of the final syllable, '-ness', and is then immediately contrasted with an impossibly sensual, languid, drawn out 'Ohh' in
bars 15–16 which leads into the second A. The effect is breath-taking.

In addition to her deployment of distinct, different timbres, Franklin
makes masterful use of vibrato, dynamics, accentuation, sibilance, recitative-
like speech and breathiness throughout her performance. Particularly effective is her use of sibilance. In bar 6 of the second A section she rests mid-phrase
on the word 'things' (see Ex. 6.7). She attacks the word at a *mf* level and immediately decrescendos to the point where her voice completely disappears
creating a break in the word between 'thing' and 's'. She then sounds the
sibilant 'ss' as the completion of the pluralized noun.

This is a sublime moment of sonic design which exists in a white noise
antecedent–consequent relationship with the sibilant sounding of the 'ss' of
'possess' one bar later. While Crosby demonstrates mastery by suppressing
any hint of sibilance in his performance, Franklin deliberately brings it out
as one of her main signifiers of emotional engagement.

Franklin is also much more adventurous in her use of vibrato, routinely
adding it at various points in a phrase in addition to its commonplace use
by all four vocalists on the held final note of each line. A good example of
this is the first syllable, 'I', of the second A section. Here the vibrato serves
as a quick 'sting' which highlights Franklin's subjectivity as the focus of
what has become in her performance an autobiographical lyric. Similarly,
Franklin typically deploys quick dynamic swells at irregular points in her
vocal phrases, emphasizing key words and images while also keeping the

Example 6.8: Bars 49–52 (bars 13–16 of the B section) of Redding's performance

listener sonically off-balance, unable to predict when and how Franklin will mark or inflect a given pitch/syllable complex. Such an approach not only signals the emotional involvement of the performer, it implicitly demands the emotional engagement of the listener, bringing the two into a continuous closed circuit of heightened emotional intensity.

Sam Cooke employs two slightly different timbres in his performance of 'Try a Little Tenderness', the first being a typically smooth and open crooner voice, and the second adding a bit of rasp.[11] For the most part, he uses the open voice, limiting the rasp to one or two isolated syllables in a given lyric line.[12] In this recording Cooke is not as mercurial, fluid or unpredictable as Franklin, as he uses small-scale timbral and dynamic variations to add shading, rather than for overt emotional display.

Otis Redding, on the other hand, makes substantial use of timbre, dynamics and playful voicedness as he constantly displaces, sets apart and ruptures the organic melodic/lyric lines originally written by Campbell, Connelly and Woods. Rather than deploy different timbres side by side, Redding takes an additive approach to his application of rasp, moving progressively over the course of the performance from a relaxed, open timbre to one that is substantially distorted. During the first A section he lightly inflects with rasp a few syllables, such as 'that', 'same' and 'shag' in 'wearing that same old shaggy [sic] dress'. In the second A, Redding heavily inflects lines 2, 3 and 4, particularly playing with rasp on the four repeats of the word 'never' in

11 'Rasp' refers to the practice of harmonic distortion in the overtone series brought about through lateral pressure on the vocal chords.
12 The only exception is the ad-libbed line that bridges the two A sections, 'oh let me tell all you fellows that', where he uses the raspy voice throughout.

117

bars 6–7. For the B section, Redding avoids the rasp for the first eight bars, while adding it back in the second half (Ex. 6.8). In the final A section Redding uses rasp as he did on the second A, while the repeating C section that concludes his performance is sung with a progressively intensified rasp which peaks in the two-bar break that ruptures the third time through C and serves as a climax of the whole performance.

Redding also makes extensive use of vibrato, dynamic swells on individual syllables and recitative-like speech, the latter being especially prominent in the B section. His distinctive use of vibrato is particularly noteworthy. While Crosby, Franklin and Cooke all hit a held syllable and immediately apply vibrato at the moment of attack, Redding will hit the held note straight and after a marked interval of time will then apply what is typically an exceedingly slow vibrato. A good example of his deployment of dynamic swells occurs on the syllables 'know' and 'wait' in the lyric line 'you know she's waiting' from bars 1–2 in the second A section.

Perhaps Redding's most effective tool in terms of playful voicedness is his sense of rhythmic play. He routinely breaks up lines by inserting rests between words that would normally, both in speech and song, flow together. This is often augmented by the repetition of a word on either side of the rest.

The net result of such effects is to convey the notion of halting speech, indicating that the singer is getting so emotionally overcome that he is unable to generate smooth, flowing 'normal' linguistic utterances, just as commonly happens with real people in real life during emotionally loaded moments.

Instrumental accompaniment

As was typically the case with Tin Pan Alley recordings of the early 1930s, Bing Crosby's recording of 'Try a Little Tenderness' has accompaniment provided by a studio orchestra. The role of the orchestra is largely that of background. Crosby's vocal phrases are accompanied by a subdued *pianissimo* string counter-melody, string bass on beats 1 and 3 and an acoustic guitar outlining the harmonies by playing running triplet quaver staccato melodic lines that emphasize the requisite chord tones. The ends of each strain are punctuated by instrumental fills by a muted trumpet after the first two A sections and by the violin section after each subsequent A section (there is no room for a fill after the B section). While the sheer presence of a studio orchestra signifies much about genre, region, class and, at that point in time, race, that articulates with the larger meanings of Crosby's performance, the orchestra, in terms of what it plays, has a very secondary role in the actual recording.

Although Aretha Franklin's rendition also features a studio orchestra (in this case composed entirely of strings), instrumental accompaniment plays a very different and much more prominent role in her performance. This is a result of a number of factors. In the first place, producer/arranger Robert Mersey has positioned the accompanying strings and piano very high in the mix. He has also written string parts which at several places feature two contrasting counter-melodies played by the violins and violas or violins and cellos which corporeally draw attention to themselves. Perhaps even more importantly, in expanding the original eight-bar A and B strains to sixteen bars, Franklin has opened up space between her vocal phrases for instrumental responses. For example, in the first A section Franklin rests for all or most of bars 1, 3, 5, 7, 9, the first half of 11, the second half of 12 and all of 15. In each of these 'spaces' either strings or piano, by default, come to the fore of the listener's consciousness and implicitly take on a responsorial role. This is in marked contrast to the Crosby recording, where the crooning vocalist sings continuously through bars 1–7, resting for an instrumental fill/turn-around only in bar 8 before beginning the next strain.

In the case of Sam Cooke's recording, accompaniment is provided by his regular touring ensemble of the time which consisted of electric guitar, string bass and drums. All three instruments are playing in a subdued, 'supper club', jazzy style: the drummer employs brushes; the bass simply keeps time and plays chordal root notes; and the guitarist either strums chords or plays chordal melodic figures. With the exception of a melodic fill based on chord tones played by the guitarist at the half-way point of the first A section, all three instrumentalists take a strictly background role. As was the case with Crosby's rendition, the actual composition and timbral palette of the performing group on Cooke's recording signifies much about genre, region and class that articulates with larger meanings, but, in terms of what the instrumentalists actually play, they fulfil a clearly secondary role.

It is in Otis Redding's Stax/Volt recording that the role of the instrumental accompaniment is most important. Starting with the four-bar

contrapuntal horn introduction,[13] the accompanying instrumentalists contribute distinctive individual parts for the duration of the performance. In
the first, extremely sparse, A section, they fulfil an additive function with
guitar and bass playing on beat 1 of each bar and every other instrument
making isolated statements as the strain unfolds. The piano plays a three-
note fill leading into bar 5, the organ serves a similar role leading into bar 8,
the piano bridges the half-way mark of the strain with a descending semiquaver run of a fifth leading into bar 9, the guitar plays two-note fills into
bars 11 and 13, a tenor sax comments on the first articulation of the refrain
'try a little tenderness' in bars 13–15 and the organ closes the strain with
ascending walking triplet crotchets that lead into the second A section.

In the second A section, drummer Al Jackson, for the first time in
the performance, lays out steady time playing crotchets on the rim of his
snare and quavers on a closed hi-hat. The rest of the ensemble behaves much
as they did in the first A section, with piano, organ and guitar contribut-
ing individual short responsorial lines at isolated, structurally important,
moments. Activity increases in the B section as the piano is much more an-
imated, playing fills with increased intensity every couple of bars, while the
organ maintains a steady presence holding chord tones for bars 1–10 before
changing to a much brighter timbre and playing a fill in bars 11–12 and ninth
chords in bars 13–16. The net effect is an increase in the rate of activity, the
overall density and harmonic content, all of which contribute to a general
intensification creating an additive effect within the strain on a micro level as
well as an additive effect on a macro level as the performance moves through
successive strains.

The final A section keeps on in this fashion and intensifies accord-
ingly, with guitarist Steve Cropper playing chordal accompaniment with a
continuous 3+3+2 Habañera rhythm, the organ and piano both playing
different comping patterns and the horns, for the first time, sustaining harmonic pads. Again, we see increases in the rate of activity of each instrument,
the number of different lines sounding at one time, the overall density of the
ensemble and the overall dynamic level. All of these changes are matched by
a concomitant increase in the intensity of rasp employed by Redding. In the

13 This horn introduction was adapted by Isaac Hayes for Redding's recording
from the string introduction Sam Cooke used on 'A Change Is Going to Come'
a couple of years earlier.

pick-up to bar 13 (the sixty-fifth bar of the piece!), the full drum kit is finally brought into play, upping the intensity level yet one more notch and serving the function of delayed gratification while avoiding a sense of closure to the strain and leading straight into section C.

Section C, as has been discussed in some detail above, further contributes to the additive nature of the performance by speeding up the harmonic rhythm, expanding the harmonic language, increasing the tempo, expanding the overall pitch range upwards, greatly increasing the overall density, volume, rate of activity, degree of syncopation, rasp and general playful voicedness. The nature of the repetition in section C can be interpreted as manifesting a circular aesthetic as the horns engage in musematic repetition at the two-beat level. With respect to the shift in tempo, note should be made of drummer Al Jackson Jr.'s, metronomic control of time. According to producer Jim Stewart and keyboardist Booker T. Jones, Jackson made a conscious decision to subtly increase the tempo of the song as the performance unfolded.[14] The gradual quality of this shift and the extraordinary consistency of Jackson's playing can be seen at a glance in the following tempo map which delineates the exact fractions of a second between each beat. Note how the time elapsed between each beat gradually shifts from an average of 0.6 seconds in the first A section (bars 5–20) to just under 0.55 seconds in the concluding C sections (bars 69–84) (see Fig. 6.2).

In Franklin's case, the responsorial fills of the strings seem anonymous and consequently chorus-like as a result of the numbers of players, the fact that they are reading sheet music,[15] the ongoing density of the arrangement and the unison part playing. In Redding's recording the members of his much smaller accompanying ensemble have the appearance of individual agency in the earlier strains as their individual contributions are largely made in isolation, in the later strains because they are playing separate and distinct lines which operate in rhythmic and melodic counterpoint with each other fitting together like nothing so much as a jigsaw puzzle. In both types of

14 Private communication.
15 Although the listener obviously is not able to actually see the orchestra reading parts, I contend that the types of lines and quality of phrasing are often significantly different when session players read from pre-written charts as opposed to when they use head arrangements. This difference is quite manifest aurally and, in my opinion, significantly affects the possible meanings of the performance.

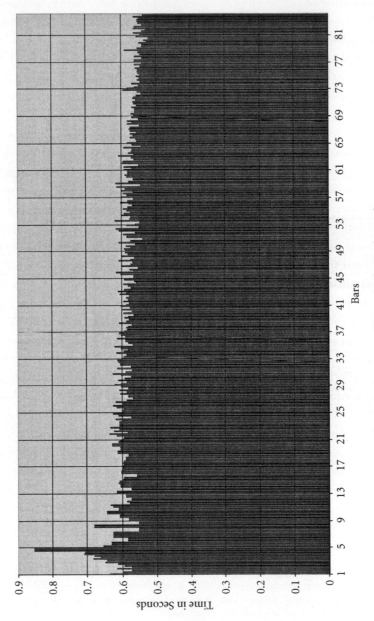

Figure 6.2: Tempo map of Otis Redding's performance of 'Try a Little Tenderness'

context, the individual band members signify notions of a community where all contribute to the good of the collective whole while still maintaining individuality and agency. In Franklin's performance, emotion is conveyed predominantly through her vocal display. This emotion is then affirmed by the plaintive string responses and piano arpeggios. In Redding's recording, much of the emotional intensity is a result of the dynamic interplay between Redding and his accompanying instrumentalists, as is commonly the case within the gospel tradition. In a sense, the instrumentalists at Stax replicate the role of background vocalists, audience or congregation as they provide affirmation for the singer or preacher's message.

Recorded 'live' in the studio,[16] the various rhythm section parts of Redding's version of 'Try a Little Tenderness' were 'improvised' on the spot. In all, three takes were recorded.[17] Listening to them is instructive. While they all build to various degrees via the deployment of additive techniques applied to multiple parameters, the exact composition of both an individual player's lines, and Redding's vocal performance, varies greatly from take to take. While the average listener would have no way of knowing this, I contend that such an approach to performance is palpable and communicates on a subconscious level value and meaning.

Making sense of difference

Characterizing the Franklin and Cooke versions is problematic. Both recordings are examples of the transculturation process. Columbia Records was attempting to market Franklin as a pop singer and consequently recorded her singing any number of Tin Pan Alley standards replete with pop string arrangements. These records were a far cry from her later Atlantic rhythm and blues hits in terms of repertoire, instrumentation, arrangement and performance style. That said, Franklin cannot and does not completely shed her gospel background and consequently, at least to a small degree, transforms the song when compared to the Crosby and Sinatra recordings.

---

16   'Live' in the sense that at Stax at this time there was no overdubbing. The five rhythm section players, the three horn players and Otis Redding simply performed the song beginning to end in 'real' time while the tape rolled.

17   The first take has been released on *It's Not Just Sentimental*, Ace Records CDSXD 041. I have a private tape of the second take.

Sam Cooke chose to perform the song at the Copa, a New York City 'society' night club, for reasons similar to those which motivated Columbia to suggest that Franklin record the song. In playing the Copa and in modifying his repertoire for the occasion, Cooke was attempting to appeal to an older white, middle- and upper-class audience. A comparison of the Copa LP with Cooke's *Live at the Harlem Square Club* LP recorded in 1963 in a black club in Miami reveals just how different his repertoire and performing style would be depending on the context in which he was performing. This is not to suggest that Cooke was not comfortable, competent and interested in performing in both styles. It simply is indicative that he had an understanding of a palpable difference in what type of repertoire and performance style would have meaning for the two different demographics that would make up the respective audiences at the Copa and Harlem Square Club.

As with many of the songs Redding covered, he completely deconstructed and reconstructed the work, in the process redefining the very possibilities and ultimately the meaning of the song. Redding's manager, Phil Walden, told me in 1986:

> Otis had an unbelievable capacity to turn something totally around. A good example is "Try a Little Tenderness". This was when we were talking about career songs where he could be on the Ed Sullivan Show or playing the Copa. These things were terribly, terribly important. They were a sign of success. I remember he called me late at night [I hadn't gone to that session] and he said, 'You know that song you've been on my ass about recording, "Try a Little Tenderness"?' I said, 'Yeah'. He said, 'I cut that motherfucker. It's a brand new song.' He could just turn things around, he could hear it in such a different way.[18]

Walden's observations speak volumes. 'Try a Little Tenderness', or any other Tin Pan Alley song, can be understood as a symbol or sign that has social meaning as an entity in and of itself outside of the specifics of lyrics or musical setting. The mere act of recording the song from Redding's and Walden's perspective would possibly serve to open the doors to certain institutions (e.g. the Ed Sullivan Show and the Copa). These institutions themselves were symbols that communicated social meaning. Without being a semiologist, Walden states as much himself when he said 'they [Sullivan and the Copa]

18 Private communication.

were a sign of success'. Again, in Walden's words, 'These things were terribly, terribly important'.

These institutions were arguably signs of success within the framework of what Antonio Gramsci (1971: 12–13ff.) has termed *cultural hegemony*, the value system of the dominant society. The fact that this value system came to bear so directly on the music-making of Aretha Franklin, Sam Cooke and Otis Redding simply makes manifest how much the dominant culture's stranglehold on the economy, the media, the school system and other institutions impinges on and influences the goals and values and consequent activities of minority cultures.[19] While the present discussion focuses on the sphere of popular music, this process clearly operates in other areas of cultural activity as well.

Meaning

Moving beyond the macro level of the Tin Pan Alley song as symbol, one concept that I find very useful in considering music as a conveyor of meaning via sound, lyrics and music-related behaviour is musicologist Christopher Small's concept of *musicking* (Small 1987: 50; 1998: 8–9). Small has taken the noun 'music' and transformed it into a verb. Instead of considering music as a product or object, he wishes to understand it as a social process. Black writer LeRoi Jones (now known as Amiri Baraka) made essentially the same point in his seminal work *Blues People* (Jones 1963: 28–9).

For Small, people are musicking when they are playing, dancing or listening to music. Small insists that music is an activity, rather than a thing. Meaning exists within the musical event rather than solely within the musical work. He also suggests that everyone is capable of musicking (learning to music is somewhat analogous to learning language – we do it unconsciously from the word go). Finally, Small suggests that the activity of musicking has

19 This is not to take a determinist position in respect of cultural production that obviates the possibility for individuals to make choices that differ or conflict with hegemonic values. It is simply to suggest that the relationship between political economy and hegemony is so tightly bound that many performers will feel internally or externally compelled either by institutions (e.g. Columbia Records in the case of Aretha Franklin) or by their own economic ambitions (e.g. Sam Cooke) to incorporate sonic gestures into their musicking which in one way or another manifest hegemonic values.

a social as well as an individual dimension. Musical forms, techniques and performance style reflect and, in turn, influence the ways in which people view themselves and their relationships to the world. Music is very important in providing individuals and groups with a sense of identity. In essence, Small theorizes that in the process of musicking all participants are unconsciously doing three things. Firstly, they are exploring, affirming and celebrating a sense of identity. Secondly, they are taking part in an ideal society that has been brought into existence for the duration of the performance. Finally, they are modelling in the actual sounds of the music the relationships of their ideal society.

Considering the various recordings of 'Try a Little Tenderness' in the light of Christopher Small's theoretical framework, the impact and social meaning of each performance is significantly different. While wishing to avoid essentializing notions with regard to race, it is important to look at the recorded versions of the song by Bing Crosby, Aretha Franklin, Sam Cooke and Otis Redding from the perspective of class, region and the rural–urban continuum. Thought of in another way, if one looks at each performer with respect to their proximity or distance from the socio-cultural matrix embodied in standard Tin Pan Alley repertoire and performance practice, a pattern emerges with Bing Crosby and Otis Redding resting at opposite ends of a continuum that posits Northern, urban, print-based, middle-class sensibilities in opposition to Southern, rural, oral-based, working-class aesthetics.

Crosby's rendition fits the Tin Pan Alley pop model where all things are neat, smooth and ordered. There are no ragged edges, nothing could even remotely be considered out of place and control is paramount, maintained over most aspects at all times. These and other social values seem to be clearly manifest in the actual sounds of the performance. While Crosby never exhibits overt emotionalism in a demonstrative manner, Redding's performance nearly defines the concept. Crosby maintains a distance as performer/entertainer in his interpretation of the song that characterized pre-World War II white pop music. Redding starts out approximating a similar aesthetic but, over the course of his performance, he transforms his role to that of somebody singing about something that he is so intensely involved in, his very life seems dependent on the outcome.

Redding's version is ultimately about the drive for and achievement of catharsis. Over the course of 3′45″ the tempo, rate of activity of each instrument, the overall density of the ensemble, the volume, height of pitch, degree of what ethnomusicologist Alan Lomax (1970) has termed *playful voicedness*, syncopation, timbral variation, harmonic rhythm and harmonic content have dramatically increased. In addition, Redding has moved over the course of the performance from linguistic/lyric sense to music/sound sense or from what is stereotypically a Euro-American aesthetic where lyrics are more important than sound to an aesthetic commonly found in African-American culture in which sound predominates in the articulation of meaning. This is quite plain by the break in the final C section where Redding dispenses with words altogether, instead uttering a series of nonsensical vocables. He has, in effect, moved beyond language to a deeper, more primordial level. Paralleling this shift from linguistic/lyric sense to music/sound sense is a move in the newly composed C section of Redding's performance to a circular aesthetic involving musematic repetition in direct contrast to the linear or narrative aesthetic embodied in the Tin Pan Alley-written A and B strains where discursive repetition is the norm.

Sam Cooke and Aretha Franklin, respectively, sit at various points between Crosby and Redding along this continuum. Cooke's performance, as detailed above, leans towards a Northern, urban, middle-class aesthetic which is consistent with the social context of the New York City society night club in which he performed the song. Franklin's performance is more complex. While the accompanying performing force signifies a Northern, urban, middle-class aesthetic, Franklin's vocal interpretation also manifests Northern sophistication which she belies via gospel practices of playful voicedness that are both historically and semiotically rooted in Southern African-American culture.[20]

The question remains as to why Franklin's and Redding's versions diverge so much from the song as originally written and from each other. The answer at least partially lies within the long-standing practice of creation and re-creation of communally owned cultural materials that characterizes much

---

20 It is interesting to note with regard to this theory of a Northern/Southern continuum that Crosby and Cooke were both born and raised in the North while Franklin, the transitional figure along the continuum, was born in the South in Memphis but was raised in both Southern and Northern cities, namely Memphis, Buffalo and Detroit. Redding, as the most rural and Southern of all these performers, was born in Dawson, Georgia and raised in Macon, Georgia.

Southern, rural-based or rural-derived African-American expressive culture. This cultural matrix has long exhibited little interest in fixed or set expressive objects. Rather, an emphasis is placed upon fluidity, individual interpretation, collective effort, improvisation, the moment and process over product. Meaning rests within the act of doing, rather than within an 'exact' realization of some abstract notion of the set cultural object itself. While this process is constituted through the collective efforts of all those engaged in bringing the musical moment into being, at the same time substantive value is placed upon individually distinct contributions.[21] Richard Middleton ties such musico-socio practices to collective-variative social practices (Middleton 1990: 270), suggesting that one of the primary ways collective-variative social practice seems to be expressed sonically is through musematic repetition, as found in the C section of Redding's performance.

Copyright

By the end of Redding's performance there is the illusion of no demonstrable distance at all between singer and song.[22] He no longer seems to be an entertainer acting out a song, rather he comes across as someone dramatizing part of his life so much so that he must have had a hand in the writing of the song. The latter, of course, is not the case. Reg Connelly, James Campbell and Harry Woods wrote the song if composition is defined as the creation of words, chord progression and melody. That is certainly the way composition is legally defined in our society and consequently that is the way that most people use the term. I contend that such a definition of composition is an outdated concept predicated upon the values of individual (one or two identified composers), as opposed to group ownership (multiple individuals

---

21 One can see parallels to this valuation of individuality in all kinds of African-American musical practices from the desire within the gospel quartet tradition to have each voice in the ensemble possess a distinct timbre that differentiates it from every other voice to the emphasis within the jazz tradition for each player to develop a unique sound on his/her horn. This aesthetic is paralleled in the emphasis within the blues, jazz, gospel, soul and funk traditions on the uniqueness of individual performances as each meets the specific exigencies of a given social moment.

22 This is especially manifest in live performances. For a good example, see the video of Redding's complete Monterey Pop performance.

who collectively take part in the musical moment), within a society based on print literacy.

Words, chords and melody are those aspects most easily written down, 'frozen' as a way of proving authorship and 'fixing' details permanently within a system of notation developed by and for the European art music tradition. When one thinks of what strata of society have tended to support that tradition and the values it maintains and what strata of society are responsible for developing and implementing our legal system, it is not surprising that those elements most easily recorded in this notation system would be those generally privileged by the legal system. Hence, the operative way that composition has come to be defined via lyrics, chords and melody, at least in the Western world, both with regards to recognition of creativity and financial reward for said creativity.

Oral culture works very differently. For the last one hundred years or so we have lived in a society where recordings have become the primary means of both the dissemination and learning of music. This is oral culture as process where nuances such as timbral variation, rhythmic articulation, pitch gesture and arrangement are at least as, if not more, important than lyrics, chord progression and melody. If this was not the case, the various versions of 'Try a Little Tenderness' would ultimately communicate essentially the same things. The lyrics, chord progression and melody, within a range of variation, are maintained between all versions. It is the performance style that is so radically changed, transforming the ultimate meaning, impact and prospective audience in the process.

In Redding's day and age, his choice of performance style simply meant that his primary audience was African American giving him a substantial hit on the rhythm and blues charts, peaking at No. 4 while he only managed to reach No. 25 on the Billboard pop charts, clearly selling considerably fewer copies to the Euro-American populace. Whoever bought the record, white or black, and whatever meanings the performance may have conveyed, for all sales royalties were paid to the publisher, Robbins Music Corporation, and ultimately to the writers of the original 1933 song.

In today's world, rap artists, in a very analogous fashion, deconstruct, reconstruct and recontextualize pre-existent compositions and recordings via sampling. Most of us have long ago accepted such refashioning of older material as new composition, as the sampled material is redefined and

129

consequently re-encoded with new meaning through its recontextualiza-
tion. The record industry has gradually stumbled its way towards working
out methods of payment that recognize the rap artist as primary composer,
while still compensating in some minor way those who created the earlier
sampled recordings. I contend that if musical composition is the arrangement
of sound materials in such a way that they convey a given set of meanings,
and that seems clearly to be the case with rap, Otis Redding with 'Try a Little
Tenderness', likewise, 'wrote' via performance style a new song that simply
'sampled' pre-existent material created by Campbell, Connelly and Woods
some thirty-three years earlier.[23]

In summary, all of this begs two related questions: 'what really constitutes composition?', and 'through what parameters is meaning communicated in music?' The way the former has been legally defined and assimilated
by most, to my way of thinking, accurately reflects the way only a small part
of the world's people create music. In the process, all domains other than
melody in the broadest sense, chord progression and lyrics are deprivileged.
Many of these other domains can be subsumed under performance style
and, ultimately, as I feel is quite manifest in the performances of "Try a Little
Tenderness" by Bing Crosby, Aretha Franklin, Sam Cooke and Otis Redding,
these other parameters may be the most important ones in creating meaning
in music.

---

23 Analogous practices have existed in jazz for several decades. An obvious and
well-known example would be John Coltrane's forty-plus-minute reworkings
of Rodgers and Hammerstein's 'My Favorite Things'.

7 Marxist music analysis without Adorno: popular music and urban geography

ADAM KRIMS

'One must always try to be as radical as reality itself...'   V. I. LENIN,
QUOTED IN MARCU (1927)

How Adorno stands in for 'Marxism' in popular music studies

The initial task of this essay will be to argue that Theodor Adorno constitutes one of the single greatest obstacles to developing a Marxist analysis of music. Lest such a contention seem paradoxical, it will be helpful, momentarily, to adopt a certain defamiliarizing perspective, and force oneself to be surprised that Adorno retains such prominence as he does nowadays in popular music studies. Even the most strenuous validations of popular music seem, at some point, out of necessity, to look back to Adorno's shadow and exorcise the weight of his critiques. His well-known, perhaps notorious, rubrics of mass production, standardization, false differentiation, and the regression of listening seem to lie inextricably as a foundational trauma in the discipline; and even those of us, perhaps the majority, in popular music studies who contest his descriptions nevertheless find it necessary to confront them. Promoting a music genre or subculture as political resistance and a disruption of discursive consensus entails explaining how that genre or subculture disrupts the deadening conformity of the music industry. Claiming the progressiveness of a community's reception of some mainstream music involves arguing the productive effects of reception against Adorno's seeming

Research for this essay was supported by a grant from the Social Sciences and Humanities Research Council (SSHRC) of Canada. I am grateful to them, and to Robert Fink, Michael Spitzer and Robert Walser for their comments on earlier versions.

131

one-way circuit from producer to consumer. And the emergence of subaltern voices in contemporary popular music must disown Adorno's vision of the homogenizing effects of the industry. The spectral presence of Adorno can be traced even in work with an apparently vast disciplinary distance from Frankfurt critical theory, such as the post-Marxist cultural studies of George Lipsitz (1994), or the populist audience-focused research of John Fiske (1987). Adorno's presence in popular music studies seems most often to resemble that of a pinball bumper, against which we all at some point fling ourselves in order to bounce somewhere else with renewed energy and theoretical momentum, but always with the horrifying threat that gravity will bring us back down in the same direction. If we need a measure of his seemingly invincible presence, we need only take a look at Keith Negus's admirable *Popular Music in Theory: An Introduction* (1997) and watch sections on Adorno open the first two chapters, with responses to his work dominating the contributions that follow.

It would perhaps be simplistic and counter-productive simply to shout 'Get over it!', as if the weight of historical constructions of popular music could simply be offloaded, and we could enjoy a newfound freedom by sheer dint of will. If Adorno is the popular music scholar's scene of primal trauma, then repression offers little relief: at least we can say that the talking cure we live out in our journals and books itself proffers more than its share of productive discussion. Furthermore, just about nobody, most likely, would want to contend that Adorno was completely wrong. Who could resist an Adornan vision of the seemingly endless worldwide proliferation of young-boy pop/r&b groups? Or who could have expected that the Backstreet Boys would come to look so good, next to the endless stream of even less interesting knock-offs? Clearly, Adorno was not wrong about everything.

But arguably today the most damaging effect of Adorno's shadow is the ways in which Marxism has come to be configured in popular music studies. Part of that story is too big to rehearse here, namely the dominating presence of so-called 'Western Marxism' in traditions of critical humanities scholarship; in many respects a set of sharp deviations from other Marxist traditions, it nevertheless remains the only tradition related to Marx that many humanities scholars encounter in any depth or detail. While just next door in the social sciences, Marxism exists in other forms and names, from David Harvey and Terry Eagleton to Ellen Maiskins Wood, our own

132

disciplinary gravitation in music scholarship draws us to the traditions of Marxism preoccupied by the problematic of the commodity fetish, a powerful but sometimes limiting problematic that often fails to convey the full cultural scope of capitalism. What is more, the notion of commodity fetish arguably becomes an ever-blunter tool precisely as our own societies come increasingly under the sway of those same commodities.

Adorno's legacy in popular music studies can be traced most prominently in the twin notions of cultural imperialism and standardization of product lines. And notably, those problematics have come, in many studies, to be equated with Marxism itself. Dominic Strinati (1995) and Peter Manuel (1993), for example, leave cultural imperialism and formal standardization as the remnants of Marxist theory in their own narratives of popular culture. A scholar, then, who wants to centralize Marxism in the study of popular music, has a tough row to hoe. I want to implement the hoeing process in two steps, which is not to say dialectically: step one is to historicize both Adorno and the present, and step two is to indicate a different route into popular music that posits that if capitalism changes in history, then a Marxist music analysis needs to change with it.

Flexible accumulation (or, Why Adorno should *not* stand in for 'Marxism' in popular music studies)

In the industrial era of capitalism, when economies of scale were transforming the landscape and the very pace and character of life, including art, Adorno's vision was extremely perceptive, even prescient for a few decades to come. If nothing else, Mike Davis's (1990) extraordinary description of the Los Angeles that surrounded Adorno should suggest that the nightmare of enlightenment had its real embodiment and a profound moment of social truth. But it is possible to recognize, from a present perspective, that the character of social life to which Adorno responded is itself historical and did not carry nearly the longevity that he imagined. What Adorno took for an inexorable process turned out to be historically specific, to have not just a birth but also a death, albeit to a varied extent throughout the mode of production. What intervened, and what Adorno could not have theorized in his lifetime, is the advent of flexible accumulation, or so-called post-Fordism, a mutation in capitalist accumulation that has inflected cultural processes sufficiently

1 shift from mass production to small-batch production
2 design intensity in production, enabled by automation
3 shift from economies of manufacturing to economies of service
4 increased consumption by individuals of services
5 vertical disintegration of larger firms, with subcontracting
6 flattening of corporate decision-making, removal of managerial layers
7 large proportion of labour in part-time, temporary jobs with little or no benefits
8 quick feedback loops from consumers, with quick integration to product and service design
9 mergers and buyouts, creating large conglomerates
10 regionalized economies
11 movement of inner-city manufacturing to suburbs, rural areas, and less developed nations

Figure 7.1: Commonly cited characteristics of Flexible Accumulation (or 'Post-Fordism')

deeply to call for new ways of theorizing music and its social effects. Flexible accumulation is not a transformation in the mode of production itself – the basic aspects of capitalism have remained constant – but rather one at the level of *regime of accumulation,* that is, specific strategies of accumulating capital.

The characteristics of flexible accumulation have been debated, both in their detail and in their scope, but for now, I will offer just a simple outline.[1] Figure 7.1 enumerates. Among the most often cited aspects are: (1) a switch in many industries from mass production to the production of a variety of products in small batches; (2) design intensity in production, while automation and programmability allow for quick and flexible design change; (3) a shift, especially in the most economically developed countries, away from manufacturing and towards the provision of services to producers (such as payroll and back-office operation); (4) increased consumption by individuals of personal services in addition to goods, examples being restaurant delivery, Internet cables, and specialized mail services; (5) vertical disintegration of large firms, as companies subcontract to independent operators what had previously been done 'in house', creating a whole sector of business service and information companies ranging from Federal Express to

---

1 Debates have raged over the scale, characteristics and historical significance of post-Fordism. Such debates are beyond the scope of this essay; some useful summaries of the major issues can be gleaned from Amin and Thrift (1994), Amin (1994a) and Elam (1994).

temp firms; (6) a flattening of corporate decision-making and the removal of managerial layers; (7) elsewhere in the labour market, the *forcing* of large numbers of workers into flexibility, with a far larger percentage of new jobs being part time, temporary, and without previously normal levels of benefits; (8) feedback loops from consumers becoming more quickly and thoroughly integrated to design; (9) mergers and buyouts forming huge multinational conglomerates, while at the same time, (10) the vertical disintegration and the outsourcing spawn specialized regional economies; and finally (11) the movement of surviving manufacturing out of inner cities either overseas or to suburbs, exurbs or rural areas.

The culture industries, especially the popular music industry, have long been privileged sites of explanation for theories of flexible accumulation, even to the extent that Scott Lash and John Urry (1994) take popular music as their exemplary instance of what they (perhaps a bit optimistically) call 'post-organized capitalism' (1987). This is one of the principal reasons why any stance towards Adorno and Marxism in popular music studies must at least address more recent theories of capitalist organization. Debates have raged about both the extent and the nature of the economic and geographic transformations involved; but very few scholars doubt that changes in technology, communications and computerized design have altered production and consumption, and even theoretically modest studies like Alfred Chandler's *Scale and Scope* (1990) mark significant departures from older industrial organization. Certainly, when one narrows the focus to the music industry itself, considerable aspects of post-Fordism have been notable for quite some time by now.[2] And so it will help to turn to those aspects of the music industry which have indeed shifted, with respect to both standardization and cultural imperialism, which, it will be recalled, remain the principal rubrics under which discussions in popular music studies tend to retain traces of Adorno.

2 In the only other study so far addressing post-Fordism and the music industry, Hesmondhalgh (1996) argues against centralizing the notion of post-Fordism in discussions of the popular music industry. The conception of post-Fordism against which he argues, however, is the optimistic 'New Times' version, in which the term is proffered as an index of liberatory cultural force. Against such a notion, Hesmondhalgh observes that the industry still moves principally through historically dominant circuits. His argument, in other words, is consistent with what is being argued in this essay, while his objections are marshalled against the more optimistic assessments of post-Fordism that range the latter against the organized force of capital.

1 *Standardization*

The extent to which changes in music technology have transformed the industry have been much remarked. The costs of professional-quality production, in the wake of ever cheaper digital technology and programming, have enabled profitable independent music production on a smaller scale than Adorno could ever have envisioned. The other face of flexible accumulation, inseparable in a broader context, is the acquisition of otherwise independent companies by ever larger entertainment conglomerates. The net result is an industry with more centralized control and greater product diversification *at the same time*. Independent record companies are inexpensive to start and can be run on shoestring budgets impossible in the era of large-scale standardized production; but the flip side is, as Stephen Lee (1995), David Hesmondhalgh (1996), Keith Negus (1997) and Robert Burnett (1996) point out, that the profitable independent labels, or their rosters, are almost always absorbed by larger companies, or enter distribution and licensing deals that transfer significant profits to the majors. The result is a configuration Adorno could not have imagined: a concentration of wealth with a deconcentration of control, an industry of a small number of majors inseparable from a veritable Lego construction of minors. This is what business economists refer to as 'organizational deconcentration', one of the hallmarks of flexible accumulation. An unprecedented proliferation of musical genres to niche markets can now be served profitably on a small scale; at all levels the industry can respond ever more rapidly to changes in consumer demand; and geographically localized and ethnically specific trends and musics can generate commercial activity whose scale, in previous years, would not have attained economic viability. Now, unlike twenty years ago, one can locate dozens, if not hundreds, of constantly mutating dance genres in specialized urban shops, just down the street from a Tower Records marketing Sarah McLachlan's singer-songwriter sincerities, next to an import shop or Internet café offering access to Swahili rap or dub poetry.

Here, already, we can see how an Adornan conception is inadequate, as the increasing industrial expansion and financial concentration – and that is precisely what has been going on for quite a few years now – does *not* necessarily mean an increasing homogenization of the product, and does *not* mean ever more standardized, falsely differentiated musical forms of deadening similarity. Listening does not have to regress to capture the variety of popular music being produced today; on the contrary, the proliferation of musics can probably be tagged as sublime in the most literal sense, producing both a pleasure at the adventures of music and a fear of being cognitively overwhelmed by the endless developments. Now, some scholars, like Robert Burnett (1996), are ready at this point to pack up their toys, declare capitalism a success in the popular music industry, and go home. And as with any celebration of capitalism, they would be partially correct. The dialectic of enlightenment has indeed taken a dialectical turn for which Adorno could not have prepared us.

2 Cultural imperialism

The music industry's ability to respond to feedback from audiences, and the increased production for small speciality markets, make an end run around the problematics of cultural imperialism and at least greatly complicate the well-worn questions of producer control versus audience inflection. Both substantial independent record companies and localized branches or affiliates of international conglomerates now design artist rosters and repertoire of staggering variety and attunement to local markets. Conversely, musics from far-flung locations like Senegal and Cape Verde can be packaged and niche-marketed globally, forming the boom in so-called 'world music' that has constituted one of the most widely remarked transformations in the music industry over the last decade. If this is a cultural imperialism – and one could easily argue that it is – it is nevertheless far from the kind envisioned in the problematic we have inherited from Adorno or, for that matter, Lenin (1996). And so-called 'active audience' theories can, to some extent, claim vindication in commercial reality: the affordability of quick, small-batch production in the music industry has rendered audience agency visible in ways that belie Adorno's nightmare of mass passivity and uniform transformations of consciousness.

But the most crucial point that needs to be made about all these affronts to Adorno's vision is that they are *fully a formation of capitalism*. The infinite variety of world musics, including that produced and consumed by subaltern subjects, has always been with us as a silent objection to the nightmare of mass consumption, but it is only the flexible-accumulation wrinkle that has allowed many of those musics wide-scale commercial representation. And while audiences have always inflected musics and integrated them to their

Real Family Income Growth by Quintile, 1950–1978

Bottom 20%	+138%
Second 20%	+98%
Middle 20%	+106%
Fourth 20%	+111%
Top 20%	+99%

Real Family Income Growth by Quintile, 1979–1993

Bottom 20%	−17%
Second 20%	−8%
Third 20%	−3%
Fourth 20%	+5%
Top 20%	+20%

source: Bluestone (1995)

Figure 7.2: The bifurcation of class under Flexible Accumulation

lives in locally unique ways, it is only with the profusion of, for example, independent dance labels that those inflections have undergone properly developed production and marketing. The coming-into-representation of audiences, including subaltern subjects, can be taken as a partial realization of a Foucauldian dream, perhaps as a challenge to Gayatri Spivak (1988), and can easily be an occasion for celebration. But the flip-side of the equation is equally important, because the same mobility of capital that enables such developments also allows the increasingly concentrated owners of that capital to outmanoeuvre the classes that struggle against it – including, by the way, many of the subjects whose representation one would have been tempted to celebrate. In other words, the material base of the situation develops in the opposite direction to our discursive liberation; here we can observe the weakening of regulatory power in collapsing nation-states, neo-liberal regimes with their devastated public sectors and, as part of the regime of flexible accumulation, labour structures that harden the lines between the haves and the increasingly trapped have-nots. Figure 7.2 shows a small part of the result, as in the United States since 1979 the rich have become richer, the poor far poorer.

In the popular music industry, the gradual disappearance of many large record companies such as Atlantic and the whittling down of the number of 'majors' suggests Adorno's very nightmare, along with concentrations of wealth and power. The independent labels normally distribute and market their products through the increasingly centralized networks of the majors. Similarly, the Internet provides exposure to a dizzying variety of sounds on lines principally owned by one conglomerate, Cisco Systems.

But the relation of increasingly centralized economic organization to diversified cultural result is *not* upside down, because there is *no essential and unchanging relation, only historical relations,* between the two. In regimes of flexible accumulation and just-in-time production, enormous inequalities in power (including but not limited to wealth) may not just be consistent with, but even may *depend* on the stylistic, ethnic and geographic mobility that we see in the cultural sphere.[3] And we can observe that dependence every day in the marketing strategies of businesses ranging from fashion through computers to circuit assemblies.

How cultural studies approaches take the same view of capital as Adorno

It is crucial to distinguish between the developments described here, and some objections to Adorno that have arisen most especially in communications and cultural theory. Those fields arguably form the closest thing to a mainstream in popular music studies, and by and large they line up against Adorno's legacy, from John Fiske to Ian Chambers (1990) to Lisa Lewis (1990). But, in the main, even those who decry Adorno's pessimistic vision base their own optimism on the same conception of capital itself. In their work, the assertion of local or subaltern voices and cultural practices becomes a rebuke to totalizing; the contamination of dominant discourse by symbolic resistance is celebrated and encouraged; and the polyvalence of the world of discourse is underlined as a challenge to domination. Whatever moment of truth lurks behind such celebrations – and surely there must be one – the fact is that the studies that embody them, working in and against the shadow of Adorno, adopt precisely his premises about the nature of capitalism and culture, differing only by arguing that the *cultural* sphere is more multiple, resistant and filled with subaltern voices and practices than Adorno allowed. Indeed, they are correct, on all counts. But what such arguments miss is that the cultural processes they celebrate are not opposed to the effects

3 Hardt and Negri (2000), in fact, theorize just such a dependence.

of capitalism, but rather are *integral parts of it*. The stumbling block here is a conception of capitalist hegemony culled from theorists like Gramsci (via Dick Hebdige and other Birmingham theorists), whose frame of civil society is inseparable from the national boundaries and cultural boundaries that flexible accumulation has been gradually displacing.

The result of all this in popular music studies is: on the one hand, Adorno, with very few adherents and viewpoints on culture based on earlier formations of capital; and on the other hand, a plethora of studies which validate the cultural processes of popular music, but do so on the basis of exactly the *same* conception of capital's relation to uniformity and discursive domination. It can probably be said that cultural theory and communications have won – very few popular music scholars accept completely Adorno's account of things, and it is usually a safe bet, theory-wise, to champion the musics of subaltern subjects and their cultural effects. But the history of capitalism, one would be tempted to submit, has in the meantime walked right past the terrain of struggle, on to a stage in which discursive domination and capitalist organization bear a strikingly different relation to each other. Under the view proposed here, capitalism is no longer a great monolithic and uniformly hierarchical force against which various liberatory cultural forces are to be aligned (even were it accepted that such was ever the case). On the contrary, the challenge now, by my conception, is how to theorize capital as *simultaneously* diversifying culturally and segregating economically and spatially.

Such a view militates against another common ground between many cultural studies approaches to music and that of Adorno, namely the desire to locate liberatory force in expressive culture. The foregoing should render it obvious that I am sceptical about such a project, but I do not want to refuse it completely. Indeed, the moment of truth in postmodern cultural studies may well lie in the mapping of how discourse and expressive culture can contaminate forms of domination in a given social formation. But too exclusive a focus on that process may blind us to how the mode of production sets possibilities and limitations for such discursive practices and may even interact with them in ways that are not often considered. Such interactions are usually mediated, and the rest of this study will elaborate one level of mediation, namely urban geography, as it plays itself out within the genre system of rap music.

Reality rap, knowledge rap, and the urban ethos

The discussion so far has argued that both the 'Adorno question' in popular music scholarship and cultural studies-inspired validations of some popular music should be sidelined in discussions of contemporary music, because both are based on a conception of culture inconsistent with the present state of capitalism. But the basic project of Marxist analysis in the humanities, as conceived here – namely, the tracing of the systematic aspects of capitalism in the production, circulation and reception of expressive culture – nevertheless retains its vital significance, in fact all the more so, as capitalism comes to characterize our societies across an ever-broader range and in deepening ways. The question then becomes, of course: what would a non-Adornan Marxism look like in music scholarship?[4] The remainder of this discussion responds to that question, albeit with only one of many possible directions such an effort could take.

In particular, the focus now shifts to urban geography and the changes wrought on city environments by the restructuring of capitalism under post-Fordist regimes of accumulation. While by no means the only possible level of mediation that one could pursue in the examination of the cultural aspects of capital in the present, urban geography is nevertheless a logical choice, for at least two outstanding reasons. First, the histories of genre within the world of popular music (which will form the framework of much of the remaining discussion below) arguably bear an intimate relation to publicly shared perceptions of the character of urban life; I argue that point at greater length in Krims (forthcoming), although a more comprehensive and systematic exposition of that point still lies in the future (and is, in my view, much needed). And second, whereas it was mentioned earlier that debates rage about the scale and scope of the transformations constituting post-Fordism, it is beyond doubt, and well documented,[5] that whatever its general reach, changes in capital accumulation over the last thirty years or so have definitely transformed cities, spatially and socially. Thus, to narrow the focus of the present discussion to urban geography both underlines a rubric of crucial significance to popular music analysis, and also may lay to rest, at

---

4 Klumpenhouwer (1998) could be taken as an earlier example, as could Krims (2000).

5 E.g. Sassen (1991) and (2000), Harvey (1989) and Smith (1996), among many others.

141

least temporarily, potentially endless debates about the nature of flexible accumulation.

David Harvey, in *The Condition of Postmodernity*, tells us that:

> the interweaving of simulacra in daily life brings together different worlds (of commodities) in the same space and time. But it does so in such a way as to conceal almost perfectly any trace of origin, of the labour processes that produced them, or of the social relations implicated in their production.
>
> (1989: 102)

The task of the following discussion of rap music and the urban ethos will be to suggest one way to restore the hidden social relations to a development in genres of rap music, tracing flexible accumulation in the very sound of the musical tracks.

It almost goes without saying that American rap music and video have always taken as a crucial locus the inner city, and that the social force of rap music has depended on this. What is less remarked in the scholarly literature (though much discussed by fans), is that images and ideas of 'the urban' in rap music and video change drastically over time, and that those changes are inseparable from the development of rap genre. The following discussion traces one instance of those changes and relates them to more fundamental developments in urban geography, to provide an illustration of non-Adornan Marxist popular music analysis.

A shift in rap genres

My earlier study of rap music (Krims 2000) describes, among other things, two musical genres that I label 'reality' rap and 'knowledge' rap.[6] Reality rap subsumes what is often called gangsta rap and some related sub-genres, and until fairly recently, it focused on a musical strategy that I label (Krims 2000: 73–9) the 'hip-hop sublime'. In music-analytic terms, the 'hip-hop sublime' is a musical strategy that deploys dense combinations of musical layers. All of the layers reinforce the quadruple metre, but in the domain of pitch they comprise a sharply dissonant combination, even by the standards of jazz, or soul, harmony. In fact, the layers tend not even

6 The two genres are discussed in Chapter 2.

142

Example 7.1: Layers from Raekwon/RZA: 'Can It Be All So Simple' (Remix)

to be 'in tune', so to speak: they are separated by intervals that can only be measured in terms of fractions of well-tempered semitones. The result is that no pitch combination may form conventionally representable relationships with others; musical layers pile up, defying aural representability for Western musical listeners.

The hip-hop sublime is achieved using a procedure that, following Tricia Rose (1994), I call *layering*.[7] Layering is the superposition of several different tracks, using either pre-existing recordings or new studio-produced recordings, to form a complex texture that serves as the musical complement to the MC's performance. Thus, to discuss the musical aspects of the hip-hop sublime, it will be instructive to illustrate how those layers are constructed to create the effect.

One song that can illustrate this is Raekwon's 'Can It Be All So Simple (Remix)', from *Only Built 4 Cuban Linx* (1995), produced by the RZA. Example 7.1 transcribes the layers that produce the effect in question. The first of them, labelled layer (a), is a sample from a pre-existing recording, namely Gladys Knight's rendition of 'The Way We Were'; it is excerpted from the bridge that provides the title of the Raekwon song ('Can it be that it was all so simple then?'). The original setting of the Knight recording, in G major, has the melody set first to IV (first bar), then to ii[7] (second bar); the melody, descending from an initial G5 through a passing F♯5 to a final E5,

---

7   Krims (2000), Chapter 2, discusses layering in a great deal more detail.

is consonant with that melodic setting (with the F♯5 a passing note). The melody is, however, removed from that harmonic context in the RZA's setting. Also, exactly at the beginning of the third beat in the second bar, Knight releases the final note by aspirating heavily the '-n-' (in a performance gesture common in both African-American charismatic religious preaching and gospel-related musical styles, such as soul); the gesture ends up being prominent in the overall texture.

The other layers are all added in the studio by the RZA. The second layer in Example 7.1, labelled layer (b), is a synthesizer line that also projects a melodic third but, in this case, a major rather than the minor third of layer (a). What is more, the melody changes both timbre and register in the middle of the line: the timbre changes from a reedy synthesizer sound in the first bar (though without the attack of a reed instrument, since the melody is played legato throughout), to a synthesized string sound an octave higher in the second half of the bar. The effect is fairly pronounced in the overall texture, because the vocal sample (i.e. layer (a)) decrescendos in the second bar and then drops quickly out of the texture (with the as-pirated '-n-' mentioned above) on the third beat. The combination of the octave transfer in the synthesizer, together with the quieting and ending of the vocal line, results in the textural replacement of layer (a) by layer (b) in the second bar.

Layer (c) consists simply of two block chords played on an electric keyboard (sounding like a Fender Rhodes, though that sound can easily be mimicked electronically). The first chord projects an a-minor triad (ii), the second a b-minor triad (iii). The layer therefore clashes somewhat with the vocal sample, whose original harmonization, it will be recalled, had been IV in the first bar, followed by ii^7. The contrast between the two would perhaps only be relevant to someone with an aural memory of the original setting (and some interest in the matter); but more salient, the new harmonic context renders the final E5 a dissonant lower neighbour to the initial F♯5 of the second bar. While the resulting unresolved dissonance in the voice is not the type of phenomenon referred to here as the 'hip-hop sublime', it lends a certain degree of harmonic tension to the mix.

Layer (d) is a bass guitar, loud and prominent in the mix (as is common in rap recording). The first bar accompanies the ii^7 harmony formed by layers

144

(a), (b) and (c) with arpeggiation from the third to the root of the chord.[8] The second bar initially supports the prevailing iii harmony projected in the electric piano. On the whole, though, the interaction of the bass with the other layers is never stable. For while the bass indeed supports the iii harmony of the piano in the first half of the second bar, the voice and synthesizer (i.e. layers (a) and (b)) together highlight the pitch-classes A and E, thus themselves suggesting a possible ii harmony; that suggestion, in turn, is reinforced by the ii harmony of the first bar. So harmonically, while the bass in layer (d) reinforces the harmony of layer (c), it conflicts with the at least implied harmony of layers (a) and (b). On the second half of beat three in the second bar, the relationship reverses. That is, the E2 struck by the bass is dissonant to the iii chord in layer (c), while reinforcing the suggested ii of layers (a) and (b).[9] Thus, there is never a time at which the layers are consonant to each other; rather, (a) and (b) together constantly exist in a state of tension with (c), while (d) alternates between the two conflicting harmonies.

But harmonic ambiguity is one thing (not uncommon in many popular styles), and the hip-hop sublime is another. For the defining aspect of these layers is that they are dramatically *out of tune*.[10] While layers (a) and (b) are roughly in tune with each other (mirroring their harmonic proximity), layer (c) is conspicuously sharper (roughly a quarter tone) than layers (a) and (b), while layer (d) is conspicuously flatter (again, roughly a quarter tone) than layers (a) and (b). Thus, even to the extent that the layers sometimes form a stable harmonic combination within their own pitch levels, they clash

8 It could be argued that the initial C3 in the bass suggests an opening IV harmony. Such a contention, though, would have to be tempered by the fact that the electric piano already sounds a ii triad. In either case, the harmony is unambiguously ii[7] by the second quaver of beat 3, when the bass guitar plays A2.

9 If one relies on harmonic theory derived from classical music, the reinforcement of layers (a) and (b) is somewhat compromised by the position of the purported harmony. However, that chord position does not bear the same ambiguous status in many popular styles, including rap, that it does in classical music.

10 In professional conversations I have had since the publication of Krims (2000), the question has occasionally arisen whether the detuning is purposeful or not. The question itself probably reveals a good deal about assumptions that some audiences make about the character of the musicians involved in rap music. The answer is that no hip-hop producer I have encountered is unaware of this effect, and that the ability to detune layers in effective ways is much prized among rap producers, at least those interested in this particular effect.

at a much more fundamental level – they are simply not from the same well-tempered universe. It is the radical disparity in their composition – their incommensurability – that comprises the hip-hop sublime being discussed here.

It should be noted that the layers just discussed are not by any means the only musical sounds in the song; they are the ones that contribute to the hip-hop sublime, as I define it. There is, of course, a drum machine beating out the $^4_4$ rhythm, and furthermore, in certain parts of the song there are other musical layers, not to mention the MCing. It is, in fact, a common practice of much rap production that there be certain 'basic' layers that are deployed throughout much or most of the song, while others are reserved for special events or effects. The ones just described form the basis for the refrains in the song.

The 'detuning' of musical layers just described has been a widely used production technique of reality rap, and I call it 'sublime' because the musical layering defeats the conceptual boundaries and unifying descriptions in our categories of pitch combination. The result may account for the widespread impression that rap music soundscapes are menacing and aggressive, quite apart from the lyrical content. But more important for present purposes, it has constituted, since roughly the early 1990s, musical 'hardness' in reality rap music, and indexically, for artists and consumers, it encodes musically the urban conditions of community devastation and danger that the lyrics in the genre describe. That encoding is a classic case of musical semiosis, and it can be seen both in interviews with rap producers and in the consistent pairing of the musical technique with semantic references to these dangers and devastation. The hip-hop sublime frames for the listener fears and pleasures of the black, inner-city ghetto that both fascinates and horrifies rap fans and our popular culture generally. In other words, this particular musical strategy has served, in rap music culture, as a figure for the view of inner-city menace and despair from the point of view of a trapped underclass; and it served that function in the music of commercially prominent artists such as the Wu-Tang Clan, Snoop Doggy Dogg, Dr. Dre, Nas, and Mobb Deep, among many others. A heady mixture of social knowledge and obscene enjoyment, the hip-hop sublime for some time anchored the 'reality' of 'reality rap' in sound, a shorthand for urban conditions inseparable from the identities of the underclass and the inner city.

Example 7.2: Layers from A Tribe Called Quest: '1nce Again'

The other pertinent genre in this story is so-called 'knowledge' rap, which presented a critical and contrasting view of the social function of rap music. Knowledge rap continues, in hip-hop culture, the centuries-old African-American tradition of music as oral history and pedagogy. More importantly, it has formed a locus of popular critique against hardcore reality rap since the emergence of the gangsta figure in the latter; and a central and consistent musical aspect of knowledge rap has thus been an *avoidance* of the hip-hop sublime and a deployment, instead, of playful invocations of jazz, r&b, and other popular, mainly black, musical styles. The song '1nce Again' by A Tribe Called Quest (from *A Tribe Called Quest* 1996) provides an informative example, as the layers (combining samples and live instruments) not only are in tune with each other, but also form a fairly conventional jazz (or pop) progression. Example 7.2 transcribes the basic repeated harmonic material of the song, namely I/bIII/bVII/V^7. Two things complicate the harmony, but only mildly. First, as the example shows, the bass guitar (lower staff) and keyboard line (upper staff) are staggered by one beat, with the former attacking on strong beats and the latter attacking on weak beats. There is, then, some fourth-species dissonant blending of adjacent harmonies; but such is not at all unusual in jazz style, or indeed in many pop styles, and the basic progression remains quite clearly projected. Second, the final dominant seventh is coloured by the presence of an added minor sixth, which is dissonant to the adjacent perfect fifth of the chord (and is prominently audible in the mix). But this, too, is well within the range of jazz harmony, even something of a characteristic gesture. In short, then, the song projects nothing of the hip-hop sublime, but rather a repeated harmonic progression consistent with mainstream (especially) jazz harmonic practices.

The situation described in Krims (2000) thus consists of the reality genre, with the hip-hop sublime, and the contrasting knowledge genre, with its sampling of older musical forms. And in the semantic realm, the reality

Reality Rap	Knowledge Rap
Hip-hop sublime; ghetto realism.	*Standard pitch combinations; education and humour.*

Figure 7.3: Reality rap vs. Knowledge rap before *c*.1996

genre, as its name implies, staked a claim to projecting the bleak conditions of inner-city life, while the knowledge genre critiqued, sometimes even ridiculed, the luridness of the purported reality. This generic relationship, as it existed previous to the mid-1990s, is modelled schematically in Figure 7.3.

But by roughly the end of 1996, that same 'reality' genre had begun shifting, with only rare exceptions, to a blatantly contrasting view of urban life. In the newly configured reality genre, the transgressive wealth that had formerly characterized a third genre, namely pimp rap, is crossed with a foregrounding of fantasy and a near obliteration of the devastated inner-city surroundings. Instead of signifying marginal subjects from a devastated inner-city neighbourhood, reality rap artists were now crime bosses decked out in illicit finery, heroes in narratives inspired by comic books or popular film, or survivors in a post-apocalyptic urban future. An informative example is the video for the song 'It's Mine', from Mobb Deep (1999), guest-starring Nas. The imagery of the video is purely that of 'Big Willy', which term refers to representations of lavish (and highly masculinist) lifestyles and object worlds. In this case, it involves expensive speedboats, a lavish mansion in a tropical setting, multiple bottles of expensive champagne, MCs decked out in fine and costly clothing, and (of course) large numbers of women dressed in scanty bathing suits and moving provocatively. All the imagery supports the mainly 'Big Willy' semantic content of the lyrics, a reality-style mixture of fantasy and gangster imagery.[11]

And importantly, this new kind of reality rap tends to preclude the hip-hop sublime, and 'It's Mine' is here, also, a case in point. The refrain of the song tropes the highly successful duet of Brandy and Monica, 'The Boy Is Mine' (from Brandy [1998]), substituting for its refrain the lyrics 'Y'all

11 More detail about this new kind of reality rap is given in Krims (2000), Chapter 2.

need to give it up / We don't give a fuck / What y'all niggaz want / Thug, life, is, mine' (repeated once). Although the singing, like much MC singing in rap music, is purposefully, even joyously, out of tune, it occurs over a strong and harmonically conventional alternation between iv and i (in g minor). What had formerly, in the reality genre, been a musical backdrop of stunningly unassimilable and immobile layers of sound – and it is worth noting that Nas and Mobb Deep had both been exemplary for the consistent sublimity of their production in their earlier careers – is now a fairly conventional soul or r&b progression.

Krims (2000) mentions this shift in persona and musical style in the context of the decline of classic gangsta rap, or at least its displacement to Atlanta and New Orleans. That context is indeed germane, but an important complementary development now can be added, namely the transfer of the project of 'realist' ghetto representation to the knowledge genre. Rather than disappearing, reality rap's earlier project of a 'hardcore' ghetto realism has been taken up within the knowledge genre that formerly had so assiduously disowned it; and rather than project the realist project musico-poetically, the knowledge genre takes its representational cues mainly in the semantic reference of the lyrics and the visual settings of cover art and videos.[12] A video by three exemplary figures in the 'knowledge' genre, Mos Def and Talib Kweli (known jointly as 'Blackstar') and Native Tongues colleague Common (formerly known as Common Sense), can serve to illustrate. The video to their song 'Respiration' (from Blackstar 1998) adopts much of the project of ghetto realism in its lyrics and visual codes. In particular, one can find there a blatant deployment of many of the music video codes which have come, within and outside rap music, to connote the project of urban realism: the architecture and street spaces of decaying neighbourhoods, the brownstone stoops which connote at the same time earlier black community life and its still-recent devastation, the struggling abject classes and decaying transportation infrastructure, and even the black-and-white photography which, in the music video world, encodes the idea that one is viewing the 'starkly real'. The musical tracks, on the other hand, are jazz-based and not

12 This is not to say that the ghetto itself has disappeared from reality rap, so much as to say that the tragic realist version of that ghetto shifted its centre of gravity to the knowledge genre.

Reality Rap	Knowledge Rap
Standard pitch combinations; fantasy characters and situations	*Greater variey of pitch combinations (not limited to hip-hop sublime); ghetto realism.*

Figure 7.4: Reality rap vs. Knowledge rap since *c.* 1996

significantly detuned: in other words, the hip-hop sublime is not there to anchor the ghetto realist project, as it had been in the reality genre.[13] More generally, the knowledge genre has, since roughly the mid- to late 1990s, hosted much of the remaining deployment of ghetto realism, from groups such as Company Flow, the Jurassic Five, and Blackstar to groups on the periphery of the genre such as the Beatnuts.

All of this is to say that after all, the project of mapping inner-city devastation has not disappeared from rap music, but rather has *shifted from reality to knowledge rap*. The two genres have retained their identity in rap music production and consumption: public reception of their work (for instance in the fan media and album reviews) has retained the identity of the genres, while simultaneously marking the changes in musical style and semantic reference of the lyrics. Figure 7.4 models the new generic relationship. There we see what, in the context of hip-hop culture, is nothing short of a striking reversal; in an earlier state of the rap genre system, the reality genre prompted Robin D. G. Kelly's neologism 'ghettocentricity', while the more explicitly didactic knowledge rap emphasized afrocentrism and even, as in the case of De La Soul, suburban spaces as loci of critique. Then in the new state of the genre system, it is precisely the avoidance of ghetto representation that characterizes the mainstream reality genre to be critiqued, while the knowledge genre presses to restore its visibility. But in terms of the musical poetics, the two genres did not exchange roles. Instead, as reality rap abandoned the hip-hop sublime for more differentiated musical strategies, the knowledge genre likewise expanded its musico-poetic possibilities, most notably in the

13 The present discussion refers to the album version of the song, not the two remixes released separately as a vinyl single; it is the album version that is used in conjunction with the video discussed here.

abundance of dance styles in the output of artists like Q-Tip and the Jungle Brothers. The genres work differentially, with the social signification only comprehensible in each with respect to the other. Thus, a simple exchange of musical style is far from the only possibility to accompany the exchange of geographic representation.

The urban ethos

Taken in isolation, such a shift could form little more than fodder for popular music trivia, an aesthetic mutation among many in the constantly shifting world of musical aesthetics. But these developments in the genre system of rap music are, in fact, part of a much larger changing field not only of popular music, but of changing cultural representations of urban life of the mid- to late 1990s. And those representations, in turn, are neither epiphenomenal nor fully autonomous; instead, they share a landscape of common material relationships that extends to the economic geography of American cities. That landscape includes objective social relations that are part and parcel of the new city order of flexible accumulation along with what I call an *urban ethos*. This term describes the character of cities and the kinds of lives lived in them, as it is represented in popular music, film, television, journalism, books (fiction and non-fiction), and other forms of public representation. Collectively, such forms of representation project a sense of the pleasures, dangers and possible experiences of urban centres. And the limits of such possibilities shift over time: could one imagine, for instance, a film with the character of *Boyz in the Hood* (1991) having been produced and disseminated in 1950? The oddity of such a notion illustrates the fundamental historicity of an urban ethos, and one argument being advanced here is that the ethos is inseparable from the changing built environment in which the social relations are lived out on a daily basis. One task of a Marxist theory of representation, as I see it, is to sort through the social relations, the built environment, and the urban ethos, constantly shifting those levels as ground to figure, then figure to ground, and always with the idea that all the shifting perspectives are retained in a larger, and fully relational, picture. I refer to this process as *telescoping*, and its purpose, in the present context, is ultimately to locate the little music-poetic shift that I have described in the relations of production in our society as a whole.

A first step will be to remark that the shifts we have seen in discourses of the 'urban' are not unique to rap music or hip-hop culture, but rather are observable across the spectrum of popular cultural production. To begin in an adjacent artistic genre, we may observe that the 'in the hood' genre of films, for instance, *Boyz 'N' the Hood* and *Menace II Society*, have all but disappeared from wide circulation, as their closest relatives have become small-run or direct-to-video fantasies of transgressive wealth like *Belly* and *I Got the Hook-Up*. Extending our vision a little further, we can observe the return of romantic urban adventure for the white bourgeoisie, for instance in television series like *Sex and the City*. Such representational changes share the landscape with objective spatial transformations in the metropolis, especially in North America and Western Europe, since roughly the early 1990s. Urban geographer Neil Smith (1996) describes these changes as a middle- and upper-class reconquest of the metropolis, coining the term 'revanchist city' to indicate the processes by which those classes have forcibly reconquered urban terrain previously threatened by the presence of more economically marginal residents. Although such activity has always gone on in major cities, Smith identifies and documents a wholesale and co-ordinated acceleration ranging from the early through the mid-1990s. Hallmarks of that acceleration include the proliferation of gated communities, aggressive enforcement of vagrancy laws, loosening of building and planning regulations, and much-vaunted jail terms for previously minor offences. Such measures have worked to increase spatial segregation and transfer marginal inner-city residents from streets to newly built and overcrowded jails and prisons; and that, in turn, has reduced the mobility and visibility of the underclasses and their perceived threat to urban existence, along with the widely vaunted drops in violent crime rates. The reconquest of Western cities by the propertied classes has changed substantially the experience of urban life for all classes, some for the better, and some for the worse. Most important, these developments were not random in their timing; after all, the middle and upper classes have always had an interest in the reconquest of the city. So, what made the revanchist city possible, starting around the early 1990s? An answer to that question can only come from a broader view of urban economic development, one that distinguishes between the 1990s economic boom and that of the 1980s – because that difference turns out to have everything to do with cultural representations of urban life.

Economic growth is significant not simply for those who profit from it, but also for those who are left behind, and for how it is that the prospering society deals with those who are left behind. These factors precisely distinguish the 1980s from the 1990s economic growth spurts. The earlier economic 'boom' of the 1980s had been publicly conspicuous for how it had left behind the black underclass of America, in the wake of the final devastations of central-city industry already mentioned above as one of the hallmarks of flexible accumulation. Sociologists and economic geographers[14] have documented just how this happened. Suddenly, the ghetto loomed large in both the American and, to some extent, the global public imagination in the 1980s and early 1990s, and it threatened the viability of gentrified neighbourhoods established in the inner city earlier in the 1980s – the very neighbourhoods that had supported the culture of the 'yuppie'. Not coincidentally, popular culture registered this mutation in urban life with well-known musical and filmic representations of what one might call the 'dangerous city'. Cultural productions like NWA (Niggaz With Attitudes), *Boyz in the Hood*, and *South Central* seemed to proliferate through popular culture, until about the time in the early 1990s when the world discovered and romanced (what was in image, more than in reality) a city with sufficient social and spatial distance from the decaying cities of the Midwest and Northeast corridor, namely Seattle. That discovery helped to announce a further development of the early 1990s and a new set of objective conditions. We are dealing here with the so-called economic 'boom' of the 1990s Clinton era, which can be characterized in several ways. The 1990s 'boom' much resembles the 1980s 'boom' in record-high levels of corporate profits and stock prices, but it differs in the far more dramatic rise in employment, which was widely represented as fulfilling the trickle-down promise of Reaganism, a softer form of capitalist prosperity that purportedly does raise all boats. A second major difference between these economic expansions, inseparable from the first difference, is constituted by some characteristics of the 1990s version: the unprecedented crackdown on inner-city 'deviance' that involves three-strike laws, mandatory minimum sentences, anti-immigrant fervour, and skyrocketing rates of incarceration for petty crimes. Emblematic of this new urban condition is the

---

14 Among those to document these changes are William Julius Wilson (1987), John Kasarda (1990) and Mark Allen Hughes (1989 and 1990).

Rudolph Giuliani 'Renaissance' in New York City, especially Times Square, which provided a prominent cultural confirmation for the American public that the underclass was then out of the way and, furthermore, had run out of excuses in the newly flourishing economy. At the same time, job statistics showed that many groups (such as inner-city African Americans) had little, if any, more access to jobs and education than ten years previously; and more to the point of flexible accumulation, a majority of the new jobs being formed were designed for the so-called 'flexible workplace', which means that they were mainly less than full-time employment and offered little or no benefits. In other words, that 'recovery' since the mid-1990s had been a flexible accumulation recovery, solidifying the subjugation of the lower end of the labour pool and the unprecedented agility of capitalism in extracting surplus value out of labour. This is not to say that flexible accumulation had nothing whatsoever to do with the 1980s economic expansion, but rather that it was the subsequent one that solidified the spatial effects in the metropolis, in effect 'cleaning up' the underclass problem for the more prosperous urban residents and workers. The black underclass that had loomed as America's cultural nightmare and morbid fascination, had lost that cultural status, as its impact on city life had been largely neutralized for the middle and upper classes.

Now, the cultural effects of the revanchist city are observable not as aspects of a crude mass psychology, but rather in the literal and representational spaces all around those who inhabit the changing metropolis. The enforcement of spatial boundaries, mass incarceration and the absorption of marginal labour into the flexible labour pool have in fact, done wonders for popular representations of urban life. One can note the visible and audible rehabilitation of the American metropolis just about anywhere in the telescoping from economic geography back to rap music, figured in anything from the new adult playground in New York's Times Square to the romanticized urban settings of recent television shows like *Queer as Folk*, whose cosy street and diner scenes, and intimate, renovated interiors revive the libidinal investments of white youth in a manner reminiscent of the early 1980s. One could also invoke, in connection with this, quite a few non-rap music videos such as Bjork's 'Big Time Sensuality', the Corrs' 'So Young', and Beck's 'Devil's Haircut', all of which deploy very different poetic strategies for imaging a contained and reconquered urban landscape. And sidelined in this new regime of representation is the very same impacted black ghetto that had loomed so large from the mid-1980s to the mid-1990s. Of course, the impacted ghetto is still there *materially*, but its relation to the dominant consumers of popular culture, and thus the culture industry, has been transformed. All of this is to say that the sidelining of the hip-hop sublime, and the corresponding playing down of the impacted ghetto in hip-hop culture, is not a mere musicological detail but rather part of a much larger cultural mutation, a *new urban ethos*.

And rap music has participated in the shifting urban ethos at a crucial point in its fortunes: in the biggest market for CDs, the United States, rap music has now overtaken country music to become the second best-selling genre, after rock (RIAA 2001). The turning of the reality genre away from the 'ghettocentricity' of hip-hop culture is thus a significant event in popular music culture overall, by dint of sheer market share, if nothing else. And while the adoption of the ghettocentric project by knowledge rap may be a less commercially visible development, it is nevertheless inseparable from the fortunes of all rap and hip-hop music, whose explosion into the mainstream of popular music bespeaks a cultural significance scholars are only beginning to explore. But of course, the argument here is for a significance that transcends the context of rap music alone and touches one of the central problematics of popular culture. The urban ethos that both responds to and constitutes a sense of the character of metropolitan life, is one of the great undertold stories of popular music in general, and of musical genre in particular.[15]

Conclusion

The arguments presented in this essay are ambitious, and the discussion has covered some distance from the original focus on Adorno; so it will be helpful to make most explicit in what sense the thesis just advanced constitutes a non-Adornan Marxism. And of course, 'non-Adornan' also means avoiding the cultural-studies mode of 'resistance' validation already argued here to be part and parcel of the problematic inherited from Adorno. In no

---

15 I am working on a monograph that elaborates the urban ethos and popular music in greater detail.

way would I wish to suggest, for example, that the more 'commercialized' reality genre represents domination and the knowledge genre the subaltern voice mustering resistance. The opposite, in fact, is the point: the earlier centrality of the ghetto in reality rap had offered its own form of surplus value for these cultural products. That surplus value has now been channelled into the knowledge genre, while the more commercially prominent reality rap merges increasingly with other aspects of (especially male) teen popular culture, such as skateboarding, video games, comic books, action fantasy and, of course, wrestling. The representational shift in the genre system has everything to do with changes in objective relations of production in our society, including what has to happen in cities like New York to protect the expansion of its communications, financial, and entertainment infrastructure into areas like Times Square.[16] None of this scenario relies on notions of co-optation or resistance, nor would I want to insert such a problematic. Furthermore, and equally important for a non-Adornan Marxism, nowhere in the situation described here must one try to map stylistic or representational homogenization to industrial centralization or integration. On the contrary, one of the happier developments in rap music since the mid-1990s has been a proliferation of new styles and generic hybrids, ranging from the Caribbean hip-hop of Wyclef Jean through the Southeastern percussive style of Outkast to well-known metal/rap hybrids of groups like Limp Bizkit and Kid Rock. All of this, one must hasten to add, has been going on against a background of increasing centralization in the music industry, as even majors like EMI continued to be gobbled up in communications mergers of record size. Something well beyond the Adornan problematic must be advanced to map all these developments; and the lesson, as so often, comes from a return to Marx himself, for whom the relation of base to superstructure is always thoroughly historical. Nobody who has learned this lesson from Marx should be surprised to see many of Adorno's observations, as insightful as they had been for a certain period, fall out of sync with later stages of capitalism.

Tracking shifts in musical representation, and tracking their complex relations to capital and both its physical and its symbolic requirements,

16 Hannigan (1998) discusses Times Square in the context of more general trends in urban restructuring. Taylor (1991) provides more detail about the specific case of Times Square.

involves abandoning the monolithic and inflexible models of capitalism that we have inherited from Adorno. It also involves casting at least a critical eye towards the cultural-studies-inspired validations of the subaltern voice and its cultural praxis; indeed, one of the hallmarks of flexible accumulation is its stunningly successful deployment of subaltern subjects, both for new forms of labour like back-office organization and low-level services, and, as Christopher Mele (1996) has shown, for cultural practices like 'world music', 'ethnic' restaurants and cultural festivals.[17] All of this is not to say that analyses from cultural studies must be set aside; in fact, they may have been enormously valuable in tracking representation in popular music. What is needed instead is a more detailed accounting of the term 'capitalism,' whose meaning in *our* analyses must change with the social system itself. Adorno's critiques have been useful and could still be useful, perhaps, with some major tinkering and updating; but it is precisely an accounting of the profound changes in capital that popular music studies must register to get past the ghost of Adorno into a more versatile, complex, and, above all, contemporary Marxism.

17 Hardt and Negri (2000) offer a convincing theorization of such cultural diversification as an aspect of the present state of capital.

8   Jethro Tull and the case for modernism in mass culture

ALLAN F. MOORE

'You can almost sing along to it [laughs]'[1]

Introduction

There seem to be two alternative ways to argue the presence of a modernist aesthetic in an art object. The first way would see it as a *necessary* response to the social conditions of modernity, as exemplified by David Harvey (Harvey 1989), such that to evade a modernistic response would be received as fraudulent. This is the essence of the position laid out by the Frankfurt theorist Theodor Adorno in his defence of Schoenberg in the face of Stravinsky, of which Adorno (1973) is the most outspoken example, and it was also adopted by such high modernist post-war composers as Boulez or Stockhausen (see Boulez 1952 and Stockhausen 1989: 140). The second way would see it as contingent, as a *possible* response to the social conditions of modernity, one among a number of other possibilities which could be represented, perhaps, by realism or postmodernism. Recalling Lyotard's (1988) emphasis on the historical concurrence of modernist and postmodernist responses, if the first articulation can only be identified chronologically (whereby modernity and modernism are instituted simultaneously), the second can be identified aesthetically, by assuming a series of modernist identifiers.

---

1   Ian Anderson quoted in Pidgeon (1991: 65). My thanks to those who offered comments on this chapter when it was delivered as a research seminar paper at the University of Leeds in late 1996.

158

Idiolect in Jethro Tull

The origins of the rock band Jethro Tull can be traced back to 1966. Almost by accident they took the name of an eighteenth-century English agriculturist in 1968 (Rees 1998), and writer/vocalist Ian Anderson assumed artistic (and subsequently financial) control of the band in 1969. In a career which has currently lasted for more than thirty years, Jethro Tull have released twenty studio albums, at least six compilations and retrospectives (usually with one or more previously unreleased tracks) and a variety of releases of live material. Their career has seen stylistic swerves from early blues, r&b and hard rock through progressive rock, folk rock and new-wave/synthesizer rock, on to heavy metal, back to quasi-blues and on to world music (if the reviewers are to be believed), but these changes of surface *style* belie a consistency of *idiolect*, analysis of which is the subject of this chapter. This idiolect's most endearing feature is, perhaps, the tendency to self-deprecation captured in Ian Anderson's own words, from an interview which took place in August 1989, in the quotation at the beginning of this chapter.

There is an important issue of theory at stake here, which can only be treated briefly in this context. In his theory of semiotic levels, Gino Stefani (1987) discusses the operation of musical *code*, from the general levels (such as social practices) down to more local levels (styles, techniques and individuated pieces of music). Richard Middleton specifies further levels within this hierarchy, from *langue* (i.e. functional tonality) through *norms* and *dialects* to *styles*, *genres*, *sub-codes*, *idiolects*, *works* and *performances*, wherein *idiolect* refers to those styles/practices 'associated with particular composers and performers' (Middleton 1990: 174). Although his terms of reference are different, Leonard Meyer (1989: 13ff.) proposes a very similar hierarchization (preferring the term *idiom* to Middleton's *idiolect*). This seems to be the established wisdom. However, one by-product of Lawrence Kramer's recent study (1995) is to challenge the simple subordination of *idiolect* to *style*, in respect of a particular example from Mozart (K.563), where he finds a marked difference between Mozart's *learned* and *popular* voices (Kramer 1995: 25–32). The issue is even clearer in considering popular music since the late 1960s. Significant musicians and writers are able to cross style boundaries without compromising their idiolectal practices: I have elsewhere argued this for Richard Thompson (see Moore 2001b), for David Bowie and Elvis Costello

(Moore 2001a: 202–11), while it will become clear below that the same position holds for Jethro Tull. Clearly, unless we are content not to distinguish stylistic practices below the levels of 'classical' or 'popular', the relationship between style and idiolect is non-inclusive.

Defining the Tull idiolect

For many fans, both in the UK and in Europe (where Jethro Tull retain a large following), the determinate album remains *Aqualung*, originally released in 1971. The album's title song still frequently forms part of their live set. This song's subject, a social outcast, is clearly a failure according to the standards of modernity, but his presence is portrayed musically as a source of enormous strength. The song's stylistic forebears are the blues as filtered through the hard rock of the late 1960s (the overdriven guitar lines and power chords, the emphatic drumming) and the observational urban 'folk' pioneered by writers such as Bob Dylan and Phil Ochs. It is noteworthy that these two styles (the electric 'rock' and the acoustic 'folk') exist within the same song, and that the acoustic, guitar-accompanied, verse returns later in hard rock guise. A number of songs of the 1970s (e.g. 'Wind Up', 'Minstrel in the Gallery', 'Black Satin Dancer', 'Heavy Horses', 'Dark Ages') use the formal device of singing the same lyrics to two totally different settings, maintaining a tension between lyrical folk introspection and hard rock declamation. There is perhaps some ambivalence as to which stylistic setting is the more appropriate each time: 'Minstrel in the Gallery' and 'Black Satin Dancer' maintain the conceit of Renaissance troubadours into which the hard rock band intrudes, while on 'Dark Ages', the rock textures appear as a clear point of arrival. Extrapolating from these songs, it can be proposed that the band's idiolect can itself be erected on the fundamental opposition of acoustic- and electric-focused ensembles: not for Jethro Tull the easily marketed, MTV-derived, equation of 'plugged' with 'unplugged', whereby the two approaches are merely alternative ways to perform the same song. In the words of one commentator, 'the clash between the individual and society, between the rural and urban worlds, between happiness (however qualified) and disillusion, is the archetypal tension…represented musically [by the opposition of] the blues/r&b and the folk tradition[s]' (Thomas 1993: 18). In 'Aqualung', this opposition is played out, beneath a rough arch form, in an alternation of chordally articulated verses founded on period structures, and open-ended structures founded on repeated riffs. In 'Orion', it is played out between the riff-based rock refrain in A Aeolian, and a gentler, acoustic verse in C Aeolian based on clear periods and accompanied by a small number of orchestral strings.

This intraopus opposition tends for many to be a first point of critical contact with the music: Jethro Tull have often been accused of being a 'folk' band with rock pretensions or, as Anderson calls them, 'a heavy rock band with mandolins' (Pidgeon 1991: 65). Despite the occasional recourse to pastiche Celtic jigs ('Flying Dutchman', 'Velvet Green', 'Broadford Bazaar', 'Warm Sporran'), the 'folk' referents are almost always English, whereas Anderson himself comes from Scotland and has his retreats there (as explored on 'Ears of Tin'). It might be suggested that 'English' folk, then, acts as his exotic 'other'. The view that 'folk' is an intrinsic, authentic constituent of Jethro Tull's idiolect is easily dispelled by their live performance of the most hackneyed possible reading of 'John Barleycorn', the only traditional song they have ever offered. Recorded on *A Little Light Music*, the version used is that found in English schools into the 1960s, its nine verses being slightly adapted from Baring-Gould *et al.* (1889) and widely known from the *Faber Book of Ballads*. In any case, I think an alternative interpretation is preferable.

The 1977 song 'Jack-in-the-Green' celebrates a character who has long featured in English rural May Day customs, where he personifies summer as 'the time of plenty' (Hole 1978: 169). There is no hard rock declamation here, but a suggested, mythical, reality alternative to that pursued under modernity. It is such an alternative, always set against the actual, that we frequently find symbolized in Tull's stylistic virtuosity. 'Cold Wind to Valhalla' represents a more overt recourse to (Nordic) myth, an option developed on *Broadsword and the Beast* which sold so well in Germany (Rees 1998: 105). On 'A Christmas Song', Anderson's attempt to act as modern, self-sufficient society's conscience is both captured in the startling quotation of the Christmas carol 'Once in Royal David's City' and questioned in the song's deflating close: 'if you wish, this is *just* a Christmas song'. In an inversion of the conventionalized position, on the early song 'Son', it is the agonies of the family that are symbolized by the ringing riff, while the anonymity achievable in massed urban spaces makes these latter a place of acoustic retreat. There is, however, a multitude of songs in which an alternative reality is not imaginable, which

Example 8.1: Reduction of 'Fylingdale flyer'

express simple bleakness in the face of continuing modernization, such as 'Nothing is Easy' (1969), 'Batteries not Included' (1980), and 'Farm on the Freeway' (1987). It is a perennial topic. 'Fylingdale Flyer', for example, in its dramatization of the misinterpretation of a harmless blip on the radar screen as a nuclear attack, celebrates the failure of the products of modernity, here represented by advanced technology. On its own, this generalized position questioning modernity signifies nothing more than that Jethro Tull were born as a rock band in the heady days before counter-cultural values became goals and, hence, idle wishes. But there is more.

'Fylingdale Flyer' typifies the rhythmic tightness which has always been a key feature of Jethro Tull's work (other good examples include 'Back Door Ladies', 'Minstrel in the Gallery' and 'Nobody's Car'). Although the textures common to the early 1980s albums mark a stylistic shift away from 'hard rock' in the direction of 'synthesizer rock', where both acoustic and electric guitars are at something of a discount, the rhythmic playing found there seems to be far more subtle than the somewhat overblown pomposity of a band like Yes. Tull's usual technique deals with metrical reconfigurations set off by displacements of a beat or half-beat, rather than the additive patterns of Yes songs like 'Awaken', but it is no less 'difficult', certainly to play, and arguably to listen to. Example 8.1 illustrates the melodic and accompanimental rhythms of the verse of 'Fylingdale Flyer'.

This almost wilful characteristic is one we find elsewhere. Discussing the early 1970s critically derided albums *Thick as a Brick* and *A Passion Play*, Thomas (1993: 26) argues that they acted to provide a challenge to the virtuosity of Anderson and his band, performing a similar function to that of *Ascension* for John Coltrane's comrades. In their frequent changes of mood, texture and tempo within an unbroken stream of music, these albums were difficult to play but, as such, maintained the 'artistic integrity' of the multiple persona that was Jethro Tull. Anderson himself is in no doubt that the 'variety' produced by such means is necessary to the live band, simply in order to stave off boredom. 'Even within the context of an individual song I still like the idea that you can have perhaps a loud riff to start the thing off, and then it goes into a gentle acoustic passage, and then it does some other big stuff and then it changes tempo and feel and goes off into something else, round the houses, a couple of guitar solos, whatever, and back to something else.'[2] But, as many music journalists of the time insisted, these particular albums (*Thick as a Brick* and *A Passion Play*), in their difficulty, courted pretension.[3] Whatever 'meaning' they might conceal, or even whatever 'enjoyment' they might enable, had to be worked at in order to be achieved, thereby denying the immediacy quintessential to 'popular' art as an ephemeral genre. Discussing the 1970 album *Benefit*, Thomas writes that some of its songs 'are sophisticated and deliberately "difficult", while still relying as a point of reference on r&b riffs and rhythms' (Thomas 1993: 19). Here, the difficulty refers less to rhythmic and textural shifts, more to interpretation of the lyrics: in the song 'Sossity', for example, Anderson appears to allegorize the individual's capacity and necessity to escape his social 'others' (the name 'Sossity' is even repronounced 'society' in the refrain) in an off-beat love song whose efforts to escape an Aeolian A are repeatedly thwarted. Thus the paradox of the hippie's idealistic social conviction as it issues in material individualism. In one sense, of course, 'difficulty' is a matter of perception, related to one's competence in the style concerned. *Melody Maker* journalist Chris Welch, who had so roundly condemned *A Passion Play*, responded to the later *Broadsword and the Beast* by claiming 'Ian Anderson expects the audience to do some work. They have to listen... But gradually... you feel you've actually undergone a course of treatment instead of a quick energy fix' (quoted in Rees 1998: 104). Against norms of regular metres and chordal patterns, however, this sense of most of an audience needing to 'work' seems clear.

To focus again on rhythmic difficulty, I move on to 'Nobody's Car'. Here, we find the sort of metrical dislocations encountered from Example 8.1,

2 Anderson, again quoted in Pidgeon (1991: 65).
3 This is documented in Rees (1998: 55–56).

Example 8.2: 'Nobody's Car' motif

which becomes...

but this time superimposed on a perfectly regular beat. Example 8.2 specifies the motif whose 'downbeat' is never clarified, and which is later foreshortened to take the process one step further.

This unorthodox strategy seems alienating in the context of Tull's usual practice, and accompanies lyrics in which the protagonist finds himself faced by facelessness – ostensibly of non-individuals in Soviet Russia, but by extension in modern society also. In his difference he is *lost*, as are other Tull characters. In the song 'Undressed to Kill', the metaphor of sexual enticement is used to dramatize the subject's state of abandonment. In the very early song 'The Witch's Promise', one of the band's few strong-selling singles, the unaddressed third party loses himself to the spell of the witch only in the very last line ('don't you wait up for him, he's going to be late'). In these songs, modern society is again personified as a seductive woman, however awkward we may feel about the metaphor. It is clearly an Anderson mainstay, a similar metaphor appearing on 'Sweet Dream', 'Some Day the Sun Won't Shine for You', 'The Clasp' and 'Strange Avenues'. In the more recent 'The Whaler's Dues', the whaler's repentance from the slaughter of his trade comes too late to 'save' him ('can you forgive me? NO'). In the earlier 'Two Fingers', a similar situation is faced with sardonic humour, and in the very early 'We Used to Know', it is faced with unutterable sadness, the expression underpinned by an unrelenting fifth-cyclic sequence in a telling marriage of affect and technique.

A key song in this sense is 'Locomotive Breath', in which Anderson took 'the idea of this train, this runaway, out-of-control train being like life. And you're on board this train, without any means of really controlling where it's going or how fast it's going or what the outcome's going to be, but nonetheless being on this train of life' (Pidgeon 1991: 64). In the same interview, however, Anderson admits that the 'message' is perhaps spurious for, to most fans, it's a foot-stamping song, 'me being rather closer to Kylie Minogue than I would like to see' (Pidgeon 1991: 64). In performance, Anderson's delight at the feel of the words skipping out of his mouth can be clearly sensed. The lyric's connotations can be disinterred, but they are not necessarily self-evident. He goes much further elsewhere. Talking of the more recent song 'Thinking Round Corners', he noted '[a] lot of lyrics ... were word associations, word-plays, little images, they're fun ... a sort of pastiche: images, things that dotted together. They don't necessarily tell a big story. They're just like lots of little ideas linked together, which maybe have a relationship and maybe don't' (Anderson 1993a: 25). Another good example of this would be the song 'Up to Me', which goes to great lengths to find alternative contexts in which those three words can complete a stanza. To extrapolate again, Jethro Tull enjoy a general refusal of formulae, of simple clichés, and even of standard genres – only think how few Jethro Tull love songs there are.

Many songs from Tull's extensive repertoire (almost 300 recorded songs aside from bootlegs) are resurrected for live performance, although only those Anderson still feels comfortable singing (rather than where he would have to 'put on a show'). One of these is, indeed, 'Locomotive Breath'. First released in 1971, it also appeared on a live album in 1992. Although recognizably the same song, it has undergone careful rearrangement. The original song was based formally on an introduction and three verses. The introduction was itself in three parts: a slow piano introduction combining gestures from nineteenth-century music (particularly Beethoven) and jazz; an upbeat piano and guitar break over a tonic pedal, reminiscent perhaps of the blues; and the introduction of the guitar's main overdriven riff. The second verse was followed by a flute break and the third was extended into the playout. On the 1992 recording, the structure remains the same. The introduction, however, is almost double the length (befitting the greater space available in live performance), while the role (and much of the material) of the piano has been taken by the flute (the 1992 tour was undertaken without a keyboard player). The most notable differences are the lack of a double-tracked guitar, which makes it far less prominent and the song far less menacing, and also the change of vocal quality necessitated by the throat problem from which Anderson suffered in the 1980s. Rather than a song of youthful angst, we now hear a song of careworn disgust.

A more surprising instance of resurrection appears on the twenty-fifth anniversary CD set, where thirteen songs received new studio recordings, in very different versions from those originally released. Now, back in 1969, before they even had a past, Jethro Tull had released the song 'Living in the Past', which warned of the seductive dangers of nostalgia (see Harris 1993: 220). Anderson claims to have no interest in awards which mark the band's historical place, to keep no platinum albums and the like (Pidgeon 1991: 67). And yet, Jethro Tull's consciousness of history is acute. The first album was entitled *This Was*. Anderson's later rationale was that it was intended to act as a picture of how they sounded then, because he already envisioned the band being stylistically mobile. Its liner notes couch this with characteristically underplayed menace: 'This was how we were playing then. But things change. Don't they.' Due to punter insistence, a version of 'Living in the Past' is now a more than occasional guest in live sets, but it is heavily rearranged because Anderson no longer feels comfortable with some of the lyrics, particularly (it would appear) those expressing apparent disinterest in others' sufferings or misunderstandings (Anderson 1993a: 9).

On a rather strange 'concept album' released in 1976 can be found the song 'From a Deadbeat to an Old Greaser'. The album as a whole dramatizes that difficult interlude between youth and death, while in this song the reminiscing deadbeat sings the line 'and the Shadows played FBI', whereon guitarist Martin Barre simply picks up the opening four-note phrase from that song with perfect Hank Marvin articulation. A similar example of explicit external reference appears on the album *War Child*, which purports through sound effects to be set amidst everyday mayhem within the Battle of Britain (or some similar conflict). The song 'Strange Avenues', which appeared in 1989, contains a telling reference to a 'wino . . . looking like a record cover from 1971'. The reference, of course, is to the album *Aqualung*. The album *Under Wraps* includes two versions of the same, title, song, one for full band and one for acoustic line-up, the two setting up a palpable sense of historical distance. The first version (for band) has prominent multiple synthesizer lines, double-tracked voice and power guitar, and a regular two-bar hypermetre throughout. The acoustic version is far shorter, has a modified

166

melody with wider leaps, and harmonies rethought in order to be more suitable to Anderson's inimitable guitar style (the song sounds almost like an out-take from *Minstrel in the Gallery*, ten years earlier). In all these cases, it appears to me that history is most invasively intervening. More recently, the song 'Rocks on the Road' is interrupted by a style completely foreign, and clearly antecedent, to it, but one suggested by the direction taken by the lyrics. They talk about enjoying a 'little light music', at which point the flute-led band shifts into a perfectly executed sloppy shuffle rhythm and comfortable melodic break, reminiscent of what we might term 'cocktail jazz'. Here, we have an obvious surface fragmentation in terms of style, one which does not require prior knowledge of the band's repertoire. The context (the identity of the song) is secure, although the sense of continuity (the shift of style articulating that song) is troubled.

This inherent waywardness has now become common live practice, whereby songs emanating from very different albums are allowed to interpenetrate. For example, the gig at Reading's Hexagon Theatre on 17 September 1996[4] used 'Thick as a Brick' as a frame for the entire show. The opening of this album-length piece led straight into the then-new 'Dangerous Veils', while in the centre of the show the main parts of 'Songs from the Wood', 'Too Old to Rock'n'Roll' and 'Heavy Horses' were allowed to interpenetrate, creating a larger entity. The encore ran from the early 'Dharma for One', through 'Cross-eyed Mary' and into the final bars of 'Thick as a Brick'. I suggested at the outset that the band's *idiolect* was marked, in part, by an encompassing of oppositions both formal and instrumental. I have also noted that frequent changes of mood, tempo and texture are fundamental. Both these aspects are marked by a troubling sense of surface continuity, although contexts remain secure. Perhaps the most dramatic instances of this occur in *Thick as a Brick* itself. Thus, in a 34″ passage from 11′56″, one gesture is gradually exchanged for another as part of an ongoing cyclic form (Josephson 1992). Three gestures are used at this point, labelled a, b and c (see Ex. 8.3).

From 11′56″, a appears and is repeated a fourth lower. This two-bar pattern is then repeated three further times with slightly differing textures, ensuring stability. These repeats are then interrupted by b and c, followed again by a. This new pattern (b and c followed by a) then repeats, after which

---

4 According to my notes taken at the time.

Example 8.3: 'Thick as a Brick' alternating gestures

b forms the basis for the ensuing section. The device appears strained on listening, although the use of c ensures that the exchange is not obvious on initial hearings. *Thick as a Brick* is also an ever-present in live shows, but it has now become just a 5–8 minute glimpse of its former self, not always used structurally as cited above. Other examples of a disturbed surface are less extreme, but take a variety of forms, from the multi-layered solo voice of 'One Brown Mouse' to the sub-psychedelic use of tape reversal on 'Play in Time' or the intricate, near-hocketed instrumental melody of 'Hunting Girl'.

Thus some aspects, at least, of the idiolect of Jethro Tull. It is now necessary to place these in a wider context.

Contextualizing the Tull idiolect

In their compendious study of the development of Western art last century, Charles Harrison and Paul Wood point to urban artists' paradoxical recourse in the first decade of the twentieth century to Nature as an 'authentic ground' for their work. They point out that '[t]he artists of the avant-garde were able to deploy these notions [Nature cults, peasant decorations, primitive fetishes] ... to justify their own critical distance from the values and priorities of their own industrialized, urbanized societies' (Harrison and Wood 1992: 125). This sense of distance, but a distance between identities which must be held in tension rather than being allowed to dissipate, seems to be at the heart of the modernist enterprise. David Harvey notes the tensions it attempted to accommodate between 'internationalism and nationalism, between globalism and parochialist ethnocentrism, between universalism and class privileges', its necessary recognition of 'the impossibility of representing the world in a single language' and its early expression of alienation from ' "bourgeois" consumerism and life-styles' (Harvey 1989: 24–5, 30, 29). We can even find it, perhaps more pertinently, in Arnold Schoenberg's frequent returns to tonality for his arranged works, and his academic interest in tonal composition. In brief, modernism appears to encompass an ambivalence towards the products of modernity. This ambivalence seems multiply represented in 'Aqualung'. It is also worth remembering that modernity frequently essentializes the pastoral as feminine and the urban as masculine. Although there is little acknowledgement of the feminine in Jethro Tull's work, where it does appear, it is often the larger whole ('society' or encompassing 'nature') which is feminine, against which the masculine individual plays out his role.

Unnecessary 'difficulty', of course, appears to many a lay audience as an obvious criterion of the 'modern'. The collapse of representation, the general abandonment of a teleological tonality, the structuralist denarrativization of the 'nouveau roman', all require of the naïve perceiver more work than he or she is frequently willing to give. If 'difficulty' thus functions as a sign of modernism, and if modernism is what David Harvey calls 'a troubled and fluctuating aesthetic response to conditions of modernity' (1989: 99), then the difficult nature of the world in which we live is, it seems, intrinsic to modernity, a position Anderson explicitly voiced in discussing 'Locomotive Breath'. This difficulty in dealing with our surroundings is allied to our alienation from them, itself fundamental to the experience of modernity, and as explored in relation to popular culture by Lawrence Grossberg (1992). Craig Thomas's description of the Jethro Tull persona, as it develops over three decades, is in this vein. He 'celebrates life, but is increasingly someone who stands apart, alienated and contemptuous, casting a bleak, cold glance, over modern society' (Thomas 1993: 19). This loss of control felt in the face of modernity is a direct result of the secularist project initiated in the Enlightenment, by which Man placed himself in control of His own destiny, a control which many find increasingly difficult to exert. There are two, distinguishable faces here: to use the same example, Aqualung who is lost in the modern world, and humanity whose modern world is itself lost, whose *telos* has been swallowed by its own *arsis*. In the songs, these ideas are represented in a variety of ways. Indeed, as early as 'Son', it had been so clearly envisioned that the idea could be turned on its head.

169

Tull's consciousness of history seems curious within the popular field, in that the past is not overturned (as punk attempted), neither is it ignored (as it is in the perpetual youth of bubblegum pop), nor preserved (as in revivals of folk, Dixieland, blues, or big band cast), but reworked in a living present. Schoenberg's recomposition of the past, or Boulez's earnest endless radicalism come to mind. For George Allan, the modernist conception of history sees its narrative as a privileged way of viewing historical succession whereby a series of events becomes causative of one historical path rather than another (Allan 1986: esp. 144–5). In this sense, history as we understand it acts as an umbilical cord to the, hence our, past. The reflexivity to which this gives rise is understood by Johan Fornäs as quintessentially 'late modern' (Fornäs 1995) although, in Jethro Tull's oeuvre, the distinction between this 'late modern' reflexivity and one more identifiably 'postmodern' is not utterly clear. The references in 'Farm on the Freeway' to those fictional paradises 'Ponderosa' and 'South Fork' may well be better understood as an example of the latter. Now, in his early thoroughgoing equation of this late modern position with postmodernism, Christopher Butler called attention to the concern, found in composers of Boulez's generation, with technique at the expense of expression, thereby making it 'very difficult for the listener to feel the presence of background conventions' (Butler 1980: 34). In the way that narrative conventions are dispensed with in a song like 'Thinking Round Corners', we see an equivalent concern with technique at the expense of content (the way certain lyrics are suggestive of other lyrics and images without attention to their overall meaning), but within a less radical basic style. A similar aim was present in the early 1980s when Anderson experimented with new synthesizer and sampler technology, aiming to utilize these as a primary requirement, again with content as secondary (Anderson 1993a: 23). Such an interpretation is strengthened by observing its corollary: an unease when concern with technique is replaced by a concern with 'communication' through providing an audience with means to 'identification' with the band. There are even early examples of this, as in the uneasy conviviality of the consciously sing-along 'Up the Pool' and the self-consciously inauthentic Hindu chant, so reminiscent of Quintessence, on the early live rendition of 'Dharma for One'. This self-consciousness is clearly typified in Anderson's self-deprecating views of his and the band's work: 'We don't always rock too much; we mainly roll. But at least it's half the battle!' and, regarding their formation, 'A comfortable and convenient step or two behind the cutting edge of "progressive rock" ' (Anderson 1993b: 6). The conceit present in the album-length pieces, particularly *A Passion Play*, suggests that 'communication' is not to the fore: hence, I think, the *almost* in the quote given at the outset.

The question of communication is paramount. Even in music, any aesthetic of communication depends on the possibility of pattern formation, patterns which, when fragmented, make communication difficult. Some years ago, in a once cult classic, the psychoanalyst Anton Ehrenzweig argued 'that modern art aimed at disrupting . . . as a matter of principle' (Ehrenzweig 1973: 84). Whereas the surface fragmentation to be found in late Mozart is normally performed as if it were in the service of a larger-scale continuity, the surface fragmentation (of tonal patterns) to be found in atonality appears to overwhelm any such continuity. In the visual arts, of course, such fragmentation is patently obvious, and is conventionally traced through painters like Monet, Cézanne, Picasso and Pollock. There is an important distinction to be made between the fragmentation of a surface within a context, and the fragmentation of a context (which latter would be identified by many as 'postmodern'), but the disturbances to the surface of *Thick as a Brick*, or 'Rocks on the Road' certainly appear to be a rock equivalent of the former practice. The security with which we can identify a Jethro Tull idiolect means that we should view this stylistic virtuosity as modernist eclecticism, rather than postmodern relativism: analogies should be drawn with Olivier Messiaen rather than John Zorn, perhaps.

Conclusion

So, with a nod towards my own predilection for an unfragmented surface but troubled depth continuity, where does all this lead? It seems to me that the exclusive equation of progressive modernity with stylistic high modernism, to which many high culture critics have been prone, is problematic. No less so, however, is the equation of modernity with the products of mass culture, and the concomitant denigration of 'stylistic high modernism', found in some critics of popular culture (most notably, perhaps, Jameson's (1984) curious identification of the Beatles and the Rolling Stones as modernist pop). On stylistic grounds, the music of Jethro Tull is unquestionably

171

popular, and directed to a mass audience. There are no high art pretensions here. And yet, in terms of subject matter and devices, there are remarkable parallels with what is accepted as modernism. To recall the distinction attempted at the opening to this chapter, I am not for one moment arguing that Jethro Tull's music is stylistically modernist but that, in its concerns, it clearly represents Harvey's 'troubled and fluctuating aesthetic response to conditions of modernity'. As such, it hints at a site wherein contemporary music practices can be conceptualized to accommodate aspects of both modernism and mass culture, enabling them to be viewed, correctly I believe, as sibling expressions of modernity.

9 Pangs of history in late 1970s new-wave rock

JOHN COVACH

In late 1977 Elvis Costello and the Attractions appeared on NBC's *Saturday Night Live*. At the time, the programme was in its early days, featuring John Belushi, Dan Ackroyd, Gilda Ratner, Jane Curtin and Garrett Morris – a cast who pushed at the boundaries of the permissible on US network television. The often-provocative show was well known to many rock listeners, especially since it regularly featured the most interesting current bands as musical guests. Any group appearing on the show during the late 1970s could expect to enjoy the attention of rock culture at least for the evening, and an appearance on the show could be especially beneficial for a new band like Costello's. But this particular appearance was distinctive in many ways. The band began a number and almost immediately broke it off, with Costello announcing that there was no reason to play that song; the group then launched into 'Radio, Radio', a tune strongly critical of the rock radio of the time; and since the show was live, there was no suitable way – short of going to black – for the show's producers to stop the band from switching tunes on the fly.[1]

Substituting tunes mid-performance was clearly a rebellious act, and this rebelliousness was underscored that evening by many other aspects of the band's presentation and music. Here was a rock singer who called himself 'Elvis', a clear reference to Elvis Presley, who at the time had only recently died, fat and drugged out, by then more a symbol of Las Vegas decadence

---

1 For an account of the history of *Saturday Night Live*, see Hill and Weingrad (1987). The early days of Costello's career, including the incident described here, are chronicled in Hinton (1999). Hinton gives the date of the performance as 17 December, and notes that the group appeared twice during the show. In his first segment, Costello and the band played 'Watching the Detectives' as planned. The second segment was supposed to feature 'Less Than Zero', which was the song begun but replaced by 'Radio, Radio' (113–14).

than youth rebellion. The band members wore straight-leg pants, narrow ties with tab collars, and sported short hair. Costello himself wore horn-rimmed glasses reminiscent of those worn by Buddy Holly. The musical instruments the group used – always something of a statement in the 1970s – were also unconventional: Costello played a Fender Jazzmaster guitar and keyboard player Steve Nieve employed a Vox combo organ. Both of these instruments were more pawn-shop bargains than music-store trophies. In light of this, what could these musicians be trying to prove, showing up looking this way in the days of bell-bottom jeans and long, shaggy hair, Fender Stratocasters and Hammond B3s, and referring to long discarded rock icons like Presley and Holly?

For US viewers that night, Elvis Costello and the Attractions were the first real taste these rock fans had of either punk or new wave. At the tail end of a long series of Sex Pistols scandals that culminated in the group's tour of unlikely venues in the American South, the music business had already begun to refashion punk into something less disruptive than what Johnny Rotten and crew had been offering. New wave was more pop-orientated, less angry and aggressive, and markedly ironic in its approach to rock music and culture. This can be gleaned easily from Costello's appearance here. The group makes clear references to rock music's past – the look, names and instruments in many ways invoke 1950s and 1960s rock culture. The pronounced irony in these references resides in the fact that new-wave bands like Costello, Police, Blondie, The B-52s, Devo, and Joe Jackson never really seemed to be advocating an actual return to earlier styles and practices; rather, they appeared to be selecting features of these earlier styles precisely because they were so at odds with mid- to late 1970s hippie culture. It was precisely what they *weren't* that counted, and in many ways this appropriation of rock's pre-*Sgt. Pepper* days – which were romanticized as days of innocence and simplicity – was a blow aimed directly at what had become of the peace-love-and-dope hippie culture of the first part of the decade.[2]

2 Savage (1992) provides a detailed study of the punk scene in the UK, while Heylin (1993) considers the American punk, focusing especially on the New York scene. Far less has been written about new-wave rock, though Joe Jackson's recent autobiography (1999) provides a good deal of insight into the irony and posturing that were clearly a component in the style; see esp. pp. 272–4.

While new-wave references to earlier pre-psychedelic rock are clear enough in the image-making and packaging of many of the bands, such references are not nearly as clear-cut in the music. One might well wonder if, in the absence of any visual clues, a listener can really hear references to earlier styles: is there an aural irony that parallels the visual one? Such music-stylistic references are indeed present in this music and the general effect of new wave depends on the listener's awareness of them. Close inspection reveals, however, that these references operate in sometimes conflicted and complicated ways. As a result, the music-stylistic distinction between new wave and the 1970s rock it hoped to replace is not always as clear as the promotional hype surrounding it might lead one to believe. After providing a brief historical introduction to new-wave music, this chapter will explore how musical references to earlier styles occur in new wave, and especially in the music of The Cars – a group that, along with Costello and Blondie, was one of the most successful and influential new-wave acts of the late 1970s. In my analysis I will employ an approach to questions of musical style that I refer to as 'musical worlding'; this notion will provide a theoretical context for understanding how references in new wave create meaning. In order to explore its stylistic distinctiveness, The Cars' music will be contrasted with that of mainstream-rockers Foreigner, whose music is taken as representative of a style often called 'corporate rock'. I will argue that despite the many music-stylistic references to pre-psychedelic rock that occur in The Cars' music, it is also grounded in seventies rock in ways that parallel the music of Foreigner. Far from the return to the perceived simplicity of the mid-sixties that it was often thought to be in the late seventies, new wave instead appropriates a grab-bag of stylistic features drawn from this earlier music, conditioned and skewed by developments in the late sixties and early seventies rock music of the intervening years.

(Post)modern reactions? The rise of new wave

If we understand new wave as primarily a reaction, it is helpful to understand what it is a reaction to. Many of the stylistic features of new wave can be seen as the opposites of what may be found in the music of popular British bands such as Pink Floyd, Jethro Tull, Led Zeppelin, and Yes or American bands such as The Allman Brothers Band, The Doobie Brothers, and Steely Dan. New wave replaces long songs and extensive instrumental soloing with short, hook-based arrangements. Hippie lyrics engaging big ideas (religion, the state, the future of mankind) or predatory sexuality are out and topics dealing with dating and romantic love (with no threat of sexual conquest) are in. Distorted, bent-string guitar solos and soaring MiniMoog synthesizer lines give way to the clean tones of rockabilly and the mechanical synth sounds of the twenty-first century. One might compare, for instance, Yes's 'Awaken' (1977) with Joe Jackson's 'Is She Really Going Out With Him' (1979): while Jon Anderson refers to 'high vibrations' and the 'workings of man', Jackson mopes over a girlfriend; and while Anderson and Rick Wakeman exchange melodic lines on the harp and church organ in a meditative central section, Jackson's spare quartet of bass, drums, guitar and piano complete their entire song in about the same length of time.

As mentioned above, all of this was part of new wave's return-to-simplicity aesthetic. Growing out of the psychedelic experimentation of the late 1960s, seventies rock had continued to explore combinations of styles and pursue greater technical sophistication, becoming increasingly complex in the process. *Sgt. Pepper* was recorded on two four-track machines, but technical advances soon made eight-, sixteen-, and twenty-four-track recording possible.[3] Indeed, as the decade wore on recording became a very sophisticated process, with albums taking months to record as care was devoted to every dimension of the multi-layered tracks. Queen's 'Bohemian Rhapsody' (1975) – which ended up employing dozens of tracks – is a good example of how studio multi-tracking can turn the three voices into an operatic chorus. Queen's blending of rock and operetta was only another instance of the fusion of rock and classical music styles that was pioneered by the Beatles. Progressive rock bands like Emerson, Lake & Palmer, Genesis, and Yes made the use of classical-sounding passages part of their trademark styles, as did more pop-orientated groups like the Electric Light Orchestra and The Moody Blues. Combining jazz and rock produced not only horn-orientated bands like Chicago and Blood, Sweat and Tears, but also the chromatically

---

3 Cunningham (1998) offers a helpful overview of the development of recording in rock music.

inflected music of Steely Dan and Paul Simon.[4] The use of Eastern musical styles – pioneered by the Kinks, Yardbirds, and Beatles – continued in significant seventies rock tracks such as Led Zeppelin's 'Kashmir', Yes's 'Close to the Edge', and much of the jazz-rock fusion of John McLaughlin's Mahavishnu Orchestra.[5] The practice of virtuosic guitar soloing developed by Eric Clapton and Jimi Hendrix in the late sixties was continued by Led Zeppelin's Jimmy Page, The Allman Brothers' Duane Allman and Dickie Betts, Carlos Santana, and Yes's Steve Howe, expanded to the keyboards by Keith Emerson and Rick Wakeman, and even extended to the bass (Yes's Chris Squire) and drums (almost every rock drummer had his solo). Psychedelic themes of spiritual, intellectual and experiential exploration were taken up in concept albums like the Who's *Tommy* and *Quadrophenia*, Jethro Tull's *Thick as A Brick*, and Pink Floyd's *The Wall*. The development of the synthesizer over the course of the decade, from monophonic to polyphonic and from analogue to digital, made the keyboards an increasingly important component in rock music.

To new-wave sensibilities, rock had become bloated and corporate – a musical style in which the musicians had become too professional and in which the expenses of recording and touring kept everyone out except those with lucrative recording contracts. What was needed, according to new wavers, was a radical stripping down to the basics. This process had already begun by mid-decade among a group of bands performing in a small New York bar called CBGB. The Ramones, Television, Talking Heads, Patti Smith, and Blondie developed a style of music that returned to the garage-band ethos of the mid-1960s.[6] One group, The New York Dolls, became Malcolm McLaren's inspiration for the formation of the Sex Pistols in Britain. While CBGB was the centre of the New York 'punk' scene, the Sex Pistols became the catalyst for UK punk.[7] By the time the group disbanded in January of 1978, 'punk' had become a dirty word inside the music business. The idea of

4 Walter Everett (1997) offers a detailed account of Paul Simon's use of chromaticism in the 1970s.
5 For a detailed analytical consideration of Yes's 'Close to the Edge', see Covach (1997). Jazz-rock is explored from a music-analytical perspective in Covach (2000).
6 See Heylin (1993), Davis (1986) and Harry, Stein and Bockris (1998).
7 See Savage (1992), Bromberg (1989) and Lydon (1994).

reducing rock music down to its simplest components, however, continued in the new-wave scene. Costello's performance on Saturday Night Live in late 1977 represents the extent to which new wave had already begun to make its way into rock culture.

As mentioned above, new wave constituted a rejection of the hippie values of the 1967–77 period. What is most interesting in this rejection is the role played by an almost acute awareness of rock's past. In order to perceive the irony so characteristic of new wave, listeners had to be familiar with music from rock's pre-1967 past. While acts like Tom Petty and the Heartbreakers, Bruce Springsteen, and Dire Straits approached rock's past as traditionalists – they really did think the earlier music was better and thus advocated a return-to-roots aesthetic – new wavers had no such investment in this earlier music. In many ways, references to earlier styles were most valuable for what they were not. Hippie music tended strongly towards a modernist stance in its faith in technology and the teleological development of the style: each new album is better when it is recorded in more sophisticated ways, employs more complex textures and performance mastery, and engages more poetic images in the lyrics. Appropriating (mostly tacitly) interpretive tropes found throughout modernist culture in the West, most bands thought of their music in terms of 'development' and 'evolution' – a path leading from the early days of groping for an individual voice to a later period of mastery and musical maturity. In appropriating the past in an ironic fashion, however, new wavers juxtaposed a postmodern aesthetic stance to the modernist one of the hippies.[8] New-wave music refers freely to a wide range of pre-1967 rock styles, creating stylistic collages that often defeat any sense of teleological development in terms of style. According to this postmodern aesthetic perspective, a band's music doesn't evolve as much as it simply changes, and rock music doesn't spiral upward as much as it simply circles back on itself: progress in rock music is a myth that has lost its ability to create meaning (except by reacting against it). Thus, while new wave follows hippie rock chronologically, it does not develop out of it. But as I will demonstrate below, the situation is not nearly so uncomplicated. New wave never completely sheds the practices of hippie

8   While the terms 'modernism' and 'postmodernism' have been used often enough
    in recent years to prompt one to avoid using them altogether, I invoke them
    because they have interpretive value here with regard to attitudes – or
    'meta-narratives' – regarding technology, history, and uses of the past.

178

rock; in some cases, it can be seen to have at least as much in common with the music that followed in the wake of *Sgt. Pepper* as it does with the 'more innocent' music that preceded it.

Musical worlding

In order to understand how new-wave musicians could invoke other styles in this process of returning to rock simplicity, we can turn to the notion of 'musical worlding'.[9] This approach is founded on the idea that listeners organize new musical experiences in terms of previous ones: any new song is heard in terms of other songs the listener knows or has at least heard. In the simplest cases, a new song that shares many musical characteristics with a number of other already known songs is easily assimilated; one that does not share such characteristics is more difficult to 'understand'. Musical worlding attempts to focus on the fact that while listeners often tend to think of any musical piece as a separate, even self-standing musical object, a closer inspection reveals that pieces are in fact much more like centre points in a web of relationships that lead off in myriad directions to many other pieces. The tendency is thus to suppress the lines that might be thought to form the outline of any given music work, thinking of the work less as an object with fixed boundaries and more as a location, or site, of musical meaning.

While listeners may hear new pieces in terms of ones already known, this process often occurs only tacitly: listeners are frequently not immediately aware of how they are hooking up works to other ones, and often a good deal of effort is required in order to specify where references lead. Sometimes characteristics are held in common among a large number of works, and thus establishing a specific reference is somewhat arbitrary or even fruitless. Such commonly held characteristics are traditionally regarded as central to the identification of musical styles. In many ways, musical worlding offers an approach to the study of musical style that suppresses the notion that pieces are distinct objects and that stylistic characteristics are properties separable from the works in which they occur. Instead, pieces merge with one another

9 See Covach (1994) for a more detailed discussion of musical worlding. Responses to that article appear in *Music Theory Online* 1/1 (January 1995). I have applied the notion of musical worlding to the atonal music of Arnold Schoenberg in Covach (1995).

until they are in some sense indistinguishable, and this erasing of boundaries gives rise to stylistic characteristics that are always understood as the result of actual pieces of music that form the basis for a listener's experience. The music-analytical task is thus to tease out the connections to other works in any given work, situating it in the richest possible network of relationships in hopes of coming to terms with how a piece creates meaning. It is important to realize that any such analysis is provisional, since each listener's experience will differ and thus each will situate any given work differently as well (and even the same listener may situate a piece differently at a later time in life); but individual experiences still converge enough for discussions of worlding to have value among listeners who hold enough musical experience in common.

In light of this discussion of musical worlding, the question in the case of new-wave rock in the late 1970s is how this music creates meaning by referring to other works or groups of works. If we can determine how this is done, we can begin to explore how – and even whether – this music distinguishes itself from the mainstream rock of the same time. In short, we can come to some conclusions about whether or not this music refers to rock music's past in ways we could detect aurally even in the absence of the short haircuts, narrow ties and naïve lyrics that serve as clear visual and verbal markers.

Foreigner

In order to investigate the musical cues in new wave, it will be helpful to establish some kind of normative model against which this newer music sets itself. There are, in fact, many rock styles in the mid- and late 1970s that represent the kind of rock music modernism described above. Almost any track from Pink Floyd, Yes, Jethro Tull or Led Zeppelin could serve as an example, as might the music of Steely Dan, the Doobie Brothers, Peter Frampton or Supertramp. But even within mainstream rock in the second half of the decade, there was a marked tendency to scale back the length and complexity found in the music of only a few years earlier. The resultant radio-friendly album-orientated rock was sometimes thought to be crafted less for musical expression than for financial profit, and was dubbed 'corporate rock' by critics. Indeed, American groups such as Boston, Styx, and Journey were among those most often thought to have sold their musical souls for more airplay and record sales.[10] But whatever critics may have thought at the time, rock fans continue to consider albums by these bands as an important component in the classic-rock style, as evinced by classic-rock format playlists across the United States today.

Despite the disagreements that may arise over the value of late seventies mainstream rock, there is little dispute that Foreigner was one of the most successful of the late seventies/early eighties rock bands.[11] In America, the band's first four albums placed within the Top 10, with six singles reaching the Top 10 as well.[12] A fresh single by a new-wave band was not likely to have to compete so much for attention with the music of Yes or Led Zeppelin (who were mostly out of the picture by the end of the decade anyway) as much as with bands like Foreigner or Van Halen, who were clearly viewed as continuing to carry the torch for modernist rock music. Thus, Foreigner will be taken as representative of late seventies mainstream rock for the purposes of this discussion; it will serve as the norm in comparison with which the irony and postmodern tendencies of new wave can be sounded out. The band's first hit single, 'Feels Like the First Time', antedates the emergence of new wave and so will serve as a good example of how mainstream rock sounded in the months just before new wave hit the US scene.

Figure 9.1 provides a formal diagram for the tune; the music is organized by sections that are marked by CD timings. The numbers that follow in each case provide a bar count for a section followed by the number of bars

10 Jerry McCulley begins his essay accompanying the Foreigner CD Anthology *Jukebox Heroes* with a paragraph that colourfully but accurately summarizes the situation:

> Foreigner has long endured two distinctly different, yet hopelessly intertwined, legacies. The public at large knows them as a multiplatinum hit machine that dominated pop radio for a decade, from the late 70s to the late 80s, with a string of successful singles and albums – the stratospheric sales of which were nearly without precedent. But to many critics and other self-appointed rock cognoscenti, they're the epitome of 'corporate rock', a soulless band of skilled musical mercenaries assembled by shadowy figures in some boardroom to plunder unsuspecting music fans with machine-tooled guitar riffs and burnished vocal hooks. (p. 3)

11 For contemporary reactions to the success of the group's first album, see Crescenti (1977), Mendelsohn (1978) and Emands (1978).

12 Of these albums, *Four* (1981) was the most successful, staying on Billboard's Top 40 chart for fifty-two weeks, ten in the No. 1 slot; the album hit No. 5 in the UK. *Four* also contained the hit singles 'Urgent' (No. 4 US) and 'Waiting for a Girl Like You' (No. 2 US/No. 8 UK).

0:00–0:27	Introduction	12 bars, 4 + *4 + **4	*synth added, stop time; **full band, in time
0:28–1:02	Verse 1	16 bars, 4 + 4 + 4 + 4	
1:03–1:21	Chorus	8 bars, 4 + 4	
1:21–1:56	Verse 2	16 bars, 4 + 4 + 4 + 4	
[1:56–2:38	Bridge 1	18 bars, 4 + 4 + 4 + 4 + 2	change of key to e minor
2:39–2:56	Chorus	8 bars, 4 + 4	
2:56–3:14	Bridge 2	8 bars, 4 + 4	guitar solo
3:14–3:48	Chorus	16+ bars, 4 + 4 + 4 + *4	*begin fade-out at 3:41

Figure 9.1: Formal diagram for 'Feels Like the First Time'

in the phrases that make up the section. Thus, the twelve-bar introduction is made up of three four-bar phrases, the sixteen-bar verse 1 is comprised of four four-bar phrases, and so on. As can be seen from Figure 9.1, 'Feels Like the First Time' loosely falls into a formal scheme common in rock music, contrasting verse–chorus form.[13] In such a form, the verse and chorus are based on different harmonic and/or melodic materials, and such is the case in this track: the verse is built on a four-bar harmonic progression that moves from I to bVII to ii back to I in G, all over a tonic pedal (see Ex. 9.1). This pattern is repeated once before moving on to an alternation between II and IV/II over a supertonic pedal and III and IV/III over a mediant pedal. A quick move to IV leads back to the tonic chord beginning the first presentation of the chorus, which falls into two four-bar phrases, each articulating the I–bVII–ii–I progression in G that opens the verse.

There are two general types of strategy that may be found in contrasting verse–chorus forms: in the first, the verse(s) and chorus follow one another without any further contrasting material, though sometimes a return to the introduction occurs after at least two verse–chorus units have been heard.

13 For more on typical formal schemes in rock music, see Covach (forthcoming).

Example 9.1: Harmonic content in the verse sections

Familiar examples of such verse–chorus schemes are the Beatles' 'Penny Lane' (1967) and the Ronettes' 'Be My Baby' (1963).[14] It was especially common in the early and mid-1970s to offer some kind of musical contrast after the second statement of the chorus, and this could be an instrumental verse (and chorus), or even a contrasting bridge section. Deep Purple's 'Smoke on the Water' (1972) provides an instance of the former, while their 'Woman from Tokyo' (1972) supplies an example of the latter. When a contrasting bridge section occurs after two verse-chorus pairs and is followed by a return of the verse–chorus (or even by the chorus only), such a form is called compound AABA, and these are common in seventies rock as well ('Woman From Tokyo' is one of these, as is Led Zeppelin's 1969 'Whole Lotta Love').

It is in comparison to such seventies practices in musical form that 'Feels Like the First Time' can be seen to provide an interesting and exceptional structural twist. Note that verse 2 begins as if the chorus should follow. But rather than moving to IV to lead back to the chorus at the end, the III is harmonically reinterpreted as V in e minor. What follows is a minor-key version of the chorus, presenting the i–VII–VI–V chaconne bass progression in a four-bar phrase is sounded four times (see Ex. 9.2). After the last iteration of this descending progression, a move to e: VI is reinterpreted as G: IV, leading back to the chorus in G that was expected before this move to the relative minor. Labelled bridge 1 in Figure 9.1, this section provides the kind of musical contrast that typically comes after the second chorus in a compound AABA form, but here it occurs *before* that chorus. In the way the music moves into bridge 1 via a reinterpretation of III, and emerges from it

14 Both of these songs are considered in more detail in my 'Form in Rock Music'.

Example 9.2: Bridge 1 as formal parenthesis

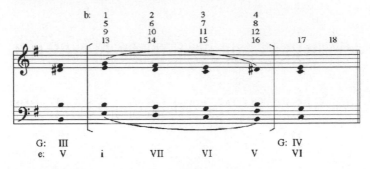

Example 9.3: Harmonic content of bridge 2

through a reinterpretation of IV, all of bridge 1 might be seen as a kind of formal parenthesis, inserted into the more common contrasting verse–chorus scheme (the brackets in Figure 9.1 reflect this). The second bridge that follows the second chorus is more conventional than the first, formally speaking, and reinforces the sense of compound AABA as the overall design. Bridge 2 is a chromatically inflected version of the g-to-d inner-voice descent found in the chorus progression (compare Exx. 9.1 and 9.3). Virtuosic slurred semiquaver triplets in the guitar fill the minor third from f♮ down to d, transforming a diatonic inner-voice melodic fourth into chromatically descending parallel minor thirds that prolong tonic harmony.[15] A return to the chorus completes the form, and the track fades as the chorus is repeated.[16] While the particular

---

15 While the f♮ is chromatic within the context of the traditional major tonality, here the f♮ arises from the use of ♭VII harmony; this is common enough in rock to count as diatonic, especially if one considers the passage as Mixolydian.

16 The single was released in an edited version. Four changes were made to the song, apparently to trim it down to slightly over three minutes to accommodate hit-radio formats: (1) the first four bars of the intro are deleted; (2) the first four

formal design in this track is novel, it relies on a conventional model in rock practice to achieve its effect – in other words, this song solves a standard seventies formal problem (adding contrast within a verse–chorus design) in an innovative way.

'Feels Like the First Time' can be situated with regard to 1970s rock in a number of other ways. Note the sparkling synthesizer that arrives early in the introduction; the synth timbres here and throughout the piece are similar to the kinds of sounds found in the early to mid-seventies progressive rock of Yes and Emerson, Lake & Palmer. The influence of British blues-rock can be heard in the distorted tone of the guitar and especially in the singing. Lou Gramm's powerful and polished tenor voice is filled with bluesy turns and ornaments drawn from the singing of Paul Rogers (Free, Bad Company) and Steve Winwood (Traffic). The back-up vocals are the kind of high, slick post-Beatles male vocals found in much seventies rock, both in the ooo's that lead out of the verses and in the anthemic choruses. The lyrics play on a double meaning. The phrase 'feels like the first time' might well refer to the first time one falls in love, but it is also meant to suggest the first time one has sexual intercourse (during bridge 2, Gramm sings: 'Open up the door. Won't you open up the door?'). While there are a number of other Foreigner songs that do not engage issues of sexuality – 'Starrider' deals with space travel à la David Bowie's 'Space Oddity' (released in 1969 but a US hit in 1973) for instance – later songs like 'Hot Blooded' (1978) and 'Dirty White Boy' (1979) clearly exploit the topic. Starting with the rumours that the Rolling Stones' 'Satisfaction' deals with masturbation (and even going back to Big Joe Turner's 'Shake, Rattle, and Roll'), sexuality has been a favourite topic for rock lyrics. Led Zeppelin's 'Whole Lotta Love' (1969) and Bad Company's 'Can't Get Enough' (1974) are other well-known rock numbers that emphasize the male swagger.

The group's second hit single, 'Cold as Ice', provides an additional example of the ways in which the band continues seventies rock practices. As Figure 9.2 shows, the track is a compound AABA structure, with a chorus–verse pair making up the first two A sections, repetitions of the

bars of bridge 1 are deleted; (3) the first four bars of bridge 2 are deleted; and (4) the fade begins on the four-bar phrase of the last chorus (at 3'02'' of the edited version).

0:00–0:07	Introduction	4 bars	piano intro with filter sweep
0:08–0:31	Chorus	12 bars, 4 + 4 + 4	
0:32–0:46	Verse	8 bars, 4 + 4	
0:47–1:16	Chorus	16 bars, (4) + 4 + 4 + 4	( ) = no vocals
1:17–1:32	Verse	8 bars, 4 + 4	
1:33–1:47	Bridge 1	8 bars, 4 + 4	guitar sol
1:47–2:13	Bridge 2	14 bars, 4 + 4 + 4 + 2	choral vocals
2:13–3:11	Chorus	32 bars, (4 + 4) + 4 + 4 + 4 + 4 + *4 + 4	*fade begins at 3:00

Figure 9.2: Formal diagram for 'Cold as Ice'

chorus making up the last one, and a pair of bridge sections making up the contrasting B section. What is somewhat unusual is that the chorus comes before the verse in the pair, and that the lyrics for the chorus change slightly during the first two occurrences, while those for the verse do not change at all. The sections designated as chorus are clearly the focus of the song, however, as the iterations after the two bridge sections make clear. There is another well-known example of the chorus preceding the verse: the Beatles' 'Strawberry Fields Forever' (1967) is organized this way, though the lyrics to the verses do change, unlike those to 'Cold as Ice'. The chorus employs a harmonic succession that moves from i to VI in e♭ minor (see Ex. 9.4), a progression perhaps most familiar from its use in the ending section of Led Zeppelin's 'Stairway to Heaven' (1971); the verses are in the relative major of G♭ (see Ex. 9.5). Like almost all progressive rock of the seventies, 'Cold as Ice' makes references to classical music, especially in the bridge sections. In bridge 1, the guitar solo evokes the melodic virtuosity of a concerto soloist, while the harmonic progression in bridge 2 – e♭: i–V$^4_3$–V$^4_2$ (see Ex. 9.6) – suggests traditional classical practice. The back-up vocals in bridge 2 – and

Example 9.4: Harmonic content of the chorus

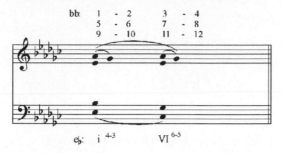

Example 9.5: Harmonic content of the verse

Example 9.6: Harmonic progression in bridge 2

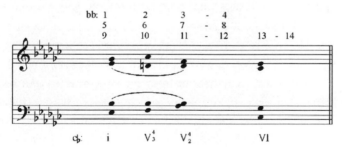

more generally throughout the track – sound much like those that can be found in late Beatles tracks such as 'Because' (1969) or those of later groups like Queen that were also strongly influenced by Beatles vocals.

The preceding discussion securely situates both 'Cold as Ice' and 'Feels Like the First Time' in the context of 1970s rock, and in the process confers on these songs a representative status for mainstream rock in 1977 (at least for the purposes of the present discussion). We can now turn to the music

187

of the Cars and investigate the ways in which it contrasts with the Foreigner tracks.

The Cars

By the summer of 1977 when the first Foreigner album was in heavy rotation on FM rock stations across the US and the Sex Pistols were wreaking havoc in the UK, a Boston disc jockey was playing tracks off a demo tape by a local new-wave band, the Cars.[17] By the end of the year the band had a contract with Elektra records, which released *The Cars* in the summer of 1978. Because of the enormous critical and commercial success of that and subsequent Cars albums, the group is widely considered to be one of the most important American new-wave bands. The band's first two hit singles were 'Just What I Needed' and the song we will consider first, 'My Best Friend's Girl'.

Similarly to 'Feels Like the First Time', 'My Best Friend's Girl' begins by featuring chords in the lower register of the guitar (see Fig. 9.3). The two-bar progression moving from I to IV and then V in F already indicates some important differences between the two tracks, however. Rather than the heavy, highly distorted guitar sound that begins the Foreigner track, the Cars opt instead for the clean (and slightly chorused) guitar sound more common in 1950s rockabilly than seventies rock. When the handclaps enter in bar 5, the reference to the Angels' girl group hit, 'My Boyfriend's Back' (early 1963) – and more generally to the Beatles' 'I Want to Hold Your Hand' (late 1963) – further distances the song from mainstream seventies rock. Ric Ocasek's lead vocals sound common and almost amateurish in comparison with those of Lou Gramm, and are filled with hiccups drawn straight from Buddy Holly. Rather than focusing on sexuality, the lyrics instead address teenage dating with a kind of faux-naïveté. When the organ enters in the first chorus, the timbre is not that of a Hammond through a Leslie speaker as in the Foreigner track, but rather the simpler sound of some kind of sixties portable organ. This timbral reference is reinforced when the quaver chords played in the organ in the second verse seem to invoke the 1966 song '96 Tears' by ? and the Mysterians. At the link between the chorus and the

17 Maxanne Santori at WBCN; see Toby Goldstein (1985: 22).

0:00–0:16	Intro	8 bars, 2 + 2 + *2 + 2	*handclaps at 0:09
0:16–0:48	Verse 1	16 bars, 4 + 4* + 4 + 4	*full band enters in fourth bar at 0:30
0:49–1:00	Chorus	6 bars, 2 + 2 + 2	
1:01–1:08	Link	4 bars, 2 + 2	rockabilly guitar leads to next verse
1:09–1:40	Verse 2	16 bars, 4 + 4 + 4 + 4	'96 Tears' organ
1:40–1:52	Chorus	6 bars, 2 + 2 + 2	
1:52–2:00	Link	4 bars, 2 + 2	leads to instrumental chorus
2:00–2:12	"Chorus"	6 bars, 2 + 2 + 2	guitar solo
2:12–2:20	Link	4 bars, 2 + 2	leads to last verse
2:20–2:51	Verse 3	16 bars, 4 + 4 + 4 + 4	repeat of verse 1 lyrics
2:51–3:03	Chorus	6 bars, 2 + 2 + 2	
3:03–3:11	Link	4 bars, 2 + 2	leads to coda
3:11–3:43	Coda	2 + 2 + *2 + 2 + *2	strings enter at 3:19, handclaps at 3:27 as fade-out begins

Figure 9.3: Formal diagram for 'My Best Friend's Girl'

verse, the rockabilly guitar lick continues the reference to that style set up earlier in the track. To end the song, the final iterations of the chorus are supported by synthetic strings that conjure up aural images of Phil Spector's pre-British invasion Wall of Sound.

There are a number of clear references to pre-hippie music in this track, and in order not to mislead, it is important to stress that not all new-wave tracks are as full of such references as this one. But even in the midst of such references, it is also possible to detect practices derived from 1970s music. The most obvious is the sonic quality of the recording itself. No attempt is made to go back to using older recording equipment or even to emulate the

189

effects of older recording equipment – this track is recorded employing as much studio technology as the Foreigner track discussed above. In fact, 'My Best Friend's Girl' (and the entire album) is produced by Roy Thomas Baker, who had produced many mainstream 1970s acts, including Queen, and though this would follow after *The Cars*, Foreigner. However much he may have smoothed out the sonic wrinkles in the Cars' music, Baker had little to do with the actual arrangements the band used on the album. The demo tapes for these tunes reveal that the arrangements were finished before the band even signed with Elektra, and the arrangement of 'My Best Friend's Girl' on the demo is almost identical to the released version.[18]

The formal diagram for the song (see Fig. 9.3) reveals that the song is in contrasting verse–chorus form, with an instrumental chorus coming after the second chorus. While contrasting verse–chorus form is a feature of both pre- and post-1967 rock, it is not a design that works to set the song apart from hippie rock. In fact, by 1977, such a design is almost the default formal pattern in rock. A much more 'retro' gesture would have been to employ the kind of simple AABA designs found in so much early Beatles and Brill Building pop like 'I Want To Hold Your Hand', 'From Me to You' (1963), or 'Will You Still Love Me?' (1960), but such designs are rare in new wave. At least in this case, all references to past styles on the surface of the track are attached to a structural scaffolding that does not break with mainstream rock in any significant way. Perhaps the guitar solo is more melodic than might be the case in most mainstream rock of the seventies, and this clearly suggests the kinds of solos found in much Beatles music.[19] But at the same time, there's more than a touch of seventies guitar distortion in some of the rhythm playing, and one only has to take the first seconds of 'Just What I Needed' to hear distortion-rich power chords. In fact, the rhythm guitar part

18 These demos are contained on the two-CD, *The Cars, Deluxe Edition*. A comparison between the two versions of 'My Best Friend's Girl' reveals that on the demo, the group employed more rockabilly-style slap-back echo in the guitars and vocal and that the back-up vocals are much more ragged. The keyboard part in the choruses is different, with keyboardist Greg Hawkes using a synthesizer line that was discarded in favour of the organ part discussed above in the text.
19 Though here again, distinctions are only loose. The harmony solo in 'Can't Get Enough' or many of the solos of Queen's Brian May could be cited as examples from mainstream rock that are just as melodic as the one found in 'My Best Friend's Girl'.

190

0:00–0:15	Introduction	8 bars	chord hits on I
0:16–0:46	Verse 1	16 bars, 4 + 4 + 4 + 4	
0:46–1:01	Interlude	8 bars, 4 + 4	synth, slow harmonic rhythm
1:02–1:31	Verse 2	16 bars	
1:31–1:49	Chorus	10 bars, 4 + 4* + 2	*last bar is 2/4
1:49–2:04	Interlude	8 bars, 4 + 4	guitar, fast harmonic rhythm
2:04–2:34	Verse 3	16 bars	repeat of verse 1 lyrics
2:34–2:51	Chorus	10 bars	
2:51–3:09	Chorus	10 bars	
3:09–3:43	Interlude with ending	16 bars, 4 + 4 + 4 + 4	synth, fast harmonic rhythm

Figure 9.4: Formal diagram for 'Just What I Needed'

throughout 'Just What I Needed' employs an overdriven guitar sound that would fit with most Foreigner numbers.

A formal diagram for 'Just What I Needed' is provided in Figure 9.4: the song is in contrasting verse–chorus form. After an eight-bar introduction featuring guitar strokes on the fourth beat of each bar, the first verse enters. The harmonic structure of the verses consists of a four-bar progression moving between the tonic and dominant, first in E major, then in the relative minor, c♯ minor (see Ex. 9.7). Bars 15 and 16 of each verse deviate from the first twelve bars by moving directly to the dominant of c♯ and then to a sonority that might be heard either as the VI of c♯ minor (creating a deceptive move in the relative) or as IV in E (making the G♯ chord that precedes it seem like III in E). The tonal ambiguity set up here between E and c♯ minor returns throughout the song. The harmonic structure of the ten-bar choruses (see Ex. 9.8), for instance, takes up this issue by placing vi unambiguously in E in bars 1–2/5–6, but then undercuts this tonal clarity by

Example 9.7: Harmonic content of verses

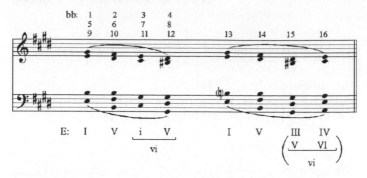

Example 9.8: Harmonic content of the choruses

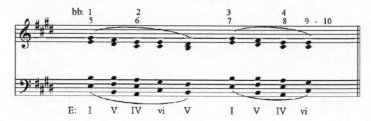

cadencing on vi in bars 3–4/7–10. A bar of $^2_4$ is injected into the otherwise consistent $^4_4$ time at bar 8, giving a little more rhythmic stress to the arrival of two bars of vi in bars 9–10.

The first chorus introduces a change in harmonic rhythm that becomes an interesting feature of the song. In the two verses and interlude leading up to the first chorus, the harmonic rhythm has stayed at one chord per bar. But beginning with the chorus, the rate of harmonic change becomes quicker. This serves to offer contrast for the chorus, but it also has ramifications for the interlude that follows. Example 9.9 shows the harmonic structure that is used in both of the first two interludes; note that the first interlude proceeds at a one-chord-per-bar rhythm while the second (shown in bar numbers above the first in the example) moves at two-chords-per-bar. This faster harmonic rhythm is a direct result of the change in this domain initiated by the chorus. The final appearance of the interlude blends features of the earlier two as well as addressing the issue of tonal ambiguity set up earlier. The first interlude features a synthesizer melody, while the second features the guitar. This last version employs the synthesizer from the first over the

192

Example 9.9: Harmonic rhythm in the interludes

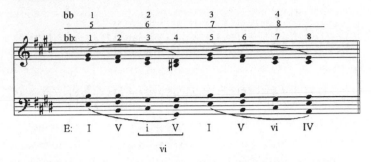

Example 9.10: Harmonic structure in the final cadence

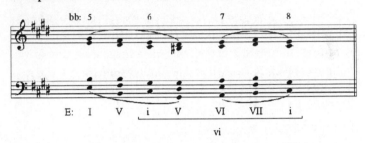

faster harmonic rhythm of the second. As Example 9.10 shows, the last four bars establish a clear cadence in c♯ minor, adding a final wrinkle to an issue that is central to the harmonic structure of the song.[20]

While the harmonic structure of 'My Best Friend's Girl' is simple – there are only two chord progressions in the entire song, I–IV–V and IV–V – the structure of 'Just What I Needed' is more complicated. The difference is not so much in an increased chord vocabulary or sophistication in chromatic usage, but rather in the crafting of the simple progressions that make up the song's harmonic structure into a design that engages a compositional issue. In this case, it is the undercutting of the primacy of E major by significant turns to the relative minor. As in 'My Best Friend's Girl', this track emerges from analysis as a mixture of seventies and pre-1967 traits. The simplicity of the harmony is a function of the new-wave return-to-simplicity aesthetic,

20 In a nice touch, the synth melody from first interlude returns to accompany verses 2 and 3; thus, despite the fact that the faster harmonic rhythm in subsequent interludes makes a literal return of this melody impossible in those sections, it continues to play a part in the tune.

but the structural features reflect the modernist bent of seventies rock, as does the contrasting verse–chorus form of the track (discussed above with regard to 'My Best Friend's Girl').

There is one distinctive feature of this track that is markedly anti-hippie but that makes no reference to pre-psychedelic rock, and this is Greg Hawkes's use of the synthesizer. Hawkes opts for very simple tones on the synth, seemingly in an attempt to make the instrument sound plain and unsophisticated. The use of very lush synthesizer settings, with pronounced filter-envelope settings creating harmonic sweeps through the overtone series, was a strong marker of the technological sophistication of seventies rock, and the use of synth in both the Foreigner tracks is representative of this practice. But Hawkes for the most part will have no part of such timbres; under the influence of Kraftwerk's *Autobahn* (1974) and *Trans-Europe Express* (1977) albums, he uses timbres that in their plainness signal their distance from the hippie sounds of Rick Wakeman and Keith Emerson.

Conclusion

This discussion is not meant to suggest that 'My Best Friend's Girl', 'Just What I Needed', the Cars' music, or even new wave generally, is basically 1970s rock with a veneer of retro references. Rather, it is to argue that analysis reveals that this song sends mixed stylistic signals; and this more restrictive point *can* be extended to cover most new wave in the late 1970s and early 1980s. In fact, many younger listeners are more likely to hear the similarities between the Cars and Foreigner than the distinctions upon which new wave depended: for these listeners, new wave is not ironic. The new-wave references to the pre-1967 era would have been easier to recognize in 1978 than they are now, and this is because the similarities between the Foreigner and Cars tunes would have been transparent to late 1970s listeners. We may tend to focus on these similarities now because, in the broader perspective of rock history, these tunes sound more like each other than they sound like other music, earlier or later. Stylistic distinctions in any era are often asserted over features that later generations will consider to be mere details.

It is crucial to understand how the Foreigner and Cars tracks discussed here create meaning; these tracks 'mean' differently because of the ways in which they 'world'. Put more simply, we appreciate these tunes differently because we situate each differently with regard to other music. The key to hearing Foreigner is situating it with regard to the 1970s rock that immediately precedes it. Thus, references in the discussion above have been to Deep Purple, Free, Bad Company, Led Zeppelin, Yes, and ELP. While one can surely make references to other music outside the realm of 1970s rock, such references tend to be viewed as influences and are not considered ironic in any way. But new wave needs to be situated in terms of earlier music – music that is meaningful precisely because it is not the same music that the Foreigner music evokes. The irony arises from the tension between the fact that in some dimensions new wave refuses to return to the past while simultaneously evoking and even celebrating rock's pre-hippie past. The experience of musical worlding thus situates Foreigner in a way that aligns with stylistic boundaries – it is heard within the style of 1970s rock – while the worlding of the Cars situates them across stylistic boundaries, and it is the crossing of the boundaries that creates irony and meaning. But when there are enough new-wave songs that cross such boundaries, one tends not to situate each song with regard to earlier music, but rather with regard to each other. Strangely enough, the more new-wave songs one knows, the less ironic they seem; this is because the relationships of these songs to one another begin to override the relationships any single one may have to earlier music. At such a point new wave stops being a reaction to hippie music and culture and becomes a distinct music and culture in its own right.

Despite its mixed signals, new-wave music does parallel the irony of new-wave fashion. There is, in other words, a general parallel between the visual and musical dimensions of new wave. But in retrospect, even new-wave images and fashion have something distinctively 'seventies' about them. Indeed, it would be strange if it were otherwise, considering the fact that most of the musicians who developed new wave grew up as hippies. In both the musical and visual dimensions, then, new wave can be thought of as a romantic vision of pre-hippie music and culture conditioned and made possible – or even necessary – by the hippie experience. The deep irony of new wave is that it is ultimately defined by the very music and culture it rejects.

10 Is anybody listening?

CHRIS KENNETT

Introduction

One of the most significant patterns in the consumption of music in the industrialized world during this century has been the trend towards ubiquity. From the shellac disc to the Rio Diamond, most advances in playback technology which were not designed to increase fidelity or frequency response have been conceived as advances in portability. In our post-Walkman world, recorded music can be played and experienced more or less anywhere – at home, in an aeroplane, under water, in a supermarket, for example – and from an ever-increasing variety of sources – terrestrial and satellite TV and radio, personal CD players, the Internet, and so on. Each of these listening environments has unique characteristics: when experiencing a recording of a drum 'n' bass tune in a busy high street clothes store, for example, some of the sonic aspects of the production values of the tune, as originally created and monitored by the artist or band in an acoustically neutral, soundproof recording studio, might not be apparent to us, due to interference from the ambient sounds of other shoppers and shop staff, sounds from outside the shop, under-powered sub-woofers struggling to cope with the extra bass response provoked by the recording, and so on.

Just as the environmental possibilities for experiencing music have expanded over time, so has the range of uses to which we put such music. For example, if we experience the same drum 'n' bass tune at a night club at 5.30 a.m., it is very likely that our primary use of that music will be as a means of expressing ourselves, however eccentrically, in dance. However, if we experience the same recording at home, in the kitchen, while frying eggs for lunch, it is less likely that we shall be using the music for the same purpose – indeed, to react to the music by dancing could prove catastrophic here, involving an avoidable emergency call to the local fire brigade.

Similarly, we might play the CD in a car on a long drive in order to make the endless motorway miles seem less monotonous, but any urge to dance succumbed to by the driver on such a journey would quite probably provoke a fatal accident.

Linked to the increased range of functions to which we assign music is a broadening of patterns of attention to that music. In none of the above drum 'n' bass examples could we be said to be listening with the same level of immersive concentration that we might employ when listening through expensive hi-fi equipment at home, perhaps with our eyes shut, waiting intently for our favourite breakbeat.[1] Nor are these differences restricted to musical situations where we have some control over the music we are experiencing: imagine the same tune assaulting our sensitive ears as background music at a funeral parlour, as we try to arrange the details of a relative's wake. Not only is the music (at best!) inappropriate in this situation: it will either be forced to the centre of our attention, in which case we may well leave under a cloud of righteous rage, vowing to find another, more sympathetic, firm of funeral directors; or we will consciously attempt to screen out the undesirable music, to the extent where, after the initial shock, we scarcely acknowledge its existence.

The facetiousness of the above examples serves to underline a rather obvious point: listening to the same music in different situations, with different purposes and with different intensity, will affect the analytical meanings which may arise from the experience. This suggests that, for music listening experiences in everyday situations at least, any exploration of analytical meaning will need to take into account the specific, unique nature of the listening experience. It also implies that the analytical text or object of study itself may be a more volatile, mutable object than has previously been accepted. As a result, for all the theoretical advances in popular music analysis research outlined in the Introduction, there remain several significant underexplored areas of the subject, particularly those concerned with the ubiquity of music in everyday life, the multitude of attendant possible listening acts, and their effects on the concept of text.

1 A 'breakbeat' is a rhythmic pattern sampled from a third-party source (generally an existing recording), which is used by those doing the sampling in a new musical context, either as the basis of a new rhythm track, or as a 'fill' pattern in the last bar of a four- or eight-bar unit.

The semiotics of the sound object

Apart from possibly the hardest-won battle in popular music analysis –
namely the by now relatively widespread acceptance of the ethics of its
existence – there have been several significant changes in musicological
perception of popular music in the past twenty years. From a bias towards critical and sociological approaches, several writers, from Tagg (1979) onwards,
have searched for an all-encompassing methodology whereby all popular
music can be discussed in predominantly textual terms, as a starting-point
from which a wider range of social and cultural factors may be brought to
bear on the analysis of what is essentially a complex process of communication. In much of Tagg's own writing (1979, 1982, 1987, 1991, 1992, 1994,
1998a), for example, he stresses the need to begin with the 'analysis object' –
the sound recording or event – as a kind of neutralist bridge between the 'guild
mentality' of 'sterile formalism' at one extreme, and the at times 'exegetic
guesswork' (1982: 41) of musical hermeneutics at the other. The analysis
object thus forms the starting-point of what Tagg calls a 'hermeneutic-
semiological method' (1982: 47), in which a thorough parsing of every
domain of the analysis object is followed by 'interobjective comparison'
(1982: 48–9) of the object with other similar objects, in order to suggest,
and attempt to corroborate as neutrally as possible, a range of possible
paramusical, associative or affectual meanings to various structural levels
of the analysis object. It follows that the wider and deeper the range of interobjective comparison, the richer the range of meanings available to the
analyst.

At the end of such textual analysis, Tagg employs 'ideological critique'
(1982: 62), a technique dealing with ways in which both producer and listener
affect 'the attitudes and implicit ideologies which seem to be encoded in
the analysed "channel"' (1982: 62). This process includes references to the
technological and industrial processes involved in the production of popular
music, and to the position of the receiver as part of a large, heterogeneous
listening audience.

Middleton, although differing in many respects, shares some common concerns with Tagg. In the chapter, 'From Me to You: Popular Music
as Message' (1990: 172–246), he explores Stefani's (1987) codal competence
hierarchy from the 'high competence' of 'Opus', down through 'Styles' and
'Musical Techniques', to the 'popular competence' of 'Social Practices' and

'General Codes', and also the incomplete homology between popular competence and popular music:

> Much popular music does de-emphasize the [Opus] level and focuses more on lower levels; it is grammar-orientated . . . Associated cultural practices tend to centre on social function and context, and on motor and emotional responses, rather than technical and aesthetic matters (for example, dance rather than criticism). Of course, this degree of correlation is historically and culturally specific. (1990: 175–6)

In other words, 'historical' or 'cultural' competence variables affect every element of an analysis, including segmentation criteria, and underline the need for 'an open-minded synthesis of available methods' (1990: 176) of analysis in order to allow for the intersubjective variations likely in analytical results.

Moore's (2001a) concerns are also largely semiotic: Moore is explicit in his description of the recording as the 'primary text' (2001a: *passim*) of investigation in popular music analysis, the starting-point for his analytical method. Moore argues for a much closer inspection of a range of domains within the primary text, splitting the text into four layers: the 'explicit rhythmic layer, where precise pitch is irrelevant', a bass-note layer, a third layer which 'corresponds to the commonsense understanding of "tune" ', and a layer of 'harmonic filler' (2001a: 33–4). Each of these, and the 'rhythmic' and 'tune' layers in particular, is given extensive analytical treatment in order to construct a style database of the patterns of rhythm, repetition, melody and harmony that are common to the majority of rock songs.

Problems of listening specificity I: time, demography, intensity

The methods of Tagg, Middleton, Moore and others[2] clearly share some common concerns: the primacy of the recording as analytical object; the parsing of the text remaining incomplete without consideration of sociological, cultural, technological and other factors; and the use of text analysis to bridge the epistemological gap between 'formalism' and 'guesswork',

---

2 Recent authors such as Brackett (1995) and Covach and Boone (1997). Brackett is unusually explicit in his choice of the sound-object as text, referring to spectrum-analysis graphs in combination with more traditional notation.

returning the concept of listening to analysis. We can use Moore as spokesman here: 'My emphasis on the listener I regard as central. We are not all performers, writers, producers, critics or followers of any of the other activities supported by rock, but we are all *listeners*' (Moore 1993: 5).

And yet, some problems arise with this approach: Moore correctly points out that 'the esthesic level is...a difficult matter, for it is simply impossible to find out from every listener what sense they make of their listening activity' (1993: 5). He then explores the problems of psychological and sociological approaches to the aesthesic level – mainly the lack of relevant experimental listening data, and the sociological 'tendency to assume monolithic listening publics' (1993: 6) – problems that persist today.[3] Almost inevitably, he concludes: 'Failing the detailed statistical exercises that are a necessary prerequisite to an adequate handling of how rock is used, I shall resort to a structure laying out possible "functions"' (1993: 6).

Moore also cites Hennion's (1983) argument that the reception of popular music is the only possible starting-point for its analysis as being 'the ideal' (Moore 1993: 24), though he suggests that a 'prior task is to determine the possible interpretations that a song or piece affords, i.e. what it is possible for a listener to make of it, and that will require a detailed investigation of the sound-constructs themselves' (1993: 24). And here is a more significant problem: the above quotation suggests that the set of 'possible interpretations that a song or piece affords' is somehow finite; my own experiences as a teacher and listener suggest that this is not the case.

A brief experimental example will clarify my point. The cover of Jimmy Smith's 1964 album, *The Cat*, shows a black cat slinking into focus against a neon-lit, night-time background. Instantly, a range of analogies might suggest themselves: links between cats/night-time, 'cats'/jazzmen, lone 'black cat'/black instrumentalist ploughing his individualist Hammond furrow, and so on. Musically, the instrumentation of the fourth track on the album, Smith's version of Elmer Bernstein's 'Theme from *The Carpetbaggers*' (brass-heavy big band, Hammond organ), might denote a range of jazz style-types. The rhythmic structure, with an interplay between the triplet-based $^9_8$ metre

---

3 The long-awaited study by Tagg and Clarida (forthcoming) into meanings assigned by 600 Swedish listeners to TV theme-tunes might remedy some of these problems. See also the discussion of the work of Hargreaves and North, below.

of the song, expressed by the bass rhythm, and the maracas exploring a 2+2+2+3-quaver scheme, might suggest some kind of Latin influence. The combination of blues-scale elements, parallel fourths and relatively sparse harmony might suggest a blues influence, and so on.

From Tagg's recent exploration of the tritone in crime drama theme-tune music (1998a), it seems that many listeners associate certain types of music ('minor-mode', 'jazz-influenced', 'chromatic' and 'tritonal' are Tagg's descriptions – 1998a: 273–81) with American TV crime dramas; indeed, when I played the Jimmy Smith tune to a group of students in a recent lecture, and asked for suggestions about the type of show the theme-tune might introduce, about 80 per cent of students suggested an American show about a 'cynical cop who breaks the rules'. However, the remaining 20 per cent suggested that it might be the theme either to an 'intellectuals-only TV arts magazine' or to 'a safari show about elephants' (probably due to the Taggian 'sonic anaphone'[4] of the muted pedal-note bass trombone). In fact, this tune was originally the theme to a film about an amoral opportunist's efforts to increase his already substantial fortune. Some years later, it was used by the BBC as the theme-tune to the weekly magazine about all things financial, *The Money Programme*.

The fact that none of the students associated the tune with opportunism or money, is problematic, and seems to suggest either that (a) the style of theme-tune was poorly chosen with regard to its original task; or (b) whoever appropriated the theme-tune (possibly because of the specialized use of the word 'carpetbagger' in the City to mean a short-term, opportunistic investor) was wrong to choose a tune with so few associative links to money; or (c) when divorced from the diegetic aspects of the film, the music is effectively meaningless; or (d) the students had acquired competence in analysing the televisual and filmic codes prevalent from the late 1950s onwards, which tend to link 'tritonal jazz' and American urban cop dramas; or (e) any links between this musical style and certain types of programming intent that may have been relevant in the 1950s or early 1970s clearly are not evident today.

Suggestion (a) is unlikely: at the time, Bernstein was an accomplished, experienced and much in demand film composer, with over forty film music

---

4 Tagg's habitual description of an analogy in sound. See Tagg (1992: 369–78) for a fuller definition of this phenomenon.

credits before *The Carpetbaggers*. The director, Ed Dymytryk, one of a group of famous directors nicknamed 'The Hollywood Ten', had had a distinguished film career with fifty credits before 1963. Regarding suggestion (b), we could argue that the production team for *The Money Programme* could have chosen a more money-denotative theme-tune, but (i) there may have been financial reasons – connected with royalty contracts, say – for the choice; (ii) there is a long tradition at the BBC of choosing background or theme music because of elements in the music's title (or lyrics, if appropriate), rather than denotative meaning in the melody, harmony, rhythm or orchestration,[5] and (iii) apart from onomatopoeic sounds of clinking coinage or cash registers in the theme-tune (as in Pink Floyd's 'Money' from the 1973 album, *Dark Side of the Moon*),[6] it is hard to suggest what sort of music *would* constitute a universally recognizable paramusical association with money. Suggestion (c) underlines the lack of inherence in any meaning we impose upon a group of musical sounds, but it does not explain the relative uniformity of codal competence evinced by four-fifths of my class, nor the codal incompetence evinced by the remainder.

All of which leaves us with (d) and (e). In other words, the current range of meanings residing in the Jimmy Smith tune is due to the levels of codal competence acquired by the students by spending their formative years osmosing associative meaning from the TV; and the reason that none of the students suggested a link with money or ambition underlines the differences between meaning structures available to nineties youth and sixties filmgoers/seventies stockbrokers. This implies both a time-specific, historical element to any competence that we might build up,[7] and also a rather arbitrary link in the first place. If the meanings that we attach to a piece of music can change over time, there can be little sense in which they *in*-here

5 The only viewers likely to realize the significance of the choice of theme-tune in this case would have been (a) jazz fans who (b) knew the title of the song, and (c) had some familiarity with the City idiolect of 'dawn raids', 'white knights' and pork-belly 'futures'. Therefore, in terms of its original target market – affluent, elitist, ambitious City investors – the esoteric choice of theme-tune would actually have been highly appropriate.
6 Which, because of the unfavourable paramusical associations the band members might have engendered among the target audience, would never have been considered as appropriate.
7 Corroborating Middleton (1990: 175–6) above.

in the text or analysis object; rather, these meanings *co*-here with an infinite variety of other meanings.

Further evidence of the 'difficulty' of the aesthesic level occurs in Tagg's extensive empirical reception test, in which 600 individual listeners described their affectual response to the arpeggiated emulations of little brooks in Schubert's *Die Schöne Müllerin* cycle. Tagg reports:

> People put down very few brooks, a lot of sea, a lot of wind in the long grass of a meadow, quite a few trees and a few cornfields . . . incidentally, some people also mentioned shampoo, but this has to do with the shampoo advert for Timotei that was popular at the time: it features a young woman with long hair in a long dress walking through the long grass of a summer meadow. All of these things – the sea, the fields, the long grass, the long hair, the long dress – have one obvious thing in common: it's the wavy movement with your hand or fingertips; it's a gesture. Logically speaking, the cornfield hasn't got much to do with someone's hair, and the sea has nothing much to do with trees really. But the movement is something that you can either internalize from the outside or project out of your body over how waves move on the sea, or you can trace the pattern of your hair or of the dress if you make the same kind of wavy gesture downwards instead of horizontally. (1998b: 7–8)

But what about other 'wavy' gestures? The insulting, masturbatory hand gesture[8] that UK football fans often use to greet an off-target shot on goal by an opposing player, when demonstrated *en masse*, subjectively to me has exactly the wavy quality as the other 'anaphones' mentioned by Tagg (albeit, perhaps, at a higher frequency); so does the rodeo-like experience of riding in an empty carriage over some sections of the London Underground's Metropolitan Line. However, it would be surprising if subjects in *any* reception test, even of an homogeneous group of Harrovian, tube-travelling football fans, were to mention either of the above types of 'waviness' as anaphonal to Tagg's Schubert example.

In addition to the time-specific and demography-specific variations implied in the above listening situations, there are significant intensity-specific variations in what music might 'afford'. For example, let us accept,

8 Formed by making a ring with the thumb and index finger of one hand, then jerking the hand along a diagonal axis with a frequency of 3–4Hz and an amplitude of 15–20 cm.

unquestioningly for a moment, Tagg's hermeneutic-semiological reading of Abba's 1976 hit single, 'Fernando':

> The verse can be said to conjure up a postcard picture of a young European woman alone against a backcloth of a plateau in the high Andes. Periodicity, vocal delivery, lack of bass and drums, and other musical aspects say that she is sincere, worried, involved in a long-ago-and-far-away environment. The words of the verse underline this mood: she has taken part, together with her 'Fernando', in a vaguely-referred-to freedom fight.   (Tagg 1982: 59–60)

Whatever our reactions to this affect analysis, it is clearly the result of a great deal of reflection, exploration and experimentation – a reading which has been evolving over several intensive, immersive listenings, with Tagg's full concentration on the sounding analysis object in hand. If we alter the listening, transplanting the experience to a supermarket, where the sound-system volume is just high enough to hear that a pop song is being played (although it is difficult to be sure of which song, because of the ambient noise of squeaky trolleys, crying children and overheard conversation), the range of meanings afforded by the recording of 'Fernando' will be of little relevance to us; nor will it make much conscious difference whether the song being broadcast is 'Fernando' or 'Waterloo', since we will probably be concentrating upon locating the olive oil rather than the epistemology of the barely audible Abba track at the time.

Problems of listening specificity II: locus, user task/producer task

All of which is not to suggest that there is *no* meaning for us in such a locus. Indeed, some companies make a good living from persuading retail outlets that their functional music[9] is more closely tailored to the

---

9 The imperfect term 'functional music' denotes any music which is transmitted and/or listened to with a specific (extra-musical) function in mind, other than that of passive entertainment. The uses of music to facilitate dancing, conversation, relaxation, burdensome work, or to modify the behaviour of a person in some way, all qualify as examples of functional music, whereas the immersive, absolutist listening to a recording on a home hi-fi does not (unless expressly for relaxation or other similar purpose). This is not to suggest that music can be 'non-functional' – the avoidance of a polar opposite to

demographic-epistemological needs of the outlets' clientele than that of competing companies. In 1991, the UK supermarket chain, ASDA Stores Limited, a wholly owned subsidiary of ASDA Group plc, unified the output of background music in its stores nationwide by employing a satellite radio broadcasting company, Hampson Associates, to create an in-house radio station, ASDA fm, to broadcast twenty-four hours a day to staff and customers of all of ASDA's UK stores. ASDA fm provides a blend of music, short features, trivia spots, cookery features and health information as well as commercials (own and national brands).[10] Advertising revenue makes the service financially self-supporting.

Each of the station library's 10,000 tracks is categorized by a range of parameters, from subject, to artist type, to age-group appeal or complexity. Hampson claim that the system facilitates demographically relevant hours of programming for children, Mother's Day, Halloween, etc. A typical half-hour's programming[11] might include singles by Michael Jackson, Cher, Genesis, and Tom Jones, generally from the current or recent charts. Every third tune is punctuated by a variety of promotional advertising.

The benefits to ASDA are obvious and practical: Hampson deal with licensing and rights clearance; musical choices are standardized, eliminating the potential for managers to evict customers with Stockhausen or Thrash Metal; and audited sales of promoted lines rise by an average of 30 per cent per advertised hour. But there are several tacit assumptions made in order to make such 'narrowcasting' seem viable: (a) that targeting customers with music will increase sales; (b) that specific musical styles – loud, micro-cultural, challenging – will actually increase sales less than other genres – quiet, macro-cultural, unchallenging; (c) that an 'ideal', ultra-narrowcast

'functional music' above underlines the difficulty in justifying such a stance – but rather to differentiate between musics with a more or less explicit physical outcome envisaged either by the transmitter, or by the receiver, or both. By this definition, the same music may be classified as 'functional' or 'absolutist', depending upon circumstantial factors which form the core of the 'cultural-acoustic' model of functional music analysis outlined in the remainder of this chapter.

10 Costley 1995 and Butler 1997 give further details of the mechanics of transmission and programming.
11 These songs were broadcast between 3.50 p.m.–4.20 p.m. on Wednesday, 31 March 1999.

interactive future might involve the data on a customer's 'smart card' pre-cipitating a change in background music content;[12] (d) that customers can actually hear the music in the first place;[13] and (e) that it is the music, rather than the promotional advertising, that is causing the increase in sales. Clearly, in order to test these assumptions, access to as wide a range of experimental listening and market research data as possible is essential. Indeed, much of the significant work being carried out by Hargreaves and North[14] into specific instances of functional music listening, in supermarkets, restaurants etc., and some aspects of the educational psychology research of Swanwick (1994) and Sloboda (1985, 1998) gives explicitly corroborable input into locus-specific aspects of the aesthesic level. More research remains to be done in this area, however.

In addition, there are two further areas of listening specificity that de-serve attention: those relating to the nature of any task which music may be employed to ameliorate, and the function of the music originally envis-aged by its producers.[15] Through their eclectic range of research projects, Hargreaves and North combine the generalized audition psychology re-search of Bruner (1990)[16] with a more specialized interest in what they call

12 Some satellite broadcasting systems are experimenting with versions of this idea. Lance Thomas, CEO of satellite broadcaster DMX Europe, claims that ' "we can instruct the smart card in every receiver in every branch of Laura Ashley, say, to fade out, change channel and fade up again at the same time", [allowing] staff to react instantly to different situations, giving appropriate music for young or old; rich or poor; heavy or weak demand' (Butler 1997: 33–4). Of course, idiocast, kafkaesque visions of a future when lifestyle information stored on our credit-card triggers a chorus of 'When I'm Sixty-Four', 'If I Were a Rich Man', or even Weird Al Yankovic's 'Eat It' (1984), to herald our every entrance into a store, remain as yet impossible.

13 The volume level of the ASDA broadcast, and the rather tinny speaker system in the north-west London store I visited, meant that I could not identify many of the tunes without stopping to listen intently.

14 See Hargreaves and North 1997; North and Hargreaves 1996a–d; 1997a–c; and North, Hargreaves and McKendrick 1997 and 1999; see also Milliman 1982; Harris, Bradley and Titus 1992; Hadlington 1998; Hamilton 1998; Huddleston 1998; McMahon 1998; Parker 1998; RNID 1998; and Thornton 1998 for related experimental data.

15 In this article, the word 'producers' denotes *all* persons with any creative or financial involvement in the production of music – composer, recording artist, sound engineer, marketing executive, etc.

16 Crozier summarizes Bruner's affective semantics experiments: 'Excitement is produced by music in the major mode . . . that is fast, of medium pitch, uneven

'tapping-on-the-wheel' aesthetic responses (North and Hargreaves 1997b: 84) – listenings as background to specific tasks, such as driving a car. From these studies of task-specific listenings, the general trend is that 'people prefer musically-evoked levels of arousal which help them to achieve a particular situational goal' (1996d: 96). Clearly, then, the nature of the task which the listener is using the music to ameliorate will have a significant input into our reading of its meaning.

Any dissonance between the task-specificity of the user and that of the producer in functional music situations also needs to be explored. Returning to my original range of uses for a drum 'n' bass tune, it is clear that, since the key elements of the drum 'n' bass style are those which most easily afford dancing – the timestretched, speeded-up rhythm samples and the sub-bass riffs in particular – a large proportion of such music is produced with a specific task[17] – dancing – in mind. When the user is not using dance music as something to dance to, but as a means to facilitate the production of lunch, style-categories based on producer task-specificity cease to have any meaning.

Towards a cultural-acoustic model of functional music analysis

None of the above problems of listening specificity should be interpreted as an argument against close textual analysis of popular music. The concept of focusing upon the recording as text in semiotically influenced popular music analysis allows for a level of analytical detail of certain aspects of musical meaning far in advance of previous, critically or sociologically biased studies – which is very well if the reception conditions can be normalized to the same extent as can the sound object (as listened to immersively, at home, on a hi-fi system, by a supercompetent listener) itself. However, such conditions *cannot* be normalized in today's world of ubiquitous functional music. The temporal, demographic, attentive, local and task-related particulars of the listening situation all conspire to dilute the analytical meanings

---

rhythm, dissonant harmony, and loud volume. Tranquillity is produced by music in the major mode, slow tempo, medium pitch, flowing rhythm, consonant harmony and soft volume' and so on (Crozier 1997: 75).

17 And, by implication, in a specific locus, at a specific time, for a specific demography, and level of intensity.

of the well-parsed text to such an extent that the absolute sound recording ceases to exist as an object of analysis; all that remains is personalized meaning, personalized using, and personalized listening – *personal text*, in fact.

Consequently, unless we are trying to describe the meanings that a piece of music creates in some ideally homogeneous group of codal experts, all of whom are giving the music their full, undivided attention, the primary analytical text in functional music situations can only be our *listenings* to it.

Any model for functional music analysis, then, must start from those specificities which define a 'personal text'. These fall into three broad categories:

Personal listenings:

- *Time-specific listening*: exploring the effects that the distance between the time-period in which the music was produced and the present time of listening may have on codal competence. A relevant contemporary example might be the exploration of the phenomenon of 'cheese' – a knowing, ironic appreciation of the songs of Burt Bacharach and others by some late nineties youth, contrasting sharply with both the eighties condemnation of the same music as irredeemably naff, and the original, late sixties naïve appreciation of 'easy listening' by middle-aged listeners;
- *Demography-specific listening*: exploring the demographic and cultural factors which might affect codal competence. Examples might include unique aspects of the listener's auditory system, issues of individual and group taste, age, social class, gender and ethnic background, and so on – a rural, eighty-year-old white widow with low-frequency deafness experiencing a dub reggae tune for the first time would be unlikely to be listening to the same text as a twenty-year-old urban black man with perfect hearing and a supercompetent appreciation of the genre.

Situational listenings:

- *Intensity-specific listening*: exploring the immersive level of the listening, and its effect on the perception of recording. When a teenager revises for exams with her/his radio tuned to a favourite station, for example, the exigencies of the situation will require the programming to be subliminally listened to, if at all;
- *Locus-specific listening*: exploring factors related to sound-source quality, ambient noise and other peculiarities of the situation in which music is being consumed, including such concerns as whether or not the listener has any control over the content, volume level or duration of the musical output.

Intentional listenings:

- *producer task-specific listening*: making explicit the producer's or broadcaster's original purpose for the production and/or broadcasting of the music (in addition to the profit motive).[18] In the domain of production, examples might include music for dancing, for relaxation, or for political reflection; in the domain of broadcasting, programming to encourage brand loyalty towards a chain-store, the purchase of promoted lines in a supermarket, or a relaxed clientele on a turbulent flight;
- *user task-specific listening*: exploring the listener's purpose for listening to the chosen music in a particular functional music situation, and the mechanisms by which the musical choice is deemed appropriate to the task by the listener. For example, in a small market town centre traffic jam, the decision to play a particular urban dance compilation tape by a rural seventeen-year-old youth in his new hatchback, at an extreme volume, is unlikely to be guided purely by musical reasons, or by the philanthropic urge to allow Saturday shoppers to share his enjoyment.

Although each listening above has been separated in order to facilitate definition, it should be noted that, in many cases, these listenings may overlap and interlock, to such an extent that it is otiose to separate them; nor should the order of the listenings outlined above be taken as definitive and normative. However, within the analyses of three different personal texts of a seminal drum 'n' bass tune which follow, I shall adhere to the above listening-group order. First, I shall briefly discuss the recording itself.

Example tune: 'Shadowboxing' by Doc Scott[19]

This tune provides a useful exemplar of the cultural-acoustic model, in that the recording contains a few archetypal elements of the drum 'n' bass style, and *nothing* else. For its 8'02" duration, the constantly repeating, obsessively edited four-bar breakbeat (with a tempo of $\downarrow = 150$) does not alter in any way, save for a 30" section in the middle of the tune, where the snare part disappears. Different amounts of reverb (some of it gated) are applied

---

18 Which is not to condemn this reasoning: indeed, it is a curious, and unfortunate, aspect of much commercial music analysis, that the 'commercial' nature of the music is given scant consideration in its analysis.

19 As featured on the 1998 compilation: *Muzik Classics: Drum & Bass*.

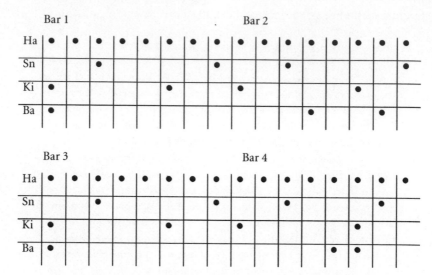

Figure 10.1: Breakbeat, 'Shadowboxing'

to each quaver beat, and different timestretchings[20] are applied to the snare and hi-hat parts. As with many such tunes, the sampled and sequenced parts are binary – either 'on' or 'off'.

The four-bar pattern is punctuated, and organized into sixteen-bar hypermetric units, by the attachment of an edited sample, possibly culled from a 'spaghetti Western' movie fight scene, to the last two bars of almost every fourth repeat of the breakbeat. A constant quaver pattern is articulated by a sample of a closed hi-hat with tambourine attached (Ha, Fig. 10.1). The kick (Ki) and snare (Sn) samples also repeat in syncopated patterns, as does the sub-bass (Ba) pattern, though this sample only plays for about a third of the tune, and there is little sense of hypermetric patterning to its 'onness' or 'offness'. Figure 10.1 summarizes the full thirty-two-quaver breakbeat.[21]

The only other element in the tune is a four-note sampled riff of a synthesized cello, moving to cello C from the G above. After the first 1'15" of the tune, this sample fades in over a period of roughly 2'45" (modified

20 Modern samplers can double the speed of a sampled breakbeat, say, or halve the speed of a vocal sample, without doubling (or halving) the frequency of pitched elements within the sample. This facility is used extensively by drum 'n' bass composers as a means of tuning each element in a breakbeat.
21 Each box represents one quaver.

gradually by an analogue sweep filter), then is replaced by an almost iden-tical sample for 2'20'', then returns for another 30''. The last minute of the recording consists only of the repeated breakbeat.

In many respects this tune represents a drum 'n' bass paradigm, being lengthy, with a slow sense of dynamic build, and a largely modular structure, whereby constituent elements are turned on or off, but rarely develop in terms of pitch or rhythm. Sub-bass frequencies form the large majority of the sonic materials, and melody and harmony barely exist.

So much for the rather minimalist recording-as-text. There follow three hypothetical personal texts of the same tune ('Shadowboxing'), in the same environment (a rural wine shop), based on the model outlined above. All three, although imaginary, are abstracted from personal observation,[22] and are summarized at the start of each analysis in a listenings profile.

Analysis I: The manager's text

Sue, the manager of a wine shop in a rural market town centre, keen to change the image of the long-established shop from fusty to funky, has been convinced by her younger deputy to experiment with a drum 'n' bass compilation as background music, in order to try to encourage more of the next generation of informed imbibers to visit. Sue likes to think she has wide musical tastes, with no particular musical dislikes; indeed, she has heard a few commercial drum 'n' bass tunes aired on her local radio station. She raises no personal musical objections to the experiment, but she is concerned that such urban, 'underground' music might cause her regular customers, who are mainly retired, financially secure, with a knowledgeable, strongly experi-mental attitude towards wine-buying, to begin to feel unwelcome, and desert her. Consequently, she has turned the volume level of her CD player down, so that the music is barely audible, and monitors the music regularly, adjusting the volume downwards or upwards as necessary, in response to the number of customers in the shop, and other factors impinging upon the level of am-bient noise – predominantly high-street traffic and customer conversation. Whilst monitoring the volume of the music, she notices how the over-boomy bass frequencies are nullified by the rather mediocre sound-system she had

---

22 Gleaned from four years' experience in the wine trade.

Personal listenings:

Time-specific:	One year after production of tune; mid-afternoon, Friday
	Current musical idiom
Demography-specific:	Female, white, rural, 40 years, retail manager; wide range
	of musical tastes
	Codal competence of idiom low

Situational listenings:

Intensity-specific:	Medium – monitoring volume of music; otherwise low –
	stock-taking
Locus-specific:	Volume kept low to avoid offending regular customer base;
	more audible due to very low environmental noise
	High frequencies privileged due to broadcast volume and
	speaker quality

Intentional listenings:

Producer task-specific:	Encourage dancing
User task-specific:	Widen demographic range of clientele;
	secure long-term future of shop

Figure 10.2: Manager's text: listenings profile

installed a few years ago, which makes the balance between treble and bass seem a lot more pleasing, although she wishes that the music wasn't *quite* so repetitive. When not actively monitoring the volume, she barely notices the music as she works, as the clink of bottles and the conversation of customers tends to get in the way. While the repetitive tune is playing, two customers enter. Sue has never seen the first customer, a young, well turned-out black man, in the shop before, though she has seen him working in the bank across the street. To her slight surprise, the man asks for a bottle of Krug '85, and speaks appreciatively to her of the choice of music, and of his love for

212

the wine. Friendly conversation about music and *prestige cuvée* champagne ensues: Sue *adores* Krug, and keeps several vintages in store, for herself as much as anything. To her delight, the man ends up buying a mixed case of '83s, '85s, and '89s. The second customer is one of the manager's most regular, and most knowledgeable customers, but he soon seems in some discomfort. He and the manager exchange the usual cordialities, but the conversation quickly turns to the music, and from the music to the graffiti on the bus shelter outside the shop, the deadly combination of youngsters and alcohol, and the decline in standards since he resigned his commission. In the end, he leaves with a single bottle of his favourite good value burgundy, showing no inclination to discuss the manager's latest buying trip to the Mâconnais.

Analysis II: The bank clerk's text

Marcel, a bank clerk, is holding a house-warming party to celebrate his recent move to the countryside from East London. A big crowd of his people, including a well-respected drum 'n' bass DJ, and useful numbers of fine ladies, have promised to show. Marcel wants the evening to go well, and needs a bottle of Krug to lubricate the social element of the evening.[23] He goes into the only wine shop in town with low expectations – of being mugged by Mozart, of an unfriendly welcome, of a dearth of fine champagne – and is amazed to notice 'Shadowboxing' playing on the sound-system. Instantly, Marcel senses a rapport with the manager, and the two discuss the music, and then champagne. He has never tried many of the vintages of Krug that the manager mentions, but he recalls how much he loved the '85, and so decides to blow a good proportion of his disposable income for the month on a mixed case. He wishes the bass response of the shop's speakers wasn't so feeble, but his fluent knowledge of the tune helps fill in the auditory gaps.

Analysis III: The Major's text

The Major is on a recce for a case of his favourite reasonably priced burgundy. He enters the town's wine shop to find some repetitive pop music

23 The drink of choice for many drum 'n' bass clubbers in London in the mid-nineties was fine vintage champagne.

Personal listenings:

Time-specific:	One year after production of tune; mid-afternoon, Friday
	Current musical idiom
Demography-specific:	Male, black, urban then rural, 22 years, bank clerk; dislikes
	classical; loves drum 'n' bass, speed garage, hip-hop
	Codal competence of idiom extremely high

Situational listenings:

Intensity-specific:	Low on entering shop – pre-formed notions about music
	Higher when tune is recognized and surprise registered
	Lower again when concentrating upon purchase
Locus-specific:	Barely audible, and out of balance due to lack of sub-bass
	frequencies from speakers

Intentional listenings:

Producer task-specific:	Encourage dancing
	Widen demographic range of clientele;
	secure long-term future of shop
User task-specific:	Not applicable at first, then
	Look forward to that night's party at home

Figure 10.3: Bank clerk's text: listenings profile

hissing out of the shop's speakers. The Major suffers from high-frequency deafness, due equally to his late middle age and his having taken one from Rommel at Alamein, and the constant thud of the drums makes it very hard to concentrate on the task in hand, not to mention being rather painful on the ear. He cannot understand why people should enjoy this sort of music, with its lack of tune, harmony or variety – all that he can hear is the drums. The manager tries to engage him in conversation, but he can scarcely hear what she is saying above the din. Out of politeness, he purchases one bottle, and hurries back to the sanctuary of his home, where he can recapture

Personal listenings:

    Time-specific: One year after production of tune; mid-afternoon, Friday

                                     Current musical idiom

    Demography-specific: Male, white, urban then rural, 70 years, army major (retired);

                                     likes light classical, big band jazz; dislikes 'any music

                                     you can't hum'

                                     Suffers from high-frequency deafness

                                     Codal competence of idiom nil

Situational listenings:

    Intensity-specific: Low on entering shop – music background assumptions

                                     Higher when loud beat is noticed and surprise registered

                                     Remaining high due to dislike and discomfort

    Locus-specific: Low frequencies emphasized due to high-frequency deafness

Intentional listenings:

    Producer task-specific: Encourage dancing

                                     Widen demographic range of clientele;

                                        secure long-term future of shop

    User task-specific: Not applicable at first, then

                                     Emphasize decline in musical and moral standards

Figure 10.4: Major's text: listenings profile

the peace and quiet that enticed him from shabby Kensington in the first place.

Conclusion

The above flight of fancy may seem a little far-fetched in some respects, but it does highlight the problems in textual analysis of drum 'n' bass, a genre which privileges extremely lengthy, non-developing repetition of the

215

simplest, most minimal materials. This is because of its primary producer-intended function as dance music. When transplanted to the thoroughly alien environment of a rural wine shop, the exigencies of local ambient sound, personal hearing acuity, personal codal competence, and the purpose to which the music is being put – to encourage young adults to buy wine – change the meaning of that music beyond recognition. This new meaning is as unique and individual as we are: it is thus that Marcel hears the full intricacies of a drum 'n' bass breakbeat, though with a frequency response unbalanced towards the quaver-patterned cymbals; the Major hears a random, discomfiting thud from the kick drum, that betokens an apocalypse of lowered moral standards; and Sue hears a balanced if repetitive song which seems to have very little meaning for her while she is working, until the music becomes foregrounded by a friendly conversation which leads to a trade-up sale. Marcel's experience might make him link drum 'n' bass music more with champagne than with dancing. Sue might link Doc Scott with Krug from now on, too; however, armed with her invaluable market knowledge, she might also link the music with her future financial security, through expansion of the shop. The Major will think of his unpurchased Mâcon-Lugny, should he ever have the misfortune to hear such cacophony again. What links the reactions of all three listeners (and personal texts) is the irrelevance of the undelineated recording, and the arbitrariness of the coherence of the texts: in other circumstances, with other listening specificities, other texts would result. Moreover, as my inaudible ASDA experience suggests, some other undelineated recording could have a hand in identical (or at least near-identical) personal texts in some functional music situations.

North and Hargreaves claim that 'artists' "explicit" and "implicit" messages are usually missed by their audience' (1996d: 92). The word 'missed' implies an accidental element to this process – a process of mislaying; but the above analyses suggest that the dissonance between producer intention and listener usage is much more deliberate, much more *creative*.

The cultural-acoustic model, then, explores the *creation* of texts from listenings. There is a databasing element to such a method, whereby results from successive listenings form a corpus of specifically corroborable personal analytical information. Such data might be financially beneficial to functional music producers and broadcasters, as well as making explicit the changes in music use and musical meaning that have occurred through the historical improvements in recording and playback technology, cultural change, ever-shifting competence patterns and so on. The holistic, interdisciplinary and empirical spirit of such research might help to underline the ways in which the ubiquity of music which is designed not to be listened to – what Lanza[24] describes as the shift 'from figure to ground' (Lanza 1995: 3) – has changed us all from analysts of 'the primary text' into those texts ourselves.

24 As yet the only thorough reference work for functional music study.

11 Talk and text: popular music and ethnomusicology

MARTIN STOKES

Introduction

The reflexive turn in recent years has dramatically repositioned the question of Theory. Despite the banality of the widespread recognition that 'Theory' is now a mass media performance art, and a global one at that, questions of what happens when garage bands read Hebdige, the Kaluli ponder *Sound and Sentiment*, and visual artists incorporate quotations from Foucault into their pictures and installations continue to press hard on issues of theoretical production. Who is 'doing theory' here? Can theory really do what it once claimed to be able to do, to explain and point the way forward? And is there any way of redrawing the line which once comfortably separated culture and theory? Clearly enough, Theory doesn't so much explain the world, but constitutes an important and inseparable part of what, itself, requires explanation and/or interpretation. Quite what it is that articulates that explanation, if no longer 'Theory', is far from clear and will no doubt remain so, to the consternation of many academic theorists. For others, both within and outside universities, the situation affords the hope that a more or less structured, more or less global, and more or less democratic conversation may emerge between those involved, and that the scope of this involvement is extended substantially beyond its current electronic horizons. In the process, clearly enough, the distinction between Theory as metadiscourse and the exclusive property of the privileged few, and Culture as a bounded field of largely implicit meaning shared by 'the rest', will disappear.

This project is, of course, well underway in a variety of musical fields. Ethnomusicologists have long since abandoned the notion that ethnomusicology is the study of people 'without music theory', and have tried to understand the ways in which notions of theory are deployed and manipulated in a variety of situations. Music theorists have taken cautious steps away from Schenkerian depth theories, increasingly seeing musical surfaces as the consequence of a multiplicity of conceptual operations, and not the rigorous and hierarchical working out of a single, 'submerged' *Urlinie* (Cohn and Dempster 1992). 'Theory', for many working in music analysis, is already becoming messy, provisional, tactical, in need of cultural and historical positioning.[1] Unfortunately, it seems unlikely to happen in the field of popular music studies, where 'Culture' and 'Theory' seem to be moving in opposite directions. The dismissal of the culturalist foundations and methods of ethnomusicology by a number of popular music scholars has been both frank and direct (Middleton 1990; Shepherd and Wicke 1997). 'Theory' in this context, is contemporary social theory, with European (predominantly Marxian and psychoanalytic) roots. Ethnomusicology, ethnography and 'the culture concept' are closely interlinked, and, as understood in these critiques, are premised on the belief that musical texts must be read 'in their cultural context'; that people know what they are doing and are capable of representing this knowledge to others; and that these representations (and only these) contain the key to the analysis of what they are doing, and how they might be understood. The problem is, following the critique, that both ethnography and the culture concept separate text and context, a process which reifies, abstracts and thoroughly impedes an understanding of text as social practice; people are not, as ethnography and the culture concept imply, the sovereign and self-aware authors of their own actions, and texts are not a transparent window on to their intentions; analysis is, or should be, a creative, even emancipatory technique for reading in ways precisely not considered or 'intended' by their various authors, audiences and so forth. Ethnomusicology, it is argued, merely re-entrenches all of these troublesome intellectual errors by dealing with remote and exotic societies that in some sense permit, or are (conveniently) powerless to resist or otherwise respond to, their neo-colonial representation and abusive commodification by outsiders.[2]

---

1 Christensen (1993), Blasius (1996) and Hyer (1989) are particularly important in this regard.
2 See Middleton (1992). Middleton's critique of ethnomusicological 'culturalism' is sketched out in Middleton (1981) with reference to Keil (1966), but is fully

This critical tack is compounded and complicated by claims made by a number of music analysts who feel that cultural analysis is, crucially, inclined to lose sight of 'the music', and that certain techniques of musical analysis, building on, modifying and inflecting those inherited from Schenker, Reti, Riemann and others in the analysis of Western art music (see Dunsby and Whittall 1988) are the appropriate means for focusing on the 'primary' material at hand, the sounds 'themselves'. This involves a binary division of the field that crosscuts others, but reinscribes a problematization of culture, and the value of a theory of culture for understanding music. For advocates of the 'primary text', the culturalist position is epitomized by a genre of high Theory drawing heavily on poststructuralism, although its ranking of primary and secondary material would consign most anthropological and ethnomusico-logical insights to the latter category; the bifurcation distinguishes 'primary' intellectual rigour ('music analysis') and interpretative free fall ('cultural studies' along with anything else that attempts to understand music by refer-ence to things that do not strictly pertain to music). The position is somewhat complicated by Shepherd and Wicke's *Music and Cultural Theory*, which also appeals to a binary division of analytical powers between those interested in the primary, material 'stuff' of musical sound, and a secondary semiology

fleshed out in his later discussion of the same material (1991: 145–6). In both cases it follows a discussion of folklore studies, and precedes an account of subcultural theory. The critique of ethnomusicology in Middleton's work in recent years has revolved explicitly, then, around the question of the structural homology. John Shepherd's work in recent years has also critiqued structural homology theories, though not necessarily tying this to a critique of ethnomusicological culturalism. Shepherd (1994: 138–9), for example, draws on Keil's and Blacking's work in a discussion of the reification of cultural repertories ('ethnographic presents') and Blacking's anthropology of the body; Shepherd and Wicke (1997) bend this critique to anthropological and ethnomusicological culturalism with particular reference to Walser (1993), a move anticipated in Shepherd's contribution to the 'Popular Music Matters' debate at the IASPM conference in Gossen, Berlin, in 1992 with Dave Harker (chaired by Peter Wicke). Arguably the real problem is a persistent language gap which ensures that popular music scholars read little ethnomusicology, and vice versa. There are some revealing asymmetries. The journal *Popular Music*, for example, does much more to review ethnomusicological publications than either *The Yearbook for Traditional Music* or *Ethnomusicology* do to review the work of British popular music scholars. On the other hand, a glance at the bibliographies of recent titles in the Chicago University Press ethnomusicology series indicates that American-based ethnomusicologists use a wider range of British popular music scholars in their bibliographies than the reverse.

220

concerned with the meanings that are, post-facto, made from this 'stuff'. Its concern, though, in comparison with the work of Moore, Hawkins and others is with the ways in which an understanding of music's semiotic peculiarities might transform, and hence ultimately participate in the cultural studies project.

The ranking of primary and secondary approaches might be understood in the context of a more general process of sub-disciplinary consolidation of popular music studies, lead by British and British-trained writers working in a variety of disciplines falling under the general rubric of 'the social' ('cultural studies' notwithstanding). In this respect, they find themselves in a somewhat self-conscious opposition to musicologists in the United States trained in universities in the sway of large and prestigious anthropology departments, specializing, generally, in 'the cultural', and with lively philosophical traditions of radical, culturalist attack on the notion of Theory with a capital 'T'.[3] Under these circumstances, poststructuralism has had a fundamentally different impact on both sides of the Atlantic. In Britain it has entrenched a tendency to enshrine Theory as the primary intellectual task, and to carve out new areas of Theoretical expertise in somewhat anxious and polemic terms.[4] Its effect in the United States has been, in some senses, more destablizing. One might distrust the motives of publishers seeking a cross-disciplinary market, and university administrators making 'inter-disciplinary' hires, but culturalism has had the effect of initiating valuable exchanges, and the liberating (if strategic and provisional) assumption of common horizons within which a common critical language might be forged.

The commitment to Theory, whether poststructuralist or music analytical, has involved an absolute distinction being made between theoretical knowledge and the operational and metapragmatic knowledges used by the people who make and listen to the music. This distinction needs to be questioned, not on the basis of a simplistic cultural relativism, but because it ignores crucial opportunities afforded for critical dialogue between both parties. This dialogue would be shaped by a more mobile theoretical language, constantly open to ideas from outside formal music theory, and the expansion

3 Quine, Whorf, Sapir and Rorty are perhaps the important names to mention (see the Bibliography).
4 The title of Keith Negus's *Popular Music in Theory* (Negus 1997) is instructive.

of the critical possibilities inherent (if not explicated) in the operational and metapragmatic knowledges possessed by those who make and listen to music. Much hinges on what kinds of knowledge musicians and listeners claim for themselves, and how, when and where they deploy this knowledge. Ethnomusicologists and popular music scholars have (on the whole) taken different approaches, both rather limiting in various ways. Ethnomusicologists have, by and large, dealt with local experts, people versed in the arts of verbal exegesis, despite recognition that experts have axes to grind and that indigenous 'theory' does not necessarily say everything that one needs to know (Baily 1981). Popular music scholars, on the other hand, have often chosen to speak about music-making in situations in which musicians and their audiences are assumed to know little, and say even less, about what they do. This situation has only more recently attracted critical reconsideration (Frith 1996), and an ethnographic approach has begun to inform valuable analyses of some key popular musical institutions (Negus 1992). The problem is partly one of assumptions still rooted in Frankfurtian mass cultural critique. Though these are widely discredited, they retain some residual theoretical force, which conveniently allow writers to clear the ground of rival opinions for an authoritative and often explicitly value-driven act of critical intervention. It is also partly that, at first glance, people often appear to have genuinely little to say about the music they are involved in. This is, in turn, partly a methodological problem (finding out how to listen to what people in fact are saying), and partly making sense of conflicting data. Faced by someone they don't know, and assume to embody superior institutional power and knowledge, people too readily act defensively, claiming 'not to know' how they go about making, interpreting and enjoying music when, in at least some senses, they demonstrably do.

Cultural subjects

The problems that are identified with anthropological notions of the culture concept by a number of writers (Middleton 1990; Shepherd and Wicke 1997; Straw 1991) might be summarized as follows. When concepts of culture are evoked to explain a musical genre, similar structural patterns are noted connecting music with other areas of cultural life. Structural homologies are juxtaposed, each explaining the other. Seen in these terms,

Middleton, for example, notes the circular nature of these kinds of arguments, their lack of historicity, the assumption of a functional 'whole', a reified context from which music might be analytically abstracted (as if one could imagine, for example, some notion of 'African-American culture' without African-American music), their failure to problematize the complex nature of musical cognition (what it is, so to speak, that makes us hear music as music and not just a restatement of patterns reiterated elsewhere) and to assume a simple 'fit' between cultures, personalities and individuals. Ethnography compounds the problem, laying stress on the self-representations of musicians and other cultural actors in ways which inhibit an awareness of the wider social and cultural forces, often unrecognized or misrecognized by the actors, that impinge on the worlds they actually inhabit. Thus blues, to continue detailing Middleton's critique, needs to be understood in its relationship to, and not simply in its difference from, other forms of musical practice (for example, the tonal harmonic procedures and the cultivation of 'clean' musical textures in Western art music), just as an understanding of the cultural dynamics of ghetto life on Chicago's south side has to be situated in and understood in relation to some conception of the forces which produce the ghetto itself.

A similar anxiety is expressed by Straw, in an oft-quoted distinction between popular musical 'community' and 'scene'. Straw is struck by the prominence of 'notions of cultural totality' and 'claims concerning the expressive unity of musical practices' in ethnomusicological writing (Straw 1991: 369), which he links with a certain tendency, particularly in subcultural theory, to posit relatively stable populations, linked organically to particular musical idioms. This he contrasts with the musical 'scene', which he defines as 'that cultural space within which a range of musical practices co-exist, interacting with each other within a variety of processes of differentiation and according to the widely varying trajectories of change and cross-fertilization' (Straw 1991: 373). Underpinning Straw's unease with the anthropological notion of culture is an old sense of the term, of 'culture' repairing the rift in communal life wrought by the ravages of 'civilization' (in the eighteenth and nineteenth centuries) and 'modernity' (in the twentieth). This nostalgic quest undoubtedly underpins not only liberal definitions of the term, but also neo-Marxian definitions, 'an essential human brotherhood, often expressed as something to be recovered as well as gained', as Raymond Williams once put it (Williams 1977: 18). Ancient Greece provided a remarkably consistent common horizon, establishing important continuities linking the ways in which Wordsworth and Arnold on the one hand, and Williams and Lukács on the other, have contributed to the culture polemic (Hartmann 1997). British new left notions of 'community', particularly in their contemporary Blairite incarnation, are, of course, entirely consistent with this nostalgic and redemptive sense of the word 'culture'. 'Culture' then, for some of its contemporary critics, expresses a vague but persistent thinking-class hope, and cannot be taken as a methodologically useful conceptual tool.

Concern with the 'culture concept' extends to popular music analysis. Shepherd and Wicke describe their book as an exercise in 'cultural theory'. Not only is the notion of cultural theory quite specific (rooted in a poststructuralist canon) as Tagg (1999) has pointed out, but culturalist methodologies, specifically those relating to anthropological or ethnomusicological practice, are entirely rejected. Culturalist explanations are deemed to confuse a first-order semiology (what is proper to the understanding of music itself) with a second-order semiology, and an assumption (identified with the work of Robert Walser) that music can only mean, 'discursively', when subordinated to the semiotic regime of language. As Shepherd and Wicke put it: 'While it is not impossible to experience the sounds of music in a manner unmediated through the effects of language, it does not follow from this that the experience is reducible to the conditions of experience instigated through language' (1997: 147). This objection is the basis of a complex argument, directed against Saussurean linguistics, and aimed at recapturing the materiality of sound as the basis for an understanding of the signifying power of sound as sound, and not simply as deficient language, or language in some 'prior' state (as according to Barthes and Kristeva). Whilst the points of reference evoked are quite different, arguments for a 'return' to popular music analysis shares with it a rhetoric of primary (important) and secondary (not so important) areas of analysis, the first connected with sounds, and the second connected to the meanings culturally, or 'discursively', attached to them (Moore 2001a). This hierarchy of analytical modes remains constant, despite recognition that actual musical experience, the experiences of people making, listening, dancing to, thinking or talking about music at specific times and in specific places, might consist of some kind of dialectic between the two 'levels', and that much music-making, for example that based on

224

Western tonal practice, is not, strictly speaking 'music' at all, but rather more like language (Shepherd and Wicke 1997).

'Culture' remains an excruciatingly complex term, and the caution I have been describing is entirely justified. Culturalist understandings of popular music have a tough time working round these complexities. Firstly, and most fundamentally, the term 'culture' bears the mark of its problematic association with the nation-state. As Elias pointed out, in a well-known discussion, the term emerged in a process of sociogenesis separating the courtly nobility, civilized on the French model, and a German-speaking middle-class stratum of intelligentsia recruited chiefly from the bourgeois 'servers of princes' or officials in the broadest sense (Elias 1982: 8–9), and casting this separation in terms of a distinction between 'Kultur' and 'Zivilization'. Kultur designated a constant process of achievement and self-making rather than the observation of modes of valued, 'civilized' behaviour, a distinction that was, since the beginning of the eighteenth century, rhetorically cast as one between 'inner' virtues, and the mere observation of form, etiquette, and so forth. Where Civilization connected individual behaviour to universal norms, Culture, 'an entire living picture of ways of life, or habits, wants, characteristics of land and sky' (Herder 1993: 188), was the incommensurable property of groups. One spoke, therefore, not of Culture, but of 'cultures' in the plural. The term was, from the outset, more or less interchangeable with 'nation'; the culture concept accompanied the emergence of the German nation-state under the tutelage of this same middle-class intelligentsia, and continues to shape the rhetoric of the most virulent forms of ethno-nationalism today (in which ethnicities, possessing cultures, are simply nations-in-waiting). Petty-nationalist culturalist thinking about music, 'folk', popular and otherwise, is certainly widespread in the Balkans (Slobin 1996). Anthropologists and ethnomusicologists often express surprise that 'their' concepts should be appropriated and lead such lively existences outside their tutelage, but in reality there is nothing particularly surprising about this at all (Handelman 1990). The cultural anthropological usage of the term, then, sits uneasily together with nationalism and the nation-state in an age in which, we are encouraged to believe, these things no longer matter, but they evidently and uncomfortably do.

Secondly, the term is compounded by the uneasy history that the culture concept shares with colonialism on both sides of the Atlantic. The definition of culture, often quite specifically with reference to music, has been a tool in politics of colonial divide and rule. It defines certain practices as valuable if, in some crucial sense, neglected, and hence positively requiring paternalistic colonial preservation, and others as deviant, 'urban', degenerate, unacceptably hybrid, and so forth. The keen perception by colonial administrators of the strong potential of the Creole elites in West African cities was based not only on their recognition of their potential power as business rivals, but the potential power of the 'Creolized' expressive culture that they patronized as the focus for fostering proto-national, anti-colonial sentiment. Colonial efforts to disentangle indigeneity from creolité can always be understood in these terms. The colonial disparagement of popular musical forms such as Jùjú and Highlife says much about the alacrity with which post-colonial elites seized on these forms of popular music as appropriate symbols of the post-colonial nation (Waterman 1990), and much about the ways in which these various processes of appropriation perpetuate the very categories from which these post-colonial elites sought to distance themselves. Ethnography, the study of culture as a lived and experienced social reality, carried out *in situ*, first became possible in a colonial or quasi-colonial context, as many critics have pointed out, and continues to encode controlling metropolitan values and definitional schemes, and the profoundly ambiguous fears, desires and plays of power involved in 'knowing others'. The connections that undoubtedly exist between colonialism, the culture concept, and ethnography thus necessitate another level of caution.

Thirdly, many would point to the continuity between colonial culturalist thinking and the multiculturalism of contemporary liberal democracies. Just as colonial administrations, particularly British colonial administrations, promoted culturalist politics to divide and rule, to establish convenient administrative units, to preserve the fiction of paternalistic preservation of what was best in colonized societies, and to militate against rival principles of oppositional political order, so too do contemporary liberal democracies turn potentially unruly sections of its citizenry into members of, in some sense, 'cultural' groups to effect much the same kind of selective inclusion and exclusion of a variety of people from the political arena. Ethnography, as Sharma, Hutnyck and Sharma argue in a discussion of the Asian dance music scene in Britain (1996), is once again implicated in the process of metropolitan othering and control, constituting a neo-colonial 'report to the centre' on a periphery which might yet be brought under the state's hegemonic control. There are, of course, close connections between the idea of culture as a form of hegemonic political control and culture as commodity form, notably in the context of mass tourism (Greenwood 1978).

Anthropologists themselves are far from unanimous on the value of the idea of culture, despite an often uneasy recognition that if the discipline has offered twentieth-century thought something, it is probably this (Barnard and Spencer 1996; Weiner 1995). British social anthropologists distinguished their project from those of Boasian cultural anthropologists in America in terms of the analytical necessity of going beyond the terms of indigenous self-representation. Culture was a constituent part of a social structure, which demanded a quite different kind of understanding – one that certainly involved taking 'culture' seriously, as providing important clues to what is going on, but never itself constituting the ground of an adequate anthropological explanation. The art of ethnography, indeed, was the art of connecting the ways in which people represented what they were doing with what, demonstrably, was 'actually going on'. Mary Douglas once dismissed the term 'culture' in a memorable put down: 'never was such a fluffy notion at large in a self-styled scientific discipline, not since singing angels blew the planets across the medieval sky or ether filled in the gaps of Newton's universe'. Rearguard action on the part of British social anthropologists continues unabated (Kuper 1999), together with a continued emphasis on participant-observer ethnography as a technique, a skill to be mastered, part of a professional cursus, without which one could hardly hope to be considered an anthropologist.

But the term is also intensely debated within US cultural anthropological circles. On the one hand, many feel that its historical baggage, and the nature of contemporary analytical reflexivity is such, that, in contemplating contemporary global realities, the term is just too much of a burden to bear (Abu Lughod 1993). On the other hand there are those, such as Annette Weiner, who are able to imagine a more radical future for the culture concept. As Weiner puts it, 'culture is no longer a place or a group to be studied. Culture, as it is being used by many others, is about political rights and nation-building. It is also about attempts by third-world groups to fight off the domination of transnational economic policies that destroy these emergent rights as they establish their own nation-states' (1995: 18). Partly, this methodological optimism is possible because the notion of culture emerged in a clear, and highly polemicized political context, still associated, in an academic context, with the radical high ground. Boas's notion of culture emerged at the end of the nineteenth century in a highly polemicized intellectual environment, primarily to counter notions that human difference could be understood in racial, and hence evolutionary terms. His students, notably Melville Herskovits, maintained this position in the extremely polarized climate of race politics in America in the 1940s and 1950s. It is this radical position that is explicitly evoked in the introduction to Keil's classic, *Urban Blues* (Keil 1966): the failure to grasp blues as culture, Keil argues, can only lead to its categorization as a pathology, and this pathologizing would, inevitably, fuel racist arguments. Though adopting the Herderian principle that cultures should be understood as unique wholes, meaningful in their own terms, Boas also stressed, in tones which have a decidedly contemporary ring to them, both their fractured historical and materially mediated nature,[5] and that ethnography should be historical and material as well as being concerned with establishing the coherence and logic of different but nonetheless ultimately interpretable and understandable 'patterns of thought'.

Weiner's formulation continues to have a forceful ring to it because, for cultural anthropologists, ethnography has always been an art of interpretation, as opposed to the radically 'technical', scientific procedure for arriving at certain sociological truths, as it was in Britain following Malinowski. In comparison to Malinowski, Boas left much less of a programme on the subject of ethnography. His fieldwork was conducted in rather formal question-and-answer situations, focusing on the transcription of texts in what Sanjek (1990) has described as 'salvage ethnography' in the context of Native American reservation life in the 1890s. Louis Henry Morgan and Frank Cushing, who worked respectively among the Iroquois and the Zuni in the preceding decades, provide a more coherent model of participant-observation, at least as far as twentieth-century practitioners are concerned, but neither Morgan, Cushing or Boas could quite condense theory and technique with anything resembling Malinowski's modernist élan (Ardener 1990). Under these circumstances it is no surprise that the radical critique of ethnography

---

5 Not so different, then, from Straw's 'scenes', or from many of the other revisions of the notion of culture that have accompanied globalization theory.

in Clifford and Marcus's seminal, but angrily debated volume *Writing Culture* should come from a predominantly American culturalist avant-garde, and should target British social anthropological practice, particularly that from the 1940s and 1950s, for its links with colonialism, its scientism, and its failure to capitalize on the radical possibilities of ethnography as a site of dialogue, reflexivity and critique. Whether this represents a descent into total cultural relativism and atomism, or whether it really succeeds in meeting its own demands for radical dialogue are open to question. Anthropologists and ethnomusicologists are, it should be stressed, keenly aware of the issues involved,[6] a fact which often escapes their critics in cultural studies.

Music and its languages

Theory *per se* necessarily excludes 'non-theoretical' knowledge of the kind that might be provided by lay participants. This exclusion is achieved through a simplified and polemicized notion of anthropological and ethnomusicological thinking on the subjects of culture and ethnography, as I have tried to demonstrate. 'Non-theoretical' knowledges can thus be excluded because, simply, that is the kind of thing that ethnomusicologists and anthropologists are concerned with. But it is also based on what post-structuralist theory claims for itself, rather than just excludes. That based on varieties of Lacanian theory (see, for example, Shepherd and Wicke 1997; Middleton 1990; Poizat 1992) is based on the ideas that subjects are made through discourse, rather than vice versa; we 'are spoken' in complex and contradictory ways. Lacanian theorists argue that discourse bears the marks of primary crises in the process of early childhood development, is always fragmented, and thus imports that fragmentation into the process of subjectification. Lacanian theory attends to properties of discourse in material terms, and the complex ways in which the subject is made through processes of looking and hearing. Although Lacanian theory provides important cues for thinking about the different ways in which the experience of sound and vision shape our subjectivity, it is muddled by its reliance on Saussurean semiology, and the way in which this semiology assigns a central role to

---

6 See Barz and Cooley (1997), and the ongoing Clifford and Marcus debate, represented most recently by James, Hockey and Dawson (1997).

verbal signification. In the work of writers such as Barthes and Kristeva, a somewhat essentialized notion of music provides a necessary kind of foil to a logocentric semiology as language's 'other'. Middleton, Poizat, Shepherd and Wicke all offer productive ways of turning this logocentrism around, in particular permitting a grasp of the ways in which music, unlike language, operates through a semiology of repetition and attraction, rather than difference and binary opposition.

The process necessitates a clear differentiation between what is 'musical' and what is 'linguistic', and this process excludes the possibility of taking any hints from people's verbal cues as to what might be analytically important. Language about music belongs exclusively to the realm of the linguistic and is *ipso facto* irrelevant. Any effort to explain 'music' by reference to 'language about music' both repeats Barthes' and Kristeva's logocentrism (the assumption that things only become properly meaningful when translated into verbal language) and also reinscribes the Enlightenment tendency to organize all experience (visual as well as musical) in terms of rationalized 'grammars' (perspective, tonality, etc.) whose ultimate model is that of spoken discourse. This act of exclusion is fraught with problems, of both a theoretical and a methodological nature. Even if one were to maintain the distinction, and accept that 'language' has been hegemonic in the history of human cognition, it ignores the consequences of a possibility which is alluded to, but never fully explored or instantiated. Thus, language about music, and indeed all 'language', broadly conceived, might bear the mark of 'musical' experience, as Blacking's musical anthropology (1977) so forcefully asserted. It is not necessarily a means of subordinating a musical to a linguistic semiology or of 'confusing' the 'primary' qualities of the first with the 'secondary' qualities of the latter. When people use words to describe, organize or manipulate musical cognition, those words might be considered adjuncts of musical discourse, part of the process by which musical experience is recognized and organized, and not in some sense alien to it or parasitic upon it.

More persistent problems with poststructural theory (including that of Foucault) focus on issues of agency, resistance and, to quote Born, 'a lack of sociological acuity' (Born 1998). Both Foucauldian and Lacanian theory describe the ways in which discourse organizes subjectivity without offering a theorization of why it 'works' in some contexts and not in others; in short: how it is that people come to operate and think differently. Resistance, then, is abstracted, atomized and mystified, a de-ontologized anarchy, or encoded in a kind of sonambulistic process of 'iteration' (Spivak 1996) or 'sly civility' (Bhabha 1994), in somewhat random processes of enunciation, as colonized subjects repeat the colonial scripts that animate them. Born stresses the need to embrace the 'lack of fit' between the psychic dimensions of subject formation and 'an encultured, socially marked and socially motivated history' (1998: 381). The social spaces of creativity, agency, resistance on the one hand, and subordination, coercion, misrecognition and alienation on the other are complex and polyphonic. These problems revolve around a decisive separation of 'theoretical' from 'everyday' knowledge, in which 'everyday' knowledge is either reduced to routine processes of subject formation, or equally routine (though, in the end, entirely unexplained) tools of transgression and subversion. Post-Lacanian music theory takes the former route. The way people talk about music in an everyday context, whether making it or listening to it, constitute an integral part of music's discursive/linguistic disciplining, which can only be reversed in a quite different (though, ironically, still linguistic) space: that of theory.

It is in everyday language that people move in, around and through discourse. It is the task of an ethnography of the everyday to determine how this happens, under what circumstances and to what extent the multiple and overlapping knowledges deployed in everyday life are socially and culturally consequential, and when they are not. If music theory were to grasp the everyday, in this sense, an important conversation between music analysis and ethnomusicology could begin afresh. Music theory has provided two significant leads. One has emerged from the Copernican destabilization of Schenkerian orthodoxy in recent years most closely associated with the work of Cohn and Dempster (1992). The suggestion that a given musical surface might emerge from a variety of different transformational operations fragments the theoretical task and relocates it on the 'surface'. The acknowledgement that a given musical surface may be the end result of quite different operations not only disrupts the reductionist logic of the *Urlinie* and its attendant depth-surface hierarchies, but an entire representational paradigm (Cook 1999), according to which an analytical model is judged according to its ability to represent what is 'in/out there'. Once this is discarded performance, for example, characteristically judged by music theorists according to the extent that it reflects good analysis, might be seen as a means of recentring the (socially and culturally situated) musician in musical analysis, engaged in a creative and critical dialogue with the musical work, rather than simply being an abstracted conduit of it. Conversely, music theory itself might be understood in terms of performativity. Cook concludes:

> the paradigm of representation... brings with it that dogmatic partisanship that characterized music theory only a few years ago, when to believe (for instance) Schenkerian analysis implied the obligation to reject all other approaches as false. If today, by contrast, we are content to let a thousand flowers bloom, then the only epistemological basis for this must be a conviction that each approach creates its own truth through instigating its own perceptions, bringing into being a dimension of experience that will coexist with any number of others. Performativity, in short, is the foundation of pluralism. (Cook 1999: 261)

Another lead has come from cognitivism. Cognitive psychology has provided a language in which music analysts have begun to embrace the possibility that 'everyday' languages about music contain important keys to processes[7] that underpin musical cognition and experience, and that these processes have to be grasped *in situ*, rather than laboratory conditions, since musical experience never occurs in an act of semiotic seclusion. This constitutes an important step, bridging the gap in ways that yet may prove extremely productive between forms of music analysis that have not been particularly attentive to issues of experience, and forms of ethnographic analysis that have not been particularly attentive to the question of what and how we hear. Its most important contribution, often lost in embattled disciplinary exchanges, is to stress the attention that needs to be paid to the variety of knowledges, embodied in different cognitive styles, that make up social and cultural experience.

Cognitivists are more inclined to enumerate, typify and identify the processes at work in these knowledges, one might argue, and less inclined to grasp them sociologically, in relation to one another, and as instrumental (though not always in a direct relationship with avowed 'intentions') in shaping social realities. The tendency is, once again, to abstract formal models from the messy inconsequence of everyday life, as though the choice, if

---

7 Such as, for example, categorization: see Zbikowski (2002).

232

it is a choice, between modelling the world in one way and modelling it in another is, literally, immaterial. An ethnography of the ways in which theory is evoked, manipulated, positioned, ironized, ignored in everyday situations might provide exactly what cognitive theory currently misses: a sense of the ways in which 'theory' actually matters in concrete musical situations, and a sense of how a complex ensemble of knowledges operates at any given moment of musical production, with particular attention to something that one might describe as cognitive 'dissonance'. Sometimes the level of dissonance will be low, when a particular musical practice is so dominant, central and historically well-entrenched that ways of 'knowing' the music operate in an everyday and unremarkable harmony (even, or perhaps particularly, when matters of aesthetics are being discussed or debated), or when it is so marginal and socially insignificant that 'meaning' is a matter of social irrelevance. Alternatively, as is the case in a great deal of 'popular' music-making, the music is positioned awkwardly between social groups who invest in it in different ways, and compete to assign authoritative readings, either positive or negative. Any process of making music will be marked to a greater or lesser extent by this cognitive dissonance, and it is likely to be most sharply focused in the processes of communication and interaction that take place amongst those most directly involved in the making of it.

Sara Cohen's detailed study of two Liverpool bands, the 'Jactars' and 'Crikey it's the Cromptons!' exemplifies just this. At first sight, there is not much material for the music analyst: the author claims no musical expertise and her interlocutors appear to make a virtue of their musical 'ignorance'. Chapter 7, the section which attends most closely to the process of composition through rehearsal contains no musical notation. The author does little to alert the reader to the kinds of conclusions drawn in the next chapter. Following a certain anthropological convention, we are simply 'there', watching and listening to it all happen, in its rich and often contradictory complexity: 'theory' comes later. However, a strong contrast emerges. The two bands demonstrate quite opposed *modi operandi*. The Jactars are quiet, mutually supportive and laid back; the music emerges from a process of gelling together with the close and apparently unshakable friendship of two band members at its core. With Crikey it's the Cromptons!, in the second half of the chapter, the reader is instantly plunged into a world of tension, irritability and gendered anomie; one band member, the lead singer, composes on his

own; a final version subsequently emerges from hours of argument, antagonism and general bickering, described in detail. The contrast serves to make
the general point that the music that emerges in both cases conforms to the
wider and more generalized indie band aesthetic of 1980s Liverpool, but also
has to be understood as the product of two quite different forms of social
interaction. The author is ultimately concerned with the more general properties of Liverpool's Rock Culture: a common homosociality and exclusion of
women, a common effort to reconcile the conflicting demands of pervasive
ideologies of democracy and individualism, the common enchantment of
creativity and performance, and the central, driving force that this affective
experience plays in everyday urban lives. 'Theory' intervenes in band life in
contrasting ways. Two brief fragments illustrate.

In the first, The Jactars are working on a new song. They have worked
out the first two riffs, and are now in the process of putting them together.
'Trav proposes that they practise "the hard bit" – the change from one riff
to another, and Tog suggests that Trav shout "change" so the others know
when to go into the second riff. They begin again but stop to confer about
how many riffs to count before the change. Dave, Trav, and Gary watch each
other while they count and occasionally Dave mouths at them "after the
next one". They agree that it works. Dave comments approvingly on Gary's
"weird" drumming and Trav suggests that Gary lead them into the change
with a drum roll.

By the next rehearsal Dave has written some lyrics. Trav tries singing
them but suggests that the "pattern" (the music) should be sorted out
first. Again a long period of thought, practice and consultation (mainly
between Trav and Dave) ensues. Trav suggests that one bit might sound too
"Jamesish"[8] but Dave thinks it is all right. Dave suggests a different drum
beat to Gary but finds it hard to describe what he means, saying that he isn't
very good at "drum talk". Trav suggests that they switch one riff to $\frac{3}{4}$ time
and leave the other in $\frac{4}{4}$ which Dave says is a "real headful". They practise it
but have problems with the counting. Dave isn't sure if he likes it or not. He
can't work out why, but says, "It's a bit too choppy like" ' (Cohen 1991: 137).

Crikey it's the Cromptons! are also approaching a new song. 'Tony (the
vocalist) plays and sings the song to the others from beginning to end and then

8 The indie band 'James', gaining national popularity at the time [ed.].

234

repeats it. Within a short space of time they devise an accompaniment but Huw breaks off to complain that Tony keeps "changing the beat". They start again but Huw tells Tony that he still keeps changing the beat and obviously doesn't know what he's doing. "I'll give you a book on time signatures so you know what I'm talking about", he says and asks Tony if he knows the difference between a $\frac{4}{4}$ beat and a $\frac{4}{6}$ [sic]. Midi thinks he does and explains it to Tony. Huw instructs Tony to count as he plays but is frustrated that even when Tony does so he still changes the beat' (Cohen 1991: 154).

There are many contrasts to be drawn. The Jactars work on 'the pattern' first, and then add the vocals at a later stage. The process of working on the pattern is collective, to a high degree, and informed by a variety of cognitive styles that operate together with a minimum of dissonance. Even the mild expressions of disagreement seem to operate as a means of establishing consensus at a higher level. Much is taken for granted, and mechanisms for dealing with problems are quickly established and agreed upon. But the structuring of a contrast between the two riffs poses a particular problem at the moment Cohen describes. Trav suggests a time change: a 'theory-driven' suggestion, in advance, we assume, of any practical sense of how this will work out, but in the conviction that this technical procedure will make for the right kind of contrast. Other kinds of language have failed. Dave cannot make himself clear to Gary, and reflects on his failure to grasp 'drum talk'; he's not happy with the result of the metrical change, but again, can't work out why. The process of using language, 'theoretical' and otherwise, to describe or prescribe music, is marked in both cases by a great deal of introspection and evident anxiety on the part of the two bands. Both need, and have evidently developed, complex ways of evaluating sounds in the context of rehearsals, and of making concrete suggestions with regard to timbre, rhythm, tempo, pitch and so forth. Yet both also adhere to the post-punk indie aesthetic, in which 'musical' talk is out of place and an obstacle to the kind of 'upfront', 'chunky', 'punchy', 'ballsy' and 'thrashy' sound they prefer (Cohen 1991: 169). The result is a complex metapragmatic repertoire, a bricolage of technical knowledge derived from trade magazines and teach-yourself books, shared points of reference from record collections, and a handful of extremely flexible evaluative terms. The contradictions implicit in this situation only fully emerge when relations between band members disintegrate. This is evidently the case with Crikey it's the Cromptons! where

235

there is a marked antagonism between Tony (the lead singer) and Huw, which frequently plays itself out in arguments about 'theory', as the example above illustrates. Tony could, one assumes, easily dismiss Huw's bookishness. At the same time, Huw evidently has the tighter grasp on the situation, and is able to intervene more effectively when things break down, or reach points at which procedural decisions need to be made. Though Tony 'composes' the songs on tape, he is, it would appear, keenly aware of the difficulties involved in translating this act of composition to group performance, and regards Huw and Dave's mobilization of notebooks and chord charts with an uneasy mixture of contempt and undisguised admiration.

From the point of view of formal music theory, whose fundamental task is one of segmentation, and whose fundamental problem, as Agawu notes (Agawu 1999), is the problem of deciding on criteria of cultural relevance for segmentation to take place, these passages provide plenty of surprisingly detailed material for reflection, in which words point to, and manipulate, the musical experiences of timbre, metre, transposition, repetition. But they also suggest that different ways of 'knowing music' are at issue, that they intervene in moments of musical production, are argued out and resolved in particular and specific ways, and that an understanding of this music cannot take place without an understanding of them. The difficulty with this example is that it might appear to privilege a specific moment of 'creativity'. The insight can, however, easily be extended to more diffuse mass-mediated situations. The world of Turkish Arabesk, the subject of my own research in the 1980s, was marked by hugely varied ways of knowing, and complex and only partially overlapping vocabularies, all of which had to deal with the central fact that the music was scorned by the intelligentsia and banned from the state's media apparatus. For many fans, the music spoke of spectacular physical presences: a sound which 'burned' one, and remote and fabulous stars who would appear and dispense grace at rare public concerts. It spoke, too, of distinct physical processes and sensations. When opening lines, free rhythm moments of particular intensity, were described to me as an 'ejaculation', it was never clear whether the musical act was being sexualized, or the physical act was being musicalized.

Most singers saw themselves as poets, nuancing and adding meaning and expression to verbal texts; a few understood Turkish *makam* (modal) theory well, and could talk at some length about the relationship of melodic structures to lyric. Lyrics were, however, the central issue. Studio session musicians were professionals, who knew the genealogies of technique relating to their particular instruments, and plundered other genres like magpies for tips, ideas and technical inspiration. They rarely played together, and, it seemed to me, inhabited extraordinarily localized musical universes. Technicians appeared to be most fascinated by issues of technical expansion: use of more channels, larger string and percussion sections, innovative uses of newer keyboards to provide backing, and so forth. Managers and recording company executives also lived in a technical universe of distribution, combating piracy, gaining surreptitious access for their stars to the state's television and radio channels. Critics saw Arabesk as an all too coherent and all too threatening counter-narrative to the state's own narrative of progressive modernism, a story of Turkish inability to fully Westernize, of a weak and passive citizenry, who identified with stories of abasement, marginalization and humiliation and masochistic lyrics to dramatize their own, more inchoate, sense of social and political failure. If this was recognized at all by anybody in the multiple and overlapping worlds of Arabesk, it was either rejected outright, or ironized.

The lack of a clearly definable cultural 'script' bears heavily on questions of musical analysis in Arabesk. The impossibility of locating an authentic site of musical production to guide an analysis, an attempt to engage with the particularities of a particular song, might lead one to abandon the whole exercise. But the fact is that songs are considered things with identities that distinguish them from other songs, that some are evidently enormously successful, and others not, that some are valued and collected objects, listened to decades after they were recorded, whilst the majority have a life span of only a few months. An understanding of how a specific song is put together in the studio, and how its listeners make it 'work' for them is clearly crucial to any understanding of Arabesk. Clearly, any act of analysis has to be a kind of assemblage of quite different representational modalities: I attempted something of the kind in *The Arabesk Debate* (Stokes 1992), with particular attention to the kind of dissonances that arise when Arabesk is understood as a kind of rural music, or conversely, as a kind of urban music.

I took my cue from a music-industry-sponsored journal, *Müzik Magazin*, that constituted the only real 'music journalism' in Turkey at the time. Each issue would take a particular hit, and devote a page to it. The vocalist would remember the circumstances of its recording. The lyricist and songwriter (relatively minor players, at least in the view of the industry and most listeners) might be mentioned with a brief biography and list of previous hits. Occasionally the singer (if he happened to be the lyricist or composer, as is sometimes the case) might take the opportunity to remember the circumstances of composition. There were two central features that would dominate the page: one was a picture of the singer, and the other a facsimile of the notation used in the studio. An additional feature was a column by an academic taking the *makam* (the modal structure), and subjecting it to a 'traditional' Middle Eastern music analysis in terms of its segmental organization into sets of tetrachords and pentachords (*terkib*), its specific tonal constitution, and its predominant melodic direction (*seyir*). This column was eventually dropped, presumably because it was just too arid and, as time went on, Arabesk producers felt less and less need to seek this kind of 'high' theoretical justification for their music.

Though these pages were in some respects little more than a means of advertising and waging an occasional battle on the part of the music industry, they provided a useful framework for considering the various overlapping and sometime competing ways in which particular Arabesk songs produced meaning. Firstly the meaning of the song was grounded explicitly in the physical presence of the musician, the lead singer. It resided particularly in a repertoire of poses and glances, with clothing and sometime visual background a secondary semiotic. Secondly, the song was understood in terms of technical procedures, as it was assembled by lyricist and songwriter and found its way to the studio. 'The notes' are central here, providing information about rhythmic and melodic mode, but also about instrumental forces and orchestration. 'Technical' sophistication or ingenuity is, then, a matter of significance, for some, if not all of those who listen to Arabesk. Thirdly, the song pages provided a written narrative. These either discussed a moment of inspiration in ways that established a genealogy[9] or connected, however fleetingly, with the story told by films and videos, of brief encounters whilst pacing the streets, or riding public transport, of odd and arresting moments of inspiration (*ilham*). These separate modes of representing Arabesk do not

---

9 How, for example, Orhan Gencebay got the title of Cennet Gözlüm from a conversation with Zeki Müren.

fit together easily. The aesthetics of disruptive physical presence (expressed both in the large pictures, but also in the opening vocalises in Arabesk performance) do not sit easily with the fascination with technical mastery and orderly studio production. The narrative of orderly studio production does not fit well with the unruly narrative of inspiration. These three elements might, however, be understood as a kind of shorthand for understanding some of the institutional pressures that bore on Arabesk production at any given moment, chief among which were the reconciliation of commodity form and popular religion in a secular republic whose elites simultaneously used but publicly disavowed both.

The attempt to grasp Arabesk 'as music' is clearly vital and republican commentators, who have repeatedly tried to understand Arabesk as a kind of social 'text', have missed the crucial point that animates Arabesk socially and politically: it is music (Stokes 1994), mediated through social space in ways which are specific to an extremely popular mass-mediated music. An attempt to confront the everyday reality of Arabesk, as a musical experience, and from an ethnographic perspective, nonetheless raises some specific questions about what an analysis of popular music might look like. Ethnography, as stated and illustrated above, entirely removes the possibility of searching for an authentic, transparent 'native model'. If anything, it provides exactly the opposite: instances of musical production in which different modes of knowing music compete, and only occasionally connect, with one another. It is, perhaps, music's semiotic multiplicity that makes it so valuable, so pleasurable, and so consequential. It also provides the strongest grounds for a convergence of ethnomusicological and music theoretical interest. A thousand flowers should, and will bloom, to return to Cook's comment, as long as that multiplicity is culturally grasped.

239

Bibliography

Abu Lughod, L. 1993: *Writing Women's Worlds* (Berkeley: California University Press).

Adorno, T. W. 1973: *Philosophy of Modern Music* (London: Sheed & Ward).

1974: *Negative Dialectics* (London: Routledge).

1978: 'On the Fetish Character in Music and the Regression of Listening', in A. Arato and E. Gebhardt (eds.), *The Essential Frankfurt School Reader* (Oxford: Oxford University Press), pp. 270–99, originally 1938.

1981: 'Perennial Fashion – Jazz', in *Prisms* (Cambridge Mass.: MIT Press), pp. 119–32.

Agawu, K. 1996: 'Analyzing Music under the New Musicological Regime', *Music Theory Online* 2/4, May.

1999: 'The Challenge of Semiotics' in Cook and Everist (1999), pp. 138–60.

Ake, D. 1998: *Being Jazz: Identities and Images* (Ph.D. Diss., UCLA; forthcoming from University of California Press).

Allan, G. 1986: *The Importances of the Past* (New York: State University of New York Press).

Amin, A. 1991: 'These Are Not Marshallian Times', in R. Camagni (ed.), *Innovation Networks and Spatial Perspectives* (London: Belhaven), pp. 105–17.

Amin, A. ed. 1994: *Postfordism: A Reader* (Oxford: Blackwell).

Amin, A. 1994a: 'Post-Fordism: Models, Fantasies and Phantoms of Transition', in Amin (1994), pp. 1–39.

Amin, A. and N. Thrift 1994: 'Living in the Global', in Ash Amin and Nigel Thrift (eds.), *Globalization, Institutions and Regional Development in Europe* (Oxford: Oxford University Press), pp. 1–22.

Anderson, I. 1993a: 'Talking Tull', in Karl Schramm and Gerald Burns (eds.), *Jethro Tull: The Complete Lyrics* (Heidelberg: Palmyra), pp. 7–25.

1993b: Liner notes to Jethro Tull: *25th anniversary* CD set (London: Chrysalis).

Antokoletz, E. 1992: *Twentieth-Century Music* (Englewood Cliffs, NJ: Prentice Hall).

ASDA 1998: annual report May 1997–May 1998, August.

Attridge, D. 1995: *Poetic Meter: An Introduction* (Cambridge: Cambridge University Press).

Austin, W. 1966: *Music in the Twentieth Century* (New York: Norton).

240

Baily, J. 1981: 'A System of Modes Used in the Urban Music of Herat', *Ethnomusicology* 25/1, pp. 1–39.

Bakhtin, M. M. 1981: *The Dialogic Imagination: Four Essays*, ed. M. Holquist, trans. C. Emerson and M. Holquist (Austin: University of Texas Press).

Barfield, O. 1988: *Saving the Appearances: a Study in Idolatry* (Hanover, NH: Wesleyan University Press), originally 1957.

Baring-Gould, S. *et al.* 1889: *Songs from the West* (London: Methuen).

Barnard, A. and J. Spencer 1996: 'Culture', in A. Barnard and J. Spencer (eds.), *Encyclopedia of Social and Cultural Anthropology* (London: Routledge).

Barnard, S. 1989: *On the Radio: Music Radio in Britain* (Milton Keynes: Open University Press).

Barthes, R. 1984: 'The Grain of the Voice', in *Image–Music–Text* (London: Fontana), pp. 179–89.

Barz, G. and T. Cooley 1997: *Shadows in the Field: New Perspectives on Fieldwork in Ethnomusicology* (New York: Oxford University Press).

Bateson, G. 1979: *Mind and Nature* (London: Wildwood House).

Bent, I. and W. Drabkin 1990: *Analysis* (London: Macmillan).

Bergero, K. and P. Bohlman (eds.) 1992: *Disciplining Music: Musicology and its Canons* (Chicago: Chicago University Press).

Berlyne, D. 1971: *Aesthetics and Psychobiology* (New York: Appleton-Century-Crofts).

Bhabha, H. 1994: *The Location of Culture* (London: Routledge).

Björnberg, A. 1998: 'Harmony Corruption: On Tonal Analysis of Contemporary Popular Styles', unpublished MS.

Blacking, J. 1977: *The Anthropology of the Body* (London: Academic Press).

Blasius, L. 1996: *Schenker's Argument and the Claims of Music Theory* (Cambridge: Cambridge University Press).

Blom, J-P. and T. Kvifte 1986: 'On the Problem of Inferential Ambivalence in Musical Meter', *Ethnomusicology* 30/3, pp. 491–517.

Bluestone, B. 1995: *The Polarization of American Society: Victims, Suspects, and Mysteries to Unravel* (New York: Twentieth Century Fund Press [http://epn.org/tcf/xxblue.html]).

Bom, G. 1998: 'Anthropology, Kleinian Psychoanalysis, and the Subject in Culture': *American Anthropologist* 100/2, pp. 373–86.

Boulez, P. 1952: 'Schoenberg is Dead', in *Stocktakings from an Apprenticeship* (Oxford: Clarendon, 1991), pp. 29–41.

Brackett, D. 1995: *Interpreting Popular Music* (Cambridge: Cambridge University Press).

Bradby, B. 1990: 'Do-Talk and Don't Talk: The Division of the Subject in Girl-Group Music', in Frith and Goodwin (1990), pp. 341–68.

Brogan, T. 1993: 'Rhyme', in Preminger and Brogan (1993), pp. 1052–64.

241

Bromberg, C. 1989: *The Wicked Ways of Malcolm McLaren* (New York: Harper and Row).

Bruner, G. 1990: 'Music, Mood and Marketing', *Journal of Marketing* 54, pp. 94–104.

Buhler, J. 1997: 'The Frankfurt School Blues: Rethinking Adorno's Critique of Jazz', Paper delivered to the American Musicological Society and Society for Music Theory, Phoenix.

Burnett, R. 1996: *The Global Jukebox: The International Music Industry* (London: Routledge).

Butler, C. 1980: *After the Wake* (Oxford: Clarendon).

Butler, D. 1997: 'Buy Me! Think You Only Buy What You Want? Think Again', *Accountancy*, September, pp. 32–4.

Carroll, D. 1987: *Paraesthetics: Foucault, Lyotard, Derrida* (London: Methuen).

Chambers, I. 1990: *Border Dialogues: Journeys in Postmodernity* (London: Routledge).

Chandler, A. 1990: *Scale and Scope: The Dynamics of Industrial Capitalism* (Cambridge: Belknap Press) with the asssistance of Takashi Hikino.

Chernoff, J. M. 1979: *African Rhythm and African Sensibility* (Chicago: Chicago University Press).

Chion, M. 1994: *Audio-Vision: Sound on Screen*, ed. and trans. Claudia Gorbman (New York: Columbia University Press).

Christensen, T. 1993: *Rameau and Musical Thought in the Enlightenment* (Cambridge: Cambridge University Press).

Clare, J. 1998: 'Calm Music Helps Pupils to Learn', *Daily Telegraph*, 19 August, p. 8.

Clifford, J. and G. Marcus 1986: *Writing Culture: The Poetics and Politics of Ethnography* (Berkeley: University of California Press).

Cohen, S. 1991: *Rock Culture in Liverpool: Popular Music in the Making* (Oxford: Clarendon Press).

Cohn, R. and D. Dempster 1992: 'Hierarchical Unity, Plural Unities' in Katherine Bergeron and Philip Bohlman (eds.), *Disciplining Music* (Chicago: Chicago University Press), pp. 156–81.

Coker, W. 1972: *Music and Meaning* (New York: The Free Press).

Cole, P. 1992: 'Peer Pressures: Kenny G', *Down Beat*, November, pp. 22–4.

Cook, N. 1998a: *Analysing Musical Multimedia* (Oxford: Clarendon).

   1998b: *Music: A Very Short Introduction* (Oxford: Oxford University Press).

   1999: 'Analysing Performance, Performing Analysis' in Nicholas Cook and Mark Everist (eds.), *Rethinking Music* (Oxford: Oxford University Press).

Cook, N. and M. Everist 1999: *Rethinking Music* (Oxford: Oxford University Press).

Cooke, D. 1959: *The Language of Music* (London: Barrie & Rockliff).

Cooke, P. and K. Morgan 1993: 'The Network Paradigm: New Departures in Corporate and Regional Development', *Environment and Planning D* 8, pp. 7–34.

242

Corbett, J. 1994: *Extended Play: Sounding Off from John Cage to Dr. Funkenstein* (Durham, NC: Duke University Press).

Costello, M. and D. Foster Wallace 1990: *Signifying Rappers* (Hopewell, NJ: Ecco Press).

Costley, J. 1995: 'Equities Pricing via Satellite', TMA News & Views – Satellite, Radio and Broadcast (web-based news and archiving service: www.tma.org.uk).

Covach, J. 1994: 'Destructuring Cartesian Dualism in Musical Analysis', *Music Theory Online* 0/11.

1995: 'Schoenberg's Turn to an "Other" World', *Music Theory Online* 1/5.

1997: 'Progressive Rock, "Close to the Edge", and the Boundaries of Style', in Covach and Boone (1997), pp. 3–31.

2000: 'Jazz-Rock? Rock-Jazz? Stylistic Crossover in Late-1970s American Progressive Rock', in Walter Everett (ed.), *Expressions in Pop-Rock Music* (New York: Garland), pp. 113–34.

forthcoming: 'Form in Rock Music: A Primer', in Deborah Stein and Cynthia Gonzales (eds.), *Essays in Musical Analysis* (Berkeley and London: University of California Press).

Covach, J. and G. Boone (eds.) 1997: *Understanding Rock: Essays in Musical Analysis* (Oxford: Oxford University Press).

Crescenti, P. 1977: 'Foreigner: An Anatomy of Success', *Circus* 165 (29 September 1977).

Crozier, W. 1997: 'Music and Social Influence', in Hargreaves and North (1997a), pp. 67–83.

Cubitt, S. 1984: ' "Maybelline": Meaning and the Listening Subject', *Popular Music*, 4, pp. 207–24.

Cunningham, M. 1998: *Good Vibrations: A History of Record Production* (London: Sanctuary Publishing).

Dalmonte, R. and M. Baroni (eds.) 1992: *Secondo Convegno Europeo di Analisi Musicale* (Trent: Università degli studi di Trento).

Davis, J. 1986: *Talking Heads* (New York: Vintage).

Davis, M. 1990: *City of Quartz: Excavating the Future in Los Angeles* (London: Verso).

Davis, M. with Q. Troupe 1989: *Miles: The Autobiography* (New York: Simon and Schuster).

Day, A. 1988: *Jokerman: Reading the Lyrics of Bob Dylan* (Oxford: Basil Blackwell).

DeMott, B. 1995: *The Trouble with Friendship: Why Americans Can't Think Straight about Race* (New York: The Atlantic Monthly Press).

DeVeaux, S. 1991: 'Constructing the Jazz Tradition: Jazz Historiography', *Black American Literature Forum* 25/3, pp. 525–60.

DiMaggio, P. 1982a: 'Cultural Entrepreneurship in Nineteenth-Century Boston: The Creation of an Organizational Base for High Culture in America', *Media, Culture and Society* 4, pp. 33–50.

243

1982b: 'Cultural Entrepreneurship in Nineteenth-Century Boston, Part II: The Classification and Framing of American Art', *Media, Culture and Society* 4, pp. 303–22.

Doise, W. 1986: *Levels of Explanation in Social Psychology* (Cambridge: Cambridge University Press).

Duncan, J. 1998: *The Making of The X-Files: Fight the Future* (London: Voyager).

Dylan, B. 1987: *Lyrics 1962–85* (London: Jonathan Cape).

Eagleton, T. 1990: *The Ideology of the Aesthetic* (Oxford: Blackwell).

Eddy, C. 1997: *The Accidental Evolution of Rock 'n' Roll: A Misguided Tour through Rock Music* (New York: Da Capo).

Ehrenzweig, A. 1973: *The Hidden Order of Art* (London: Granada).

Eisen, J. (ed.) 1969: *The Age of Rock: Sound of the American Cultural Revolution* (New York: Vintage).

Elam, M. 1994. 'Puzzling out the Post-Fordist Debate: Technology, Markets and Institutions', in Amin (1994), pp. 43–70.

Elias, N. 1982: *The Civilizing Process* (New York: Pantheon).

Emands, B. 1978: 'The Awful Truth About Foreigner', *New Musical Express* (16 September).

Euripides 1986: *The Bacchae and Other Plays* (Harmondsworth: Penguin).

Everett, W. 1997: 'Swallowed by a Song: Paul Simon's Crisis of Chromaticism', in Covach and Boone (1997), pp. 113–53.

(ed.) 2000: *Expression in Pop-Rock Music* (New York: Garland).

Feld, S. 1990: *Sound and Sentiment: Birds, Weeping, Poetics, and Song in Kaluli Expression*, 2nd edn (Philadelphia: University of Pennsylvania Press).

Fischer, Michael M. J. 1986: 'Ethnicity and the Post-Modern Arts of Memory', in James Clifford and George E. Marcus (eds.), *Writing Culture: The Poetics and Politics of Ethnography* (Berkeley: University of California Press), pp. 194–233.

Fiske, J. 1987: *Television Culture* (London: Routledge).

Flanagan, B. (ed.) 1990: *Written in My Soul: Candid Interviews with Rock's Greatest Songwriters* (London: Omnibus).

Fleeman, J. D. 1971: *Johnson: The Complete English Poems* (Harmondsworth: Penguin).

Fomäs, J. 1995: *Cultural Theory and Late Modernity* (London: Sage).

Forte, A. 1995: *The American Popular Ballad of the Golden Era 1924–1950* (Princeton: Princeton University Press).

Frith, S. 1983: *Sound Effects* (London: Constable).

1988: 'Why do Songs have Words?' in *Music for Pleasure: Essays in the Sociology of Pop* (Cambridge: Polity), pp. 105–28.

1996: *Performing Rites: On the Value of Popular Music* (Oxford: Oxford University Press).

Frith, S. and A. Goodwin (eds.) 1990: *On Record: Rock, Pop, and the Written Word* (London: Routledge).

Gabbard, K. 1993: 'The Jazz Canon and its Consequences', *Annual Review of Jazz Studies* 6, pp. 65–98.

Gallagher, T., M. Campbell and M. Gillies 1995: *All Men Have Secrets* (London: Virgin).

Goehr, L. 1994: *The Imaginary Museum of Musical Works* (Oxford: Clarendon).

Goldstein, T. 1985: *Frozen Fire: The Cars* (Chicago: Contemporary Books).

Goodwin, A. 1990: 'Sample and Hold: Pop Music in the Digital Age of Reproduction', in Frith and Goodwin (1990), pp. 258–76.

    1998: 'Drumming and Memory: Scholarship, Technology, and Music-Making', in T. Swiss, J. Sloop and A. Herman (eds.), *Mapping the Beat: Popular Music and Contemporary Theory* (Oxford: Blackwell), pp. 121–36.

Gracyk, T. 1996: *Rhythm and Noise* (London: I. B.Tauris).

Gramsci, A. 1971: *Selections from the Prison Notebooks*, ed. and trans. Q. Hoare and G. N. Smith (New York: International).

Gray, M. 1981: *Song and Dance Man: The Art of Bob Dylan*, 2nd edn (London: Hamlyn).

    1996: *It Crawled from the South: An R.E.M. Companion*, 2nd edn (London: Fourth Estate).

Greenwood, D. 1978: 'Culture by the Pound: An Anthropological Perspective on Tourism as Cultural Commodification' in V. L. Smith (ed.): *Hosts and Guests: The Anthropology of Tourism* (Oxford: Blackwell).

Griffiths, D. 1992: 'Talking about Popular Song: In Praise of "Anchorage"', in Dalmonte and Baroni (1992), pp. 351–8.

Grossberg, L. 1990: 'Is There Rock After Punk?', in Frith and Goodwin (1990), pp. 111–23.

    1992: *We Gotta Get Outta This Place* (London: Routledge).

Guck, M. A. 1994: 'Rehabilitating the Incorrigible', in Pople (1994), pp. 57–73.

Hadlington, S. 1998: 'How the Right Music Makes You Run Faster', *Independent on Sunday*, 5 July, p. 5.

Hall, S. and T. Jefferson (eds.) 1976: *Resistance Through Rituals* (London: Hutchinson).

Hamilton, A. 1998: 'Piper Calls the Tune in March against Muzak', *The Times*, 12 December, p. 6.

Hamm, C. 1979: *Yesterdays* (New York: Norton).

    1983: *Music in the New World* (New York: Norton).

Handelman, D. 1990: *Models and Mirrors: Towards an Anthropology of Public Events* (Cambridge: Cambridge University Press).

Hannigan, J. 1998: *Fantasy City: Pleasure and Profit in the Postmodern Metropolis* (London: Routledge).

Hardt, M. and A. Negri 2000: *Empire* (Cambridge, Mass.: Harvard University Press).

Hargreaves, D. and A. North (eds.) 1997a: *The Social Psychology of Music* (Oxford: Oxford University Press).

Hargreaves, D. and A. North 1997b: 'The Social Psychology of Music', in Hargreaves and North (1997a), pp. 1–21.

Harris, C., R. Bradley and S. Titus 1992: 'A Comparison of the Effects of Hard Rock and Easy Listening on the Frequency of Observed Inappropriate Behaviours: Control of Environmental Antecedents in a Large Public Area', *Journal of Music Therapy* 29, pp. 6–17.

Harris, J. F. 1993: *Philosophy at 33 1/3 rpm* (Chicago: Open Court).

Harrison, C. and P. Wood (eds.) 1992: *Art in Theory, 1900–1990: An Anthology of Changing Ideas* (Oxford: Blackwell).

Harry, D., C. Stein and V. Bockris 1998: *Making Tracks: The Rise of Blondie* (New York: Da Capo).

Hartman, G. 1997: *The Fateful Question of Culture* (New York: Columbia University Press).

Harvey, D. 1989: *The Condition of Postmodernity* (Oxford: Blackwell).

Hawkins, S. 1993: 'Perspectives and Problems within the Analysis of Popular Music: "Lost in Music"', Paper presented at 5th British Music Analysis Conference/ 28th Annual RMA Conference, Southampton University (March).

Headlam, D. 1997: 'Blues Transformations in the Music of Cream', in Covach and Boone (1997), pp. 59–92.

Hebdige, R. 1979: *Subculture: The Meaning of Style* (London: Methuen).

Heckman, D. 1996: Review of Kenny G's *The Moment*, *Los Angeles Times*, 5 October, p. F6.

Hennion, A. 1983: 'The Production of Success: An Anti-musicology of the Pop Song', *Popular Music* 3, pp. 32–40.

Herder, J. G. 1993: *Against Pure Reason: Writings on Religion, Language and History*, ed. and trans. M. Bunge (Minneapolis: Fortress).

Hesmondhalgh, D. 1996: 'Flexibility, Post-Fordism and the Music Industries', *Media, Culture & Society* 18/3, pp. 469–88.

Heylin, C. 1993: *From the Velvets to the Voidoids: A Pre-Punk History for a Post-Punk World* (London and New York: Penguin).

1996: *Behind Closed Doors: The Recording Sessions 1960–1994* (Harmondsworth: Penguin).

Hill, D. and J. Weingrad 1987: *Saturday Night: A Backstage History of Saturday Night Live* (New York: Vintage Books).

Hinton, B. 1999: *Let Them All Talk: The Music of Elvis Costello* (London: Sanctuary Publishing).

Hirst, P. and J. Zeitlin 1991: 'Flexible Specialization Versus Post-Fordism: Theory, Evidence and Policy Implications', *Economy and Society* 20/1, pp. 1–56.

Hodgart, M. (ed.) 1965: *The Faber Book of Ballads* (London: Faber).

Hole, C. 1978: *A Dictionary of British Folk Customs* (London: Granada).

Horkheimer, M. and T. W. Adorno 1986: *Dialectic of Enlightenment* (New York: Continuum).

Hoskyns, B. 1994: Interview with Joni Mitchell, *Mojo*, 12A (December), p. 49.

Huddleston, N. 1998: 'Shop Till You Bop', *Off-Licence News*, 24 November, pp. 10–11.

Hughes, M. A. 1989: 'Misspeaking Truth to Power: A Geographical Perspective on the "Underclass" Fallacy', *Economic Geography* 65/3, pp. 187–207.

    1990: 'Formation of the Impacted Ghetto: Evidence from Large Metropolitan Areas, 1970–1980', *Urban Geography* 11/3, pp. 265–84.

Hughes, W. 1994: 'In the Empire of the Beat: Discipline and Disco', in Ross and Rose (1994), pp. 147–57.

Huyssen, A. 1986: *After the Great Divide: Modernism, Mass Culture, Postmodernism* (Bloomington: Indiana University Press).

Hyer, B. 1989: 'Tonal Intuitions in *Tristan und Isolde*'; Ph.D. diss., Yale University.

Jackson, J. 1999: *A Cure for Gravity* (New York: PublicAffairs).

James, A., J. Hockey and A. Dawson 1997: *After Writing Culture: Epistemology and Praxis in Contemporary Anthropology* (London: Routledge).

James, M. 1997: *State of Bass: Jungle: The Story So Far* (London: Boxtree).

Jameson, F. 1979: 'Reification and Utopia in Mass Culture', *Social Text* 1/1, pp. 130–48.

    1984: 'Postmodernism, or the Cultural Logic of Late Capitalism', *New Left Review* 146, pp. 53–92.

Jones, L. 1963: *Blues People: Negro Music in White America* (New York: William Morrow).

Josephson, N. S. 1992: 'Bach meets Liszt: Traditional Formal Structures and Performance Practices in Progressive Rock', *Musical Quarterly* 76/1, pp. 67–92.

Kasarda, J. 1990: 'Structural Factors Affecting the Location and Timing of Urban Underclass Growth', *Urban Geography* 11/3, pp. 234–64.

Keil, C. 1991: *Urban Blues* (Chicago: Chicago University Press), originally 1966.

    1994: 'Motion and Feeling through Music', originally 1964, in Keil and Feld (1994), pp. 53–76.

Keil, C. and S. Feld 1994: *Music Grooves* (Chicago: University of Chicago Press).

Kempster, C. (ed.) 1996: *History of House* (London: Sanctuary Publishing Ltd).

Kerman, J. 1980: 'How We Got Into Analysis, and How To Get Out', *Critical Inquiry* 7, pp. 311–31.

1985: *Musicology* (London: Fontana), published in the USA as *Contemplating Music* (Cambridge, Mass.: Harvard University Press).

Klumpenhouwer, H. 1998. 'Commentary: Poststructuralism and Issues of Music Theory', in Adam Krims (ed.), *Music/Ideology: Resisting the Aesthetic* (New York: Gordon and Breach), pp. 289–310.

Kohlhasse, B. 1997: 'Marking a Decade of All That Smooth Jazz', *Los Angeles Times*, 4 August, pp. F8, F11.

Koppl, R. 1998: 'Mark Snow: Scoring *The X-Files*: A Challenging Transition', *Music from the Movies* 21, pp. 6–13.

Kramer, L. 1995: *Classical Music and Postmodern Knowledge* (Berkeley: University of California Press).

Krims, A. 1998: 'Introduction: Postmodern Musical Poetics and the Problem of "Close Reading"' in Adam Krims (ed.): *Music/Ideology: Resisting the Aesthetic* (New York: Gordon and Breach), pp. 1–15.

2000: *Rap Music and the Poetics of Identity* (Cambridge: Cambridge University Press).

forthcoming: 'Disco Seen From a Changing City', in Mitchell Morris (ed.), *Disco's Distinctions: Essays in Music, Sexuality, and Commerce* (Berkeley: University of California Press).

Kuper, A. 1999: *Among the Anthropologists: History and Context in Anthropology* (London: Athlone).

Lakoff, G. and M. Johnson 1980: *Metaphors We Live By* (Chicago: University of Chicago Press).

Langlois, T. 1992: 'Can You Feel It? DJs and House Music Culture in the UK', *Popular Music*, 11/2, pp. 229–38.

Lanza, J. 1995: *Elevator Music: A Surreal History of Muzak, Easy-Listening and Other Moodsong* (London: Quartet).

Lash, S. and J. Urry 1987: *The End of Organized Capitalism* (Cambridge: Polity).
1994: *Economies of Signs and Space* (London: Sage).

Lebrecht, N. 1998: 'Fans Celebrate as Prokofiev Scores', *Daily Telegraph*, 11 March, p. 1.

Lee, S. 1995: 'Re-Examining the Concept of the "Independent" Record Company: The Case of Wax Trax! Records', *Popular Music* 14, pp. 13–31.

Lenin, V. I. 1996: *Imperialism, the Highest Stage of Capitalism: A Popular Outline*, trans. and ed. Norman Lewis and James Malone (London: Junius).

Lerdahl, F. and R. Jackendoff 1983: *A Generative Theory of Tonal Music* (Cambridge, Mass.: MIT Press).

Levine, L. W. 1988: *Highbrow/Lowbrow: The Emergence of Cultural Hierarchy in America* (Cambridge, Mass.: Harvard University Press).
1993: *The Unpredictable Past: Explorations in American Cultural History* (New York: Oxford University Press).

1996: *The Opening of the American Mind: Canons, Culture, and History* (Boston: Beacon Press).

Lewis, L. 1990: *Gender Politics and MTV: Voicing the Difference* (Philadelphia: Temple University Press).

Lipsitz, G. 1990: *Time Passages: Collective Memory and American Popular Culture* (Minneapolis: University of Minnesota Press).

1991: 'High Culture and Hierarchy', review of Levine: *Highbrow/Lowbrow*, *American Quarterly* 43/3, p. 520.

1994: 'We Know What Time It Is: Race, Class, and Youth Culture in the Nineties', in Ross and Rose (1994), pp. 17–28.

1995: *Dangerous Crossroads: Popular Music, Postmodernism and the Poetics of Place* (London: Verso).

1998: *The Possessive Investment in Whiteness: How White People Profit from Identity Politics* (Philadelphia: Temple University Press).

Lindsay, J. 1979: *Javanese Gamelan* (Oxford: Oxford University Press).

de Lisle, T. 1996: 'Just Don't Call Them Jingles', *Daily Telegraph*, 26 March, p. 25.

Lomax, A. 1970: 'The Homogeneity of Afro-American Musical Style', in N. Whitten and J. Szwed (eds.), *Afro-American Anthropology: Contemporary Perspectives* (New York: Free Press), pp. 181–201.

Lowry, B. 1995: *The Truth Is Out There: The Official Guide to The X-Files* (London: HarperCollins).

1996: *Trust No One: The Official Third Season Guide to The X-Files* (London: HarperCollins).

Lydon, J. (Johnny Rotten) 1994: *Rotten: No Irish, No Blacks, No Dogs: The Authorized Biography of Johnny Rotten of the Sex Pistols* (New York: St Martin's Press).

Lyotard, J.-F. 1984: *The Postmodern Condition: A Report on Knowledge*, trans. B. Massumi (Manchester: Manchester University Press).

1988: *The Differend: Phrases in Dispute* (Manchester: Manchester University Press).

1993: *Libidinal Economy* (London: Athlone).

Machlis, J. 1979: *Introduction to Contemporary Music*, 2nd edn (New York: W. W. Norton).

Manuel, P. 1993: *Cassette Culture: Popular Music and Technology in North India* (Chicago: University of Chicago Press).

Marcu, V. 1927: *Lenin: 30 Jahre Russland* (Leipzig: List).

Marcus, G. and M. Fischer 1986: *Anthropology as Cultural Critique: An Experimental Moment in the Human Sciences* (Chicago: University of Chicago Press).

Marsh, D. 1989: *The Heart of Rock and Soul: The 1001 Greatest Singles Ever Made* (Harmondsworth: Penguin).

Martin, P. 1995: *Sounds and Society: Themes in the Sociology of Music* (Manchester: Manchester University Press).

Martin, S. 1986: *Art, Messianism and Crime: A Study of Antinomianism in Modern Literature and Lives* (Basingstoke: Macmillan).

Matteson, S. 1998: 'Gag Me with a Soprano Sax', *New Times Los Angeles*, 11–17 June, p. 3.

McClary, S. 1991: *Feminine Endings: Music, Gender and Sexuality* (Minneapolis: University of Minnesota Press).

1994: 'Same As It Ever Was: Youth Culture and Music', in Ross and Rose (1994), pp. 29–40.

McClary, S. and Walser, R. 1990: 'Start Making Sense! Musicology Wrestles with Rock', in Frith and Goodwin (1990), pp. 277–92.

McCrystal, C. 1998: 'Wield that Baton – Want to Control a Riot? Play Them Vivaldi', *Observer Review*, 15 March, p. 1.

McMahon, B. 1998: untitled story from 'This is America' column, *Evening Standard*, 7 August, p. 21.

Mele, C. 1996: 'Globalization, Culture, and Neighborhood Change: Reinventing the Lower East Side of New York', *Urban Affairs Review* 32/1, pp. 3–22.

Mellers, W. 1965: *Music in the New World* (New York: Knopf).

1973: *Twilight of the Gods: The Beatles in Retrospect* (London: Faber).

Meltzer, R. 1970: *The Aesthetics of Rock* (New York: Da Capo).

Mendelsohn, J. 1978: 'Foreigner's Road Map: Destination Top Ten', *Rolling Stone* 264 (4 May).

van der Merwe, P. 1989: *Origins of the Popular Style* (Oxford: Oxford University Press).

Meyer, L. 1956: *Emotion and Meaning in Music* (Chicago: University of Chicago Press).

1989: *Style and Music: Theory, History and Ideology* (Philadelphia: Pennsylvania University Press).

Michaelson, J. 1996: 'The Wave's on Crest of Popularity', *Los Angeles Times*, 6 August, pp. F1, F6.

Middleton, R. 1972: *Pop Music and the Blues* (London: Gollancz).

1981: 'Reading Popular Music', in *Form and Meaning* 2 (Buckingham: Open University Press).

1990: *Studying Popular Music* (Buckingham: Open University Press).

1992: Review of S. Blum, P. Bohlman and D. Neuman: *Ethnomusicology and Modern Music History*, *Popular Music* 11/3, pp. 371–3.

1993: 'Popular Music and Musicology: Bridging the Gap', *Popular Music* 12/2, pp. 177–90.

2000: *Reading Pop: Approaches to Textual Analysis in Popular Music* (Oxford: Oxford University Press).

Miles (ed.) 1978: *Bob Dylan in His Own Words* (London: Omnibus).

Milliman, R. 1982: 'Using Background Music to Affect the Behaviour of Supermarket Shoppers', *Journal of Marketing* 46, pp. 85–91.

Mishel, L. and J. Bernstein 1994. *Is the Technology Black Box Empty? An Empirical Examination of the Impact of Technology on Wage Inequality and the Employment Structure* (Washington, DC: Economic Policy Institute).

Moelants, D. 1997: 'A Framework for the Subsymbolic Description of Meter', in M. Leman (ed.), *Music, Gestalt, and Computing* (Berlin: Springer), pp. 263–76.

Monelle, R. 2000: *The Sense of Music* (Princeton: Princeton University Press).

Moore, A. F. 2001a: *Rock: The Primary Text*, 2nd edn (Aldershot: Ashgate).

    2001b: 'Questioni di stile, genere e idioletto nel rock', *Musica realtà* 64, pp. 85–102.

Morgan, R. P. 1991: *Twentieth-Century Music: A History of Musical Style in Modern Europe and America* (New York: Norton).

    1998: *Source Readings in Music History: The Twentieth Century*, rev. edn (New York: Norton).

Negus, K. 1992: *Producing Pop* (London: Edward Arnold).

    1997: *Popular Music in Theory: An Introduction* (Hanover, NH: University Press of New England).

Neuenfeldt, K. 1999: 'The Yanni Phenomenon: Musical Exotica, Memories, and Multi-Media Marketing', in P. Hayward (ed.), *Widening the Horizon: Exoticism in Post-War Popular Music* (London: John Libbey).

Nietzsche, F. 1993: *The Birth of Tragedy Out of the Spirit of Music* (Harmondsworth: Penguin).

North, A. and D. Hargreaves 1995: 'Subjective Complexity, Familiarity, and Liking for Popular Music', *Psychomusicology* 14, pp. 77–93.

    1996a: 'The Effects of Music on Responses to a Dining Area', *Journal of Environmental Psychology* 24, pp. 55–64.

    1996b: 'Responses to Music in a Dining Area', *Journal of Applied Social Psychology* 24, pp. 491–501.

    1996c: 'Situational Influences on Reported Musical Preferences', *Psychomusicology* 15, pp. 30–45.

    1996d: 'Responses to Music in Aerobic Exercise and Yogic Relaxation Classes', *British Journal of Psychology* 87, pp. 535–47.

    1997a: 'The Musical Milieu: Studies of Listening in Everyday Life', *The Psychologist* 10, pp. 309–12.

    1997b: 'Experimental Aesthetics and Everyday Music Listening', in Hargreaves and North (1997a), pp. 84–103.

    1997c: 'Music and Consumer Behaviour', in Hargreaves and North (1997a), pp. 268–89.

North, A., D. Hargreaves and J. McKendrick 1997: 'In-store Music Affects Product Choice', *Nature* 390, p. 132.

    1999: 'Music and On-hold Waiting Time', *British Journal of Psychology* 90, pp. 161–4.

Oliver, M. L. and T. M. Shapiro 1995: *Black Wealth/White Wealth: A New Perspective on Racial Inequality* (New York: Routledge).

Parker, M. 1998: Letter to the editor, *Guardian*, 30 May, p. 22.

Perrons, D. 1998a: 'Perspectives on Gender Inequality in European Employment', *European Urban and Regional Studies* 5/1, pp. 5–12.

    1998b: 'Gender Inequality in the Regions of Western Europe', *European Urban and Regional Studies* 5/1, pp. 13–26.

Pidgeon, J. (ed.) 1991: *Classic Albums* (London: BBC Books).

Pietrykowski, B. 1994: 'Consuming Culture: Postmodernism, Post-Fordism, and Economics', *Rethinking Marxism* 7/1, pp. 62–81.

Piore, P. and C. Sabel 1984: *The Second Industrial Divide* (New York: Basic Books).

Pippin, R. 1991: *Modernism as a Philosophical Problem* (Oxford: Blackwell).

Poizat, M. 1992: *The Angel's Cry: Beyond the Pleasure Principle in Music* (Ithaca: Cornell University Press).

Pope, R. 1998: *The English Studies Handbook* (London: Routledge).

Pople, A. (ed.) 1994: *Theory, Analysis and Meaning in Music* (Cambridge: Cambridge University Press).

Preminger, A. and T. V. F. Brogan (eds.) 1993: *The New Princeton Encyclopedia of Poetry and Poetics* (Princeton: Princeton University Press).

Price, S. 1999: *Everything (A Book about Manic Street Preachers)* (London: Virgin).

Pride, D. 1993: 'Kenny G Conquers the World', *Billboard*, 3 July, pp. 40–1, 43.

Quine, W. 1987: *Quiddities: An Intermittently Philosophical Dictionary* (Cambridge, Mass.: Harvard University Press).

Rees, D. 1998: *Minstrels in the Gallery: A History of Jethro Tull* (Wembley, Middx.: Firefly).

Reich, R. 1991: *The Work of Nations* (New York: Alfred A. Knopf).

Reynolds, S. 1990: *Blissed Out: The Raptures of Rock* (London: Serpent's Tail).

    1998: *Energy Flash: A Journey through Rave Music and Dance Culture* (London: Picador).

RIAA (Record Industry Association of America). 2001. Press release, 'U.S. Consumer Trends', 13 March 2001.

Ricks, C. 1984: 'American English and the Inherently Transitory', in *The Force of Poetry* (Oxford: Oxford University Press).

Rietveld, H. C. 1997: 'The House Sound of Chicago', in S. Redhead (ed.), *The Clubcultures Reader: Readings in Popular Cultural Studies* (Oxford: Blackwell), pp. 124–36.

    1998: *This Is Our House: House Music, Cultural Spaces, and Technologies* (Hants: Ashgate).

Rivenburg, R. 1998: 'Off-Kilter', *Los Angeles Times*, 20 April, p. E4.

Rorem, N. 1968: 'The Music of the Beatles', *New York Review of Books*, reprinted in Eisen (1969), pp. 149–59.

252

Rorty, R. 1991: *Objectivism, Relativism and Truth* (Cambridge: Cambridge University Press).

Rose, T. 1994: *Black Noise: Rap Music and Black Culture in Contemporary America* (Hanover, NH: University Press of New England).

Ross, A. and T. Rose (eds.) 1994: *Microphone Fiends: Youth Music and Youth Culture* (London: Routledge).

Royal National Institute for Deaf People (RNID) 1998: 'Music to Whose Ears?' (RNID).

Russell, T. and S. Tyson (eds.) 1995: *And Then I Wrote: The Songwriter Speaks* (Vancouver: Arsenal Pulp Press).

Ruwet, N. 1987: 'Methods of Analysis in Musicology', trans. M. Everist, *Music Analysis* 6/1–2, pp. 3–36.

Marquis de Sade 1990: *The One Hundred & Twenty Days of Sodom and Other Writings* (London: Arrow).

Sanjek, Roger 1990: *Fieldnotes: the Making of Anthropology* (Ithaca: Cornell University Press).

Sanjek, Russell 1983: *From Print to Plastic: Publishing and Promoting America's Popular Music (1900–1980)* (New York: Institute for Studies in American Music, Conservatory of Music, Brooklyn College of the City University of New York, Monograph 20).

Sapir, E. 1949: *Selected Writings in Language, Culture and Personality*, ed. D. Mandelbaum (Berkeley: University of California Press).

Sassen, S. 1991: *The Global City: New York, London, and Tokyo* (Princeton: Princeton University Press).

2000: *Cities in a World Economy* (Thousand Oaks: Pine Forge Press).

Savage, J. 1992: *England's Dreaming: Anarchy, Sex Pistols, Punk Rock, and Beyond* (New York: St Martin's Press).

Savan, L. 1993: 'Commercials go Rock', in S. Frith, A. Goodwin and L. Grossberg (eds.), *Sound and Vision: The Music Video Reader* (London: Routledge), pp. 85–90.

Schönberg, A. 1983: *Structural Functions of Harmony* (London: Faber).

Schwarz, D., A. Kassabian and L. Siegel (eds.) 1997: *Keeping Score: Music, Disciplinarity, Culture* (Charlottesville: Virginia University Press).

Seeger, A. 1987: *Why Suyá Sing: A Musical Anthropology of an Amazonian People* (Cambridge: Cambridge University Press).

Seeger, C. 1959: 'Whither Ethnomusicology?' *Ethnomusicology* 3, pp. 101–2.

1961: 'Semantic, Logical, and Political Considerations Bearing upon Research in Ethnomusicology', *Ethnomusicology* 5(2), pp. 77–80.

1970: 'Toward a Unity Field Theory for Musicology', *Selected Reports* 1/3, pp. 171–210.

253

1977: *Studies in Musicology, 1935–1975* (Berkeley: University of California Press).

1994: *Studies in Musicology II: 1929–1979*, ed. A. Pescatello (Berkeley: University of California Press).

Sharma, S., J. Hutnyk and A. Sharma 1996: *Dis-orienting Rhythms: The Politics of the New Asian Dance Music* (New Jersey: Zed Books).

Shepherd, J. 1991: *Music as Social Text* (Cambridge: Polity).

1994: 'Music, Culture and Interdisciplinarity: Reflections on Relationships', *Popular Music* 13/2, pp. 127–42.

Shepherd, J. and P. Wicke 1997: *Music and Cultural Theory* (Cambridge: Polity).

Sieburth, S. A. 1994: *Inventing High and Low Literature, Mass Culture, and Uneven Modernity in Spain* (Durham, NC: Duke University Press).

Simms, B. R. 1986: *Music of the Twentieth Century: Style and Structure* (New York: Schirmer).

Slobin, M. 1996: *Retuning Culture: Musical Changes in Central and Eastern Europe* (Durham: Duke University Press).

Sloboda, J. 1985: *The Musical Mind: An Introduction to the Cognitive Psychology of Music* (Oxford: Oxford University Press).

1992: 'Psychological Structures in Music: Core Research 1980–1990', in J. Paynter; R. Orton, T. Seymour and T. Howell (eds.), *A Compendium of Contemporary Musical Thought* (London: Routledge), pp. 803–39.

1998: 'Does Music Mean Anything?' *Musicae Scientiae* 2/1, pp. 21–32.

Small, C. 1977: *Music – Society – Education* (London: John Calder).

1987: *Music of the Common Tongue* (London: John Calder).

1998: *Musicking: The Meanings of Performing and Listening* (Hanover, NH: Wesleyan University Press).

Smith, N. 1996: *The New Urban Frontier: Gentrification and the Revanchist City* (London: Routledge).

Spivak, G. 1988: 'Can the Subaltern Speak?' in Cary Nelson and Lawrence Grossberg (eds.), *Marxism and the Interpretation of Culture* (Urbana: University of Illinois Press), pp. 271–313.

1996: 'Revolutions that as yet have no Model: Derrida's "Limited Inc."' in Donna Landry and Gerald MacLean (eds.): *The Spivak Reader* (London: Routledge), pp. 75–106.

Stefani, G. 1987: 'A Theory of Musical Competence', *Semiotica* 66/1–3, pp. 7–22.

Stockhausen, K. 1989: *Stockhausen on Music*, ed. R. Maconie (London: Marion Boyars).

Stokes, M. 1992: *The Arabesk Debate: Music and Musicians in Modern Turkey* (Oxford: Clarendon).

1994: 'Deceit, Desire and the Arabesk Stage': *New Formations*, pp. 66–96.

Straw, W. 1991: 'Systems of Articulation, Logics of Change: Communities and Scenes in Popular Music', *Cultural Studies* 5/3, pp. 368–88.

Street, J. 1986: *Rebel Rock* (Oxford: Blackwell).

Strinati, D. 1995: *An Introduction to Theories of Popular Culture* (London: Routledge).

Swanwick, K. 1984: *Musical Knowledge: Intuition, Analysis and Music Education* (London: Routledge).

Tagg, P. 1979: 'Kojak – 50 Seconds of Television Music: Towards the Analysis of Affect in Popular Music', Ph.D. Diss., University of Gothenburg.

1982: 'Analysing Popular Music: Theory, Method and Practice', *Popular Music* 2, pp. 37–67.

1985: 'Why IASPM? Which Tasks?' *Popular Music Perspectives* 2, Papers from the Second International Conference on Popular Music Studies, Reggio Emilia 1983, IASPM, pp. 501–7.

1987: 'Musicology and the Semiotics of Popular Music', *Semiotica* 66/3, pp. 279–98.

1991: *Fernando the Flute: Musical Meaning in an Abba Mega-hit* (Liverpool: Institute of Popular Music).

1992: 'Towards a Sign Typology of Music', in Dalmonte and Baroni (1992), pp. 369–78.

1994: 'From Refrain to Rave: The Decline of Figure and the Rise of Ground', *Popular Music* 13/2, pp. 209–22.

1998a: 'Tritonal Crime and "Music as *Music*" ', in S. Miceli, L. Gallenga and L. Kokkaliari (eds.), *Norme con Ironie: scritti per I settant' anni di Ennio Morricone* (Milan: Suvini Zerboni), pp. 273–312.

1998b: Interview by Prof. Martha Ulhôa at Pontllyfni, Wales on 11 April, unpublished, available at Tagg's website: www.liv.ac.uk/IPM/tagg/tagghmpg.htm.

1998c: Review of John Shepherd and Peter Wicke: *Music and Cultural Theory*, *Popular Music* 17/3, pp. 331–48.

Tagg, P. and R. Clarida forthcoming: *Ten Little Title Tunes*.

Taylor, W. 1991: *Inventing Times Square: Commerce and Culture at the Crossroads of the World* (New York: Russell Sage Foundation).

Théberge, P. 1997: *Any Sound You Can Imagine: Making Music/Consuming Technology* (New Haven: Wesleyan University Press).

Thomas, C. 1993: Liner notes to Jethro Tull: *25th anniversary* CD set (London: Chrysalis).

Thomson, V. 1981: 'Why Composers Write, or the Economic Determinism of Musical Style', in *A Virgil Thomson Reader* (New York: E. P. Dutton), pp. 122–47, originally 1939.

Thornton, J. 1998: 'The Man Behind the Muzak', *Sunday Telegraph*, 22 March, p. 15.

255

Thornton, S. 1995: *Club Cultures: Music, Media and Subcultures* (Cambridge: Polity).

Tickell, A. and J. Peck 1992: 'Accumulation, Regulation and the Geographies of Post-Fordism: Missing Links in Regulationist Research', *Progress in Human Geography* 16/2, pp. 190–218.

Tomlinson, G. 1991: 'Cultural Dialogics and Jazz: A White Historian Signifies', *Black Music Research Journal* 11/2, pp. 229–64.

1993: 'Musical Pasts and Postmodern Musicologies: A Response to Lawrence Kramer', *Current Musicology* 53, pp. 18–40.

Walser, R. 1992: 'Eruptions: Heavy Metal Appropriations of Classical Virtuosity', *Popular Music* 11/3, pp. 263–308.

1993: *Running With the Devil: Power, Gender, and Madness in Heavy Metal Music* (London: Wesleyan University Press).

1995: 'Rhythm, Rhyme and Rhetoric in the Music of Public Enemy', *Ethnomusicology* 39/2, pp. 193–217.

1999: *Keeping Time: Readings in Jazz History* (New York: Oxford University Press).

Waterman, C. 1990: *Jùjú: A Social History and Ethnography of an African Popular Music* (Chicago: Chicago University Press).

Watkins, G. 1988: *Soundings: Music in the Twentieth Century* (New York: Schirmer).

Weber, W. 1977: 'Mass Culture and the Reshaping of European Musical Taste, 1770–1870', *International Review of the Aesthetics and Sociology of Music* 8/1, pp. 5–22.

Weiner, A. 1995: 'Culture and our Discontents', *American Anthropologist* 97/1, pp. 14–20.

Wesling, D. 1980: *The Chances of Rhyme: Device and Modernity* (Berkeley: University of California Press).

Whitburn, Joel 1986: *Pop Memories 1890–1954* (Menomonee Falls, WI: Record Research).

Whorf, B. 1991: *Language, Thought and Reality*, ed. J. Carroll (Cambridge, Mass.: MIT Press).

Wideman, J. E. 1995: 'Doing Time, Marking Race', *The Nation*, 30 October, pp. 503–5.

Williams, R. 1977: *Marxism and Literature* (Oxford: Oxford University Press).

Wilson, W. J. 1987: *The Truly Disadvantaged: The Inner City, the Underclass, and Public Policy* (Chicago: University of Chicago Press).

Wimsatt, W. K. 1954: 'One Relation of Rhyme to Reason', *The Verbal Icon: Studies in the Meaning of Poetry* (Lexington: University of Kentucky Press), originally 1944.

Winkler, P. 1978: 'Toward a Theory of Pop Harmony', *In Theory Only* 4, pp. 3–26.

Zbikowski, L. 2002: *Conceptualizing Music: Cognition, Theory and Analysis* (New York: Oxford University Press).

Zinn, H. 1990: *The Politics of History*, 2nd edn (Urbana: University of Illinois Press).

Zollo, P. 1997: *Songwriters on Songwriting*, expanded edn (New York: Da Capo).

Discography

Abba 1976: 'Fernando' (Epic).
Beatles 1962: *Please Please Me:* 'Please Please Me' (Parlophone).
Belle and Sebastian 1998: *The Boy with the Arab Strap* (Jeepster).
Björk 1995: *Post:* 'You've Been Flirting Again' (One Little Indian).
Björk 1996: *Telegram:* 'Enjoy – Outcast' (One Little Indian).
Black Star 1998: *Black Star* (Priority).
Brandy 1998: *Never Say Never* (Atlantic).
Jackson Browne 1974: *Late for the Sky:* 'Fountain of Sorrow' (Asylum).
Jackson Browne 1985: *Lives in the Balance:* 'Lives in the Balance' (Asylum).
John Cale 1975: *Helen of Troy:* 'Leaving It Up to You' (Island).
The Cars 1999: *The Cars, Deluxe Edition* (Rhino).
John Coltrane 1959: *Giant Steps* (Atlantic).
John Coltrane 1965: *Ascension* (Impulse).
Sam Cooke 1964: *Sam Cooke at the Copa:* 'Try a Little Tenderness'
    (RCA).
Julian Cope 1991: *Peggy Suicide:* 'Safesurfer' (Island).
Elvis Costello 1978: *This Year's Model:* 'No Action', '(I Don't Want to Go to) Chelsea'
    (Radar).
Elvis Costello 1982: *Imperial Bedroom:* 'Beyond Belief' (F-Beat).
Bing Crosby 1933: 'Try a Little Tenderness' (with a studio orchestra;
    ARC-Brunswick).
Bob Dylan 1976: *Desire:* 'Hurricane' (Columbia).
Bob Dylan 1981: 'The Groom's Still Waiting at the Altar' (Columbia).
The Fall 1981: 'Lie Dream of a Casino Soul' (Kamera).
Foreigner 1977: *Foreigner* (Atlantic).
Foreigner 1981: *Four* (Atlantic).
Foreigner 2000: *Jukebox Heroes* (Rhino).
Aretha Franklin 1962: *The Tender, the Moving, the Swinging Aretha Franklin:*
    'Try a Little Tenderness' (Columbia).
Kenny G 1992: *Breathless:* 'The Joy of Life' (Arista).
Gang of Four 1979: *Entertainment!:* 'Ether' (EMI).
Hole 1994: *Live Through This:* 'Doll Parts' (Geffen).
Ice Cube 1992: *The Predator:* 'When Will They Shoot?' (Priority).

Jethro Tull 1968: *This Was:* 'Some Day the Sun Won't Shine for You', 'Dharma for One' (Chrysalis).

Jethro Tull 1969: *Stand Up:* 'Nothing is Easy', 'We Used to Know' (Chrysalis).

Jethro Tull 1970: *Benefit:* 'Son', 'Play in Time', 'Sossity' (Chrysalis).

Jethro Tull 1971: *Aqualung:* 'Aqualung', 'Cross-eyed Mary', 'Up to Me', 'Locomotive Breath', 'Wind Up' (Chrysalis).

Jethro Tull 1972a: *Thick as a Brick* (Chrysalis).

Jethro Tull 1972b: *Living in the Past:* 'Sweet Dream', 'The Witch's Promise', 'Up the Pool', 'Dharma for One' (live), 'A Christmas Song' (Chrysalis).

Jethro Tull 1973: *A Passion Play* (Chrysalis).

Jethro Tull 1974: *War Child:* 'Back Door Ladies', 'Two Fingers' (Chrysalis).

Jethro Tull 1975: *Minstrel in the Gallery:* 'Minstrel in the Gallery', 'Cold Wind to Valhalla', 'Black Satin Dancer' (Chrysalis).

Jethro Tull 1976: *Too Old to Rock'n'Roll, Too Young to Die:* 'Too Old to Rock'n'Roll, Too Young to Die', 'From a Deadbeat to an Old Greaser' (Chrysalis).

Jethro Tull 1977: *Songs From the Wood:* 'Songs From the Wood', 'Jack-in-the-Green', 'Velvet Green', 'Hunting Girl' (Chrysalis).

Jethro Tull 1978: *Heavy Horses:* 'One Brown Mouse', 'Heavy Horses' (Chrysalis).

Jethro Tull 1979: *Stormwatch:* 'Orion', 'Dark Ages', 'Flying Dutchman', 'Warm Sporran' (Chrysalis).

Jethro Tull 1980: *'Fylingdale Flyer'*, 'Batteries not Included' (Chrysalis).

Jethro Tull 1982: *Broadsword and the Beast:* 'The Clasp' (Chrysalis).

Jethro Tull 1984: *Under Wraps:* 'Under Wraps #1', 'Nobody's Car', 'Under Wraps #2' (Chrysalis).

Jethro Tull 1987: *Crest of a Knave:* 'Farm on the Freeway' (Chrysalis).

Jethro Tull 1989: *Rock Island:* 'Undressed to Kill', 'The Whaler's Dues', 'Ears of Tin', 'Strange Avenues' (Chrysalis).

Jethro Tull 1991: *Catfish Rising:* 'Rocks on the Road', 'Thinking Round Corners' (Chrysalis).

Jethro Tull 1992: *A Little Light Music:* 'John Barleycorn', 'Locomotive Breath' (Chrysalis).

Jethro Tull 1993a: *25th Anniversary Boxed Set* (Chrysalis).

Jethro Tull 1993b: *Nightcap:* 'Broadford Bazaar' (Chrysalis).

Jethro Tull 1995: *Roots to Branches:* 'Dangerous Veils' (Chrysalis).

Rickie Lee Jones 1981: *Pirates:* 'Living It Up' (Warner).

Gladys Knight and the Pips 1976: 'Midnight Train to Georgia' (Buddah).

Manic Street Preachers 1992: *Generation Terrorists:* 'Motorcycle Emptiness' (Columbia).

Massive Attack 1994: *Protection:* 'Karmacoma' (Circa).

Metallica 1991: *Metallica:* 'Enter Sandman' (Elektra).

Mobb Deep 1999: *Murda Muzik* (Loud).

Van Morrison 1971: *Tupelo Honey:* 'Tupelo Honey' (Warner).

Niggaz with Attitude 1988: *Straight Outta Compton:* 'Fuck the Police' (Priority).

Nirvana 1991: *Nevermind:* 'Polly' (Geffen).

Pet Shop Boys 1993: *Very:* 'Can You Forgive Her?' (Parlophone).

Pink Floyd 1973: *Dark Side of the Moon:* 'Money' (Harvest).

Pirates of the Mississippi 1990: *Pirates of the Mississippi:* 'Feed Jake' (Liberty).

Portishead 1994: *Dummy:* 'Glory Box' (Go!).

Quintessence 1970: *Quintessence* (Island).

Raekwon 1995: *Only Built 4 Cuban Linx* (BCA).

Otis Redding 1966: *Complete and Unbelievable: The Otis Redding Dictionary of Soul* (Volt).

Lou Reed 1972: *Transformer:* 'Walk on the Wild Side' (RCA).

Lou Reed 1989: *New York:* 'There is No Time' (Sire).

Lou Reed and John Cale 1990: *Songs for Drella:* 'Trouble with Classicists' (Sire).

REM 1992: *Automatic for the People:* 'Nightswimming' (Warner).

Sex Pistols 1977: *Never Mind the Bollocks:* 'Pretty Vacant' (Virgin).

Jane Siberry 1995: *Maria:* 'See the Child' (Reprise).

Frank Sinatra 1945: 'Try a Little Tenderness' (with Alex Stordahl's Orchestra; Columbia).

Sleeper 1995: *Smart:* 'Inbetweener' (Indolent).

Jimmy Smith 1964: *The Cat* (MGM).

Patti Smith 1974: 'Piss Factory' (MER).

Patti Smith 1975: *Horses* (Arista).

Smiths 1984: *The Smiths:* 'This Charming Man' (Rough Trade).

Squeeze 1981: *East Side Story:* 'Labelled with Love' (A&M).

A Tribe Called Quest 1996: *Beats, Rhymes, and Life* (Jive/Novus).

Underworld 1993: *dubnobasswithmyheadman:* 'Dirty Epic' (Junior Boy's Own).

Underworld 1995: 'Born Slippy' (Junior Boy's Own).

Underworld 1996: *Second Toughest in the Infants:* 'Pearl's Girl' (Junior Boy's Own).

Underworld 1999: *Beaucoup Fish:* 'Moaner' (Junior Boy's Own).

Whale 1995: *We Care:* 'Tryzasnice' (Virgin).

Cassandra Wilson 1993: *Blue Light 'Til Dawn:* 'Tupelo Honey' (Blue Note).

Weird Al Yankovic 1984: 'Eat It' (Scotti Bros).

Yes 1977: *Going for the One:* 'Awaken' (Atlantic).

various 1987: *Les Mystères des Voix Bulgares* (Nonesuch).

Film/Videography

The Carpetbaggers (dir. by Edward Dmytryk, 1963).

Index